I0038518

Common Law Torts in Business and How to Avoid Them: A Handbook for Managers

Frank J. Cavico and Bahaudin G. Mujtaba

ILEAD Academy, LLC
Davie, Florida. United States of America
www.ileadacademy.com

Frank J. Cavico and Bahaudin G. Mujtaba, 2021. *Common Law Torts in Business and How to Avoid Them: A Handbook for Managers*

Cover Design by: Cagri Tanyar

All rights reserved. No part of this publication may be reproduced or transmitted in any form or by any means electronic or mechanical, including photocopy, recording, or any information storage and retrieval system, without permission in writing from both the copyright owner and the publisher.

© ILEAD Academy, LLC

ISBN-13: 978-1-936237-18-0

ISBN-10: 1-936237-18-0

Subject Code & Description
BUS008000 - Business & Economics: Business Ethics
LAW051000 - Law: International
BUS010000 - Business & Economics: Business Law
PHI005000 - Philosophy: Ethics & Moral Philosophy

The purpose of the common law is to protect the weak from the abuse and insults of the strong.

English Jurist, William Murray,
First Earl of Mansfield
(1705-1793)

Table of Contents

Preface

The essence of management is decision-making; and one critical aspect of decision-making in business is to ensure that the decisions are legal ones. This book focuses on one area of the law that impacts business-decision-making – tort law. Tort law is part of civil law and is based on the common law, that is, judge-made decisions. Tort law is an old body of law harkening back to very early English law; yet nonetheless tort law can have serious ramifications for managers and business today. Tort law violations are civil law infractions and not criminal ones. However, it is certainly possible for the commission of a tort, for example, assault and battery, to also be a crime. This book will stay on the civil side of the law. Accordingly, the purposes of this book are to educate managers as to the essential principles and rationales behind tort law and to demonstrate how tort law violations can be avoided. After providing a foundation as to basic legal definitions and concepts, the authors explicate and illustrate in the context of business and employment three main bodies of tort law – intentional torts, the tort of negligence, and strict liability torts. The authors also explore the relationship among tort law and agency and employment law. Throughout the book the authors supply suggestions and recommendations to managers on how to reduce and eliminate legal liability for tort violations. The authors, moreover, supply a glossary of key terms, followed by a bibliography, and ending with the authors' brief biographies.

The authors have titled this book a "handbook"; that is, the book is a succinct summary and explanation in understandable language of important tort legal principles; the book is not an exhaustive legal treatise. In addition, the authors want to point out that this book takes a general approach to tort law in the United States; yet tort law in the U.S. is very state specific, predominantly based on the decisions by the highest court in the state, the state supreme court, and state appellate courts. Case examples are furnished from many states in the United States. Nevertheless, if a tort controversy arises in a certain state then perforce reference must be made to the law of that specific state to resolve the dispute. As such, the book is not a substitute for an attorney and his or her legal opinion based on the law of the pertinent state. However, the authors hope and trust that their handbook will help educate managers to the principles of tort law, how torts can arise in a business and employment setting, and, most significantly, how to avoid tort violations. The book will also educate managers as to the language and concepts of the law and thus aid managers in their discussions with legal counsel. The authors, therefore, want the discerning reader – business manager or otherwise – to be conscious of the scope, complexity, and variety of this one basic *corpus* of law – tort law. Although the focus of this book is the application of tort law to the private sector, many of the principles can be extrapolated to the public sector and accordingly there are also public sector case examples in the book. The authors wish to make the reader recognize legal situations in business, the public sector, as well as everyday life, and the authors especially want to impart an awareness of potential legal problems pursuant to tort law and how to avoid them.

In addition to the analysis of tort law in this book, the authors go "above and beyond" the law by discussing several concepts related to the law which also are very important for managers to be aware of and handle effectively. As such, the authors build on the law by examining the fields of ethics, social responsibility, and sustainability. The objective, the authors emphasize, is for a business to act not "merely" in a legal manner, but also in an ethical, socially responsible, and sustainable manner; and the task of managers as business leaders is to establish the "right" corporate culture – one that values legality, morality, diversity, respect, social responsibility, and sustainability. Such an approach, the authors maintain, given efficacious management decision-making, will lead to personal and business success and sustainable success.

This "handbook" can be used academically, of course, as a supplement to a traditional business law course or as the basis for a specialized law course; but the book is primarily designed as a corporate training and educational tool for managers. For a more comprehensive examination of tort law as well as other bodies of law affecting business, the authors would recommend our other books: *Business Law for the Entrepreneur and Manager* (4th Edition 2020), published by ILEAD Academy, LLC, which treats in addition to tort law other basic business law principles, such as contract and sales law, business organizations, agency law, the law of creditors and debtors, and commercial paper law; *Legal Challenges for the Global Manager and Entrepreneur* (Second Edition 2014), published by Kendall-Hunt Publishers, which treats government regulation of business legal subject matters, such as consumer law, securities law, anti-trust law, environmental law, and civil rights law; and finally, *Business Ethics: The Moral Foundation of Effective Leadership, Management, and Entrepreneurship* (Third Edition 2013), published by Pearson Publishers, which treats philosophical ethics, applied business ethics, social responsibility, and sustainability.

The quote from Lord Mansfield that commences this book reflects the essential rationale of tort law, that is, to protect people and their property from injury and harm. As such, the authors maintain that treating people and their property with dignity and respect as well as in a careful and judicious manner will go a long way to achieving the goal of acting in a legal, moral, socially responsible, and sustainable manner. The authors hope that you, the reader, will find their handbook a beneficial and useful educational and practical tool, especially in a management, business, and employment context, and that you also will find the book intellectually stimulating, thought-provoking, challenging, as well as enjoyable. The authors want you to be very successful personally, professionally, in business and management, and as leaders. You and your organization's success bring us the greatest satisfaction and pleasure.

Sincerely,
Frank and Bahaudin

CHAPTER I - INTRODUCTION AND OVERVIEW

This first chapter to the book provides an *introduction and overview* to the work. The book is predominantly an examination of one important component of the law – tort law, which is based predominantly on the common law, that is, judge-made decisions, in the context of business management and employment. The commission of a tort is a civil wrong, though the same act can be both a tort and a crime (but with different evidentiary standards). The focus of this book is the civil wrong of a tort. Moreover, the focus is on the private sector, though many of the principles explicated and illustrated herein can have public sector ramifications. The objective of the book is to educate managers as to certain fundamental principles of tort law, to demonstrate how torts can arise in a business and employment setting, and to show managers how to avoid legal liability under tort law. Accordingly, throughout the book the authors have provided suggestions and recommendations to managers on how to reduce and eliminate tort liability. The three main tort fields analyzed in the book are intentional torts, the tort of negligence, and the tort of strict liability for products. In addition to the legal materials presented in the book the authors include a discussion of the related fields of ethics, applied business ethics, social responsibility, and sustainability, as well as corporate culture and leadership. Each chapter has a brief introduction as well as a summary and conclusion.

The second chapter to the book, *Fundamental Common Law Concepts*, introduces the reader to basic legal concepts and definitions, such as the differentiation among civil and criminal law, the common law and civil law, and the common law and statutory law. Two critical components of common law legal systems – the use of precedents and the doctrine of *stare decisis* – are explained. Moreover, the distinctions among a tort, a crime, and a breach of contract are stated and explained. Finally, the distinction between the doctrines of legal misfeasance and legal nonfeasance is presented, including the important general rule dealing with nonfeasance being explained and illustrated.

The third chapter, *Intentional Torts*, is a very substantive one, as several intentional torts are presented, explicated, and illustrated. These torts are as follows: battery and the related tort of assault; false imprisonment, including a discussion of merchant's protection laws; intentional infliction of emotional distress, including "bullying" in the workplace; invasion of privacy, including the intrusion and disclosure types; intentional interference with contract or business relations; defamation, consisting of slander and libel, including the essential "publication" requirement; and fraud (in the old common law sense of deceit, that is, purposefully and knowingly lying). Next, the breach of loyalty in the employment relationship will be covered, especially since some jurisdictions consider this breach to be also a breach of a fiduciary duty, which is equivalent to fraud. Similarly, the public policy doctrine will be examined since in some jurisdictions the violation of public policy will be deemed to be the equivalent of an intentional tort violation. In addition, the tort of wrongful institution of legal proceedings as well as intentional torts to property, including trespass to land, trespass to chattels, and conversion, will be succinctly covered. Finally, defenses to intentional torts generally and to certain specific intentional torts will be presented and described, especially the very important qualified privilege protection under defamation law.

The fourth chapter, *Negligence*, deals with the common law tort of negligence, which is a very old legal principle harkening back to the early Middle Ages in England, yet which is still a very viable tort today for business, employment, and otherwise. The elements of the tort of negligence – duty, breach of duty, causation, and damages - will be stated, explained, and illustrated. Factual causation will be distinguished from legal causation, also known as proximate causation. The role of the judge and the jury will be differentiated. The tort of negligence will be fully explicated and illustrated in three major employment settings – hiring, supervising, and retaining employees. Moreover, certain specialized negligence doctrines will be explained, to wit: the doctrine of *res ipsa loquitur*, negligence *per se*, and negligent infliction of emotional distress, which will be differentiated from the intentional tort version by highlighting the "impact" requirement. In addition, the authors will provide a concise analysis of negligence principles regarding premises liability and the types of people who can come upon one's land – invitees, guests, and trespassers – and the legal duties owed thereto. Finally, defenses to the tort of negligence will be presented with the focus on the two main ones – comparative negligence and assumption of the risk.

The fifth chapter, *Strict Liability Torts*, will focus mainly on strict liability for products and the rationales for this "strict" type of liability. The authors will focus on the critical requirements for liability of the seller as an entity on the marketing chain as well as the critical finding of the product being "defective." The three types of potential product defects, based on having a "flawed" product, a product with no or an inadequate warning, as well as a product defectively designed, will be explained, and examples will be provided. The components of the legal test for a design defect – state-of-the-art, practicality of use, and economic feasibility – will also be explained and illustrated. Defenses to strict liability will be offered. Finally, strict liability for ultra-hazardous activities will be briefly mentioned.

The sixth chapter, *Torts and Agency Law*, deals with the intersection of tort law with agency law. Agency law is a broad term encompassing three very important legal relationships – principal and agent, employer and employee, and employer and independent contractor. These three relationships will be defined and examined in the context of intentional tort as well as negligence liability. The factors in determining whether a person hired is an employee or an independent contractor will be addressed. The critical doctrines of vicarious and imputed liability and the ancient, though still very valid, doctrine of *respondeat superior*, will be explicated and illustrated. Essential to the aforementioned doctrines is the very important "scope of employment" rule, which will be explained and illustrated too, including the quaint, but still consequential, "frolic and detour" exception. The exceptional circumstances where there is imputed liability for intentional torts will be stated, and examples provided, especially regarding the liability of a principal for the intentional tort of fraud by his or her agent.

The seventh chapter, *Law, Ethics, and Social Responsibility*, goes "above and beyond" the foregoing legal presentation as the authors present and explain the field of ethics, first as a branch of philosophy with the four main ethical theories in Western Civilization – Ethical Egoism, Ethical Relativism, Utilitarianism, and Kantian ethics – differentiated and explained. Next the authors demonstrate how ethics can be applied to business so that managers can be sure their firms are acting not only legally but also morally. Examinations of whistleblowing, codes of ethics, and corporate governance in the context of law and ethics are presented. Next, the authors go "above and beyond" ethics by treating the field of social responsibility, which is known as "corporate social responsibility" when the concept is applied to business. Social responsibility is examined first in its traditional conception of charity, philanthropy, and community and civic-minded activities and endeavors, as well as in its more modern configuration of "sustainability," that is, environmental responsibility. The objective of the authors is to get managers to think and act not "merely" legally, but also morally based on ethics as well as in a socially responsible and sustainable manner. By so acting, the authors maintain, assuming good management decision-making, managers and their organizations will obtain success and will be able to sustain that success in the long-term, thereby benefiting themselves, their organizations, communities, and society as a whole.

The final chapter, *Summary and Conclusion*, provides a brief summary of the book as well as the final conclusion, followed by a Glossary of key terms, a bibliography, and brief biographies of the authors.

CHAPTER II - FUNDAMENTAL COMMON LAW CONCEPTS

This chapter to the book deals with certain very important fundamental common law concepts. First, definitions of the law, including the distinctions between civil and criminal law, and common law, also called case law, and statutory law, will be provided. Two doctrines critical to the operation of the common law – the system of precedents and the doctrine of *stare decisis* – will be explained. The definition and nature of a tort, the distinction between intentional torts and negligence, as well as the differentiation of torts from crimes and breach of contract, will be provided. The authors will next distinguish legal misfeasance, that is, acting in a wrongful illegal manner, from legal nonfeasance, that is, not acting at all, as well as discuss the legal liability ensuing from both doctrines. Suggestions and recommendations to managers and employers will be offered regarding potential liability under the legal nonfeasance doctrine.

Definition and Nature of the Law

The "law" is complex; consequently, it has many definitions. Fundamentally, the *law* is the entire body of principles that governs conduct, and which can be enforced by the courts or other government tribunals. If there were no society-made laws, many people would still act in a "proper" manner based on societal norms, moral beliefs, conscience, or religion. However, not all people would act in such a "good" manner. Therefore, a basic purpose of the law is to provide a degree of order and control to human activities. The law thus serves as an instrumentality of control by means of substantive legal rules, legal procedures, and mechanisms of legal promulgation, adjudication, implementation, and enforcement.

When most people think of the term, the "law," they usually are thinking of a statute enacted by a legislative body, such as the United States Congress or a state legislature. *Statutory law* encompasses, in addition, the legislative ordinances enacted by constituent government elements of states in the United States, that is, ordinances and codes promulgated by counties and municipalities. Law also includes constitutional law, such as in the United States the federal, that is, national, constitution as well as state constitutions. Constitutional law in the U.S. as in most legal systems is supreme. Law further includes regulatory law, that is, the laws, in the forms of rules and regulations promulgated by administrative agencies, which have been delegated sovereign law-making powers by the legislative bodies. In the United States, a good part of the law that regulates business stems from government administrative agencies on not only the federal level but also the state and local level. Law consists, moreover, of *case law*, called the "*common law*" in the Anglo-American judicial tradition, which is the law expressed by judges in court decisions. The tort law affecting business discussed herein is primarily based on the common law. Treaties are another source of the law. As a matter of fact, in the United States, the federal constitution explicitly gives the President the power with the advice and consent of the Senate to enter into treaties with foreign governments. Executive orders, finally, are yet one more source of the law. These are orders from the executive branch of government, for example, in the U.S. by the President or the governor of a state. The authority to issue executive orders is either expressly granted to chief executive officers or implied from the federal or state constitutions.

There are many different classifications to the law. Generally, law can be divided into "public" law and "private" law. *Public law* impacts the "people" as a whole who are directly involved with the law; the aim of public law is to serve the societal interest as well as to seek to achieve justice; and the "people's" interests are represented by government agencies and officers. Prime examples are constitutional law, administrative law, and criminal law. Whereas "*private*" *law* deals with the legal problems, relations, and interests among private individuals; society and "the people" are not involved as-a-whole. Prominent illustrations of private law are the laws of contracts, torts, and property. Related to public and private law, though narrower in focus, are the criminal law and the civil law. The *criminal law* deals with legal wrongs committed ultimately against society, since society cannot function unless people and their property are protected. Criminal infractions are punished by society, particularly by the sanction of imprisonment; and in so doing the wrongdoer makes amends to society. Whereas the *civil law* deals with legal wrongs committed by one private party against another private party, for example, a lawsuit for breach of contract or for the tort of negligence, where the payment of money is the usual means of redress. The term "civil law," however, has another meaning. In many legal systems, the sole or primary source of the law is found in detailed statutes, called codes. Court decisions have a secondary importance, and, as a matter of fact, in some legal systems do not even have the force of law. The civil law in this sense is premised on the Napoleonic Code, but harkens back even further to the Roman law. Today, most European countries and all Latin American countries have "civil law" systems, as well as, to some extent, the state of Louisiana in the United States due to its Spanish and French origins and former rule. Civil law, moreover, must be differentiated from the "common law," which is a system of law which relies substantially on judicial-made case law for the law. Great Britain and the United States are two examples of common law systems. In a common law system, there of course will be statutory law too; and accordingly the function of the courts will be to not only make law but also to interpret statutory law and to review statutory law. One final important classification to the law is the distinction between *substantive law* and procedural law. The former defines the legal relation of people with other people or people with the state, and sets forth their respective rights and duties; whereas *procedural law* is the legal method, means, or process by which the substantive law is administered and the parties' and society's rights and duties are enforced.

Precedents and *Stare Decisis*

In the Anglo-American legal tradition, it is necessary to explicate the meaning of the core legal concept – the "*common law*" – as well as to explore the relationship between the common law and statutory law. In early English days, the kings and their royal representatives officiating as courts made up the law on a case-by-case basis; yet not from a subjective starting point, but rather rooted in the customs and prevailing mores in the community. Over time, as more and more cases were decided, discrete bodies of law were developed. Moreover, after time, courts looked to earlier cases to see what legal principles were enunciated; and then, most significantly, followed these prior legal principles in deciding present cases. Following these foundational legal principles became the heart of the common law of England. The English common law was of course adopted by courts in the United States.

In common law systems, two concepts are critical: one is a "precedent," and the other and related one is the doctrine of "*stare decisis*." A *precedent* is an earlier case with the same or similar facts which has enunciated certain legal rules; and the system of "*stare decisis*" means that a court will follow established precedents in resolving the present case "at bar." If a similar case is found, a court will stick to the same rule in settling the present case. The strength of "*stare decisis*" is that the system brings order, uniformity, certainty, and predictability to the law. When a rule is applied to more and more cases with the same or similar issues, the greater the likelihood that the rule will be followed in the future; and thus an attorney will be better able to advise his or her client of how a court will decide in the client's potential case. Nevertheless, there are some problems with precedents and the system of "*stare decisis*." First, the more dissimilar the issues and factual patterns between the precedent case and the current legal controversy, the more the uncertainty as to legal result ensues; and, consequently, the present court now has some flexibility in resolving the dispute. Second, if there are no cases or very few cases with the same or similar issues and facts, then a court similarly will possess more latitude in determining what rule of law to apply. Third, if there are no cases on point anywhere, then a court is free to decide the dispute, yet again based on prevailing customs or if none on what is deemed to be just. The next "precedent" problem arises when there is a "bad" or "unfair" rule that is "stuck" in the system and as a result is applied again and again. Fortunately, this happenstance has not been a regular occurrence, and there have not been that many "bad" laws; and, of course, a court is not bound to keep to precedent slavishly but rather ultimately to do justice. Finally, the original reason behind a precedent may no longer exist, but the courts may keep on applying the rule; yet again this has not been a widespread problem, as courts are cognizant of changed conditions. As an example of the latter situation, in the old common law, hospitals were regarded as charities and thus were "cloaked" with charitable immunity, meaning that a hospital was not legally responsible for the wrongs committed by its employees. Now, obviously, hospitals can be legally responsible due to heightened public policy concerns as well as the fact that hospitals have become "big business" and business that is protected by insurance too.

Torts, Crimes, and Breach of Contract

In United States law, *a tort* is a wrongful act against a person or property for which a legal cause of action may be brought for the harm sustained. The term "tort" is a very old one, harkening back to the early common law in England, and even before that to the Norman-French conquest of England. A tort is a private wrong, the violation of private duty created by the law, and the violation of which results in a private injury. To compare, a *crime* is a public wrong, the violation of a publicly created duty, and the violation of which results in harm to the "state." Yet it is important to note initially that the same act may constitute both a tort and a crime, for example, an assault and battery, which the state can prosecute as a crime and the victim can also sue for intentional tort damages. A breach of contract is a private wrong too, resulting in a private injury, but the breach arises from the violation of a duty created consensually by the parties. Torts can be personal torts, arising from an injury to a person's body, feelings, or reputation; and torts can be property torts, arising from harm to land, real estate, or personal property. The purposes of tort law are to provide protection to certain legally recognizable interests, to afford a remedy if these interests are wrongfully harmed, and to allocate the risk and cost of injury on a just basis. Speaking very generally, people are free to act as they please in the United States so long as their actions do not infringe on or invade the interests of others.

Misfeasance vs. Nonfeasance

There is, finally, a distinction of great consequence that the common law makes between *nonfeasance* and *misfeasance*. Misfeasance means acting in an illegal manner and violating the civil or criminal law. Misfeasance should not be confused with malfeasance, which is illegal conduct by public officials, such as bribery or embezzlement. *Nonfeasance*, however, means not acting; and most significantly as a general rule under the common law there is no legal duty imposed on a person to affirmatively act to help, aid, rescue, or benefit another person. As a result, generally, nonfeasance, that is, not acting, is not legally actionable as the tort of negligence. The failure to act in contract, moreover, that is, the breach of a contractual promise, will not give rise to tort liability under the nonfeasance doctrine, and consequently the aggrieved party can only sue for economic loss based on a breach of contract theory (*Doe v. Yackculic*, 2019, applying Texas law). However, when one acts and undertakes the performance of a positive and assertive act then the omission of a proper aspect of performance of that act will be regarded as misfeasance (*Mems v. LaBruyere*, 2019, applying Texas law). Similarly, if there is a "special relationship" between the parties, such as common carrier and customer, innkeeper and guest, or school personnel and students, then there is an affirmative duty to help and aid, and thus the failure to do so will result in legal liability (*Doe v. Hotchkiss Sch.*, 2019, applying Connecticut law). An example of the lack of a special relationship is the Michigan appeals court case of *Estate of Kermath v. Independent Oxford, LLC* (2020), where the elderly resident, with dementia and a deteriorating mental state, of a residential facility wandered off the facility at night in only her nightgown, suffered frostbite and hypothermia, and died. Her estate sued contending the residential facility owed her a duty of care due to the existence of a special relationship. However, the appeals court ruled that no special relationship existed because the facility was only a private residential facility for seniors and not a nursing home. Although some limited services and assistance were provided to the residents, the facility was geared for seniors who wished to live independently. Moreover, the family of the elderly resident had contracted with a third-party medical provider to provide medical services to the resident. Thus, the

Michigan appeals court stated that the nonfeasance doctrine applied, and consequently there was no liability for the residential facility because of the lack of a special relationship. Similarly, simply walking by a pharmacy where one usually shops on the way home did not create a special relationship between the pharmacy and walker, and thus the pharmacy was not liable for a light that was out and the resulting darkness and the criminal attack on the walker by a third person since the pharmacy had no legal duty to protect the walker from the criminal conduct (*Dunn v. Garfield Beach CVS, LLC*, 2020, applying California law).

The "classic" nonfeasance case is a drowning example, where the expert swimmer in a boat with a rope and life preserver does nothing and watches the victim drown. The old English precedents dealt with drowning cases; and as such so long as one did not cause the risk of drowning, for example, by pushing another person into the water, there is no legal liability for not rescuing a drowning person. Sad-to-say, one does not have to go back to the old English common law for precedents, because in Ft. Lauderdale, Florida in the summer of 2017 occurred a horrendous case. Apparently, a person with disability fell into pond and was struggling to survive. Five young men, between the ages of 14 and 16, not only did not help the victim or call for help, but also mocked and ridiculed him as he struggled. Moreover, and this is hard to believe happened in a civilized society, they in fact videotaped him on a cell phone while watching him drown and die. The young men, moreover, showed no remorse. The local prosecutor condemned their actions and inaction as "callous" (which seems too mild a word); but stated there would be no prosecution since there was no duty to rescue based on the nonfeasance doctrine (Valencia and Sayers, 2017). A civil lawsuit would be precluded based on the same rationale. As a general rule the state of Florida as well as other states, based on the doctrine of nonfeasance, do not have laws obligating citizens and residents to render aid, help anyone in distress, or even call for help. Therefore, legally, there is no liability; morally, however, is another question.

Management Implications and Recommendations:

Managers must be aware that there are many exceptions to the general nonfeasance rule. Even if one does not have a duty to act, once one decides to act and affirmatively undertakes to do so for the assistance or benefit of another, one then has a duty to act carefully. Consequently, if the careless "rescuing" causes injury then tort liability for negligence may exist. Similarly, if the defendant's own negligence places another in danger, the defendant is now under an obligation to use reasonable care to aid or rescue that person. Another example stems from the old common law whereby common carriers and innkeepers are under an affirmative legal duty to warn and to aid and assist passengers and guests and to prevent injuries to them and to third parties. As noted, statutes supersede the common law. As such, a state statute may impose a duty to act affirmatively, for example, requiring school administrators and faculty to report child abuse, or for a health-care worker to report elder abuse at any time. Finally, members of a profession may be obligated not by the law, but by the codes of ethics of their profession, to affirmatively act to aid people, for example, a registered nurse who is morally bound by the code of ethics of the nursing profession and the Florence Nightingale Oath to provide medical assistance.

Summary

This chapter to the book dealt with certain very important fundamental common law concepts. Initially, definitions of the law, including the distinctions between civil and criminal law, and common law, also called case law, and statutory law, were provided. Two doctrines critical to the operation of the common law – the system of precedents and the doctrine of *stare decisis* – were explained. The definition and nature of a tort, the distinction between intentional torts and negligence, as well as the differentiation of torts from crimes and breach of contract, also were provided. The authors next distinguished legal misfeasance, that is, acting in a wrongful illegal manner, from legal nonfeasance, that is, not acting at all; and then the authors discussed the legal liability ensuing from both doctrines. Suggestions and recommendations to management and employers were supplied regarding potential liability under the legal nonfeasance doctrine. In the next chapter of the book we will cover intentional torts, mainly to the person, but also to property.

CHAPTER III - INTENTIONAL TORTS

A "*tort*" as recognized in the common law is a civil legal wrong where redress can be obtained in the form of monetary damages. The three major categories of torts in the United States are intentional torts, the tort of negligence, and the doctrine of strict tort liability. In a civilized society, a person cannot intentionally injure another person or harm his or her property. Each person in society is entitled to have certain interests, such as freedom from bodily injury, protected. If another person intentionally invades such a protected interest, the perpetrator violates a legal duty to the injured person who as a result has the legal right to sue for damages for the intentional wrong. Moreover, in a civilized society, everyone is held to a legal duty to exercise reasonable care when one acts. Thus, the victim of one who acts in a careless manner can bring a lawsuit for damages to compensate for the injury caused by the violation of the duty to exercise reasonable care. Such a lawsuit is premised on the tort of negligence. Finally, society by means of the legal system may create doctrines that impose liability without fault for types of activities that the law brands as "ultra-hazardous." In such a case, the person so acting is held accountable, even without any intentional wrongdoing or even negligent conduct, for any resultant harm. This type of tort liability without fault is called "strict liability" and is premised on utilitarian rationales.

Intentional torts provide a legal remedy for those people whose protected personal or property interests are purposefully invaded or harmed by another. The required elements, or components, to an intentional tort lawsuit generally are: 1) a purposeful wrongful act by another, 2) requisite intent, 3) causation, and 4) damages. The victim as the plaintiff must establish all these elements to the tort in order to have a *prima facie* (or initial) case against the defendant actor. A purposeful act that is committed volitionally, that is, voluntarily, by the defendant is first required. Thus, if one strikes another during the throes of a medical seizure, or if one is pushed by a wrongdoer into a third party who suffers harm, one has not committed a volitional act. This act, of course, must intentionally invade a legally protected interest and consequently be a wrongful act. The requisite intent can be specific or general. Specific intent exists when a person's objective is to cause a certain result or consequences; whereas general intent exists when a person does not have a specific goal or result, but acts knowing with substantial certainty that certain consequences will ensue. An example of the latter intent would occur when a person does intend to push another person, who falls and injures himself or herself. The actor may not have intended that specific harm; but is liable nonetheless due to the substantial certainty of the victim falling and injuring himself or herself. An interesting old common law doctrine concerning intent and intentional torts is called the "*transferred intent*" doctrine, usually found in assault and battery cases. Transferred intent is a legal device that is used when a defendant intends to cause harm to one person, but he or she in fact injures another person. The defendant's intent to commit the wrongful act is thus transferred from the intended "target" to the actual victim, who then can sue for the appropriate intentional tort. The causation requirement means that the harmful result giving rise to liability must have been caused by the defendant's wrongful act. The causation test will be met when the conduct of the defendant is a substantial factor in bringing about the plaintiff's injury. Finally, there must be some type of injury or harm, which can be minor, but nevertheless will support an award of damages, including punitive damages.

This chapter to the book will first cover the older common law intentional torts of battery and assault and false imprisonment. The authors will cover the civil law aspects of these torts, though their commission may also be a crime. The authors will mention an important business ramification to these torts, which deals with the defense afforded to merchants under the common law, and now mainly by statute, typically called Merchants Protection statutes, to detain and to make reasonable investigations of suspected shoplifters. Next, the authors will examine the tort of intentional infliction of emotional distress, which will be differentiated from the tort of negligent infliction of emotional distress. Although rare in a business context the tort of intentional infliction of emotional distress may arise, particularly in the context of "bullying" and harassment in the workplace. The authors then will analyze four intentional torts with clear business consequences – invasion of privacy, interference with contract or business relations, defamation, and fraud. Note that fraud will be treated in the old common law sense of "deceit," that is, purposeful, knowing misrepresentations. Note too that regarding defamation the important qualified privilege will be covered in detail in the context of employment. Next, the authors will cover the breach of loyalty by employees which in some states is considered the breach of a fiduciary duty and thus the equivalent of an intentional tort. The authors then will cover the violation of public policy doctrine, which similarly in some states is viewed as an intentional tort violation. Brief mention will be made of the tort of *wrongful institution of legal proceedings*, also called "*malicious prosecution*," as well as the related but broader tort of "*abuse of process*." Although the bulk of this chapter deals with intentional torts to the person, the authors will briefly cover the three main intentional torts to property – trespass to land, trespass to chattels, and conversion, which also can be crimes. Specific defenses to certain preceding intentional torts will be stated as will be general defenses applicable to all intentional torts. Finally, the authors will provide suggestions and recommendations to employers and managers on how to avoid liability for these intentional torts.

Battery

The first intentional tort to the person is a "*battery*." A battery is a purposeful, intentional act by the defendant that causes a harmful or offensive contact to the person of the plaintiff. "Harmful" or "offensive" conduct is measured by the standard of a reasonably prudent person, that is, a person of ordinary sensibilities and not an overly sensitive person. The "person" of the plaintiff refers to not only the physical body of the plaintiff, but his or her clothes, or a purse or laptop suspended from the body. It is noteworthy to point out that there is no apprehension requirement for a battery; thus, a plaintiff may recover for a battery even though he or she was not even conscious of the harmful or offensive conduct, for example, in the "classic" case of the "kissing bandit" who kissed his (or was it her?) "victims" while they were sleeping and who placed a rose on their chests. There is no requirement of an actual injury, for example, a supervisor purposefully slapping an employee even if the supervisor did not intend to harm the employee (Legal Aid, 2020). The Georgia court of appeals stated in *Carnegay v. Wal-Mart Stores* (2020) that the touching can be "minimal" so long as it is offensive. As such, for a battery the plaintiff can recover nominal damages even though there are no material damages sustained by the plaintiff. Moreover, nominal damages can serve in many jurisdictions as a predicate for a punitive damage recovery. For example, a male supervisor deliberately patting a female colleague on the rear may not cause her actual physical harm, but it certainly is "offensive" conduct by any ordinary standard of reasonableness, and thus grounds for a battery, including potentially punitive damages, as well as being the basis for a sexual harassment lawsuit (Legal Aid, 2020).

Assault

Closely related to a battery is its "cousin," the "*assault*." An assault is an act by a defendant which causes a reasonable apprehension of fear in the victim of an immediate harmful or offensive contact to the victim's person, that is, the fear of a battery. "Apprehension" is measured by the "reasonableness" test; and as such the fear of harm must be a reasonable expectation and not an exaggerated one. Moreover, as opposed to a battery, in order to have this fearful apprehension or expectation, the plaintiff must have been aware of the defendant's act. However, a person may be placed in a situation of reasonable apprehension of immediate harmful or offensive conduct, even though the defendant is not actually capable of committing a battery on the plaintiff. This circumstance is called the "apparent ability" doctrine; and the classic example arises when the wrongdoer points an unloaded gun at the victim who does not know that the gun is unloaded. Legally, it is sufficient if the defendant has the apparent ability to bring about the contact. Words alone, as a general rule, no matter how violent, do not constitute an assault; rather some overt act is necessary, such as a co-worker raising his or her arm as if to strike or making a fist, thereby causing one to have a reasonable belief that one is going to be struck (Legal Aid, 2020). Another workplace example regarding assault and battery claims might be when a supervisor and an employee are "horsing around" and the situation gets a bit out of hand (Legal Aid, 2020). Words, however, may form the basis of other independent intentional torts, as will be seen. Finally, with assault there is a requirement of immediacy. That is, the apprehension must be of immediate harmful or offensive conduct; consequently, neither the threat of future harmful contact nor a conditional threat is sufficient for an assault. Also, assault and battery claims typically are not covered by Workers' Compensation statutes since the conduct involved is not part of the course or scope of the employer's normal business operations and routine (Legal Aid, 2020).

False Imprisonment

The next intentional tort to the person is "*false imprisonment*." This tort occurs when a defendant acts or fails to act and thereby confines or restrains the plaintiff to a bounded area. Confinement or restraint can be effectuated by physical barriers or by physical force directed at the plaintiff or a member of his or her family as well as physical force being directed at the plaintiff's property. Threats of physical force or harm by words, acts, or gestures to oneself or one's family or one's property will be sufficient for the tort so long as there is a reasonable apprehension that force will be used if the plaintiff does not submit (*Carnegay v. Wal-Mart Stores*, 2020, applying Georgia law). Also constituting false imprisonment will be the failure to provide a means of escape or egress, even when the plaintiff originally has come under the defendant's control. Generally, moral pressures and conditional threats will be insufficient means of confinement or restraint. There is, however, no need to resist the physical force used to confine or restrain the plaintiff. Moreover, the time of confinement and restraint are immaterial for the cause of action, though material as to the amount of damages. Moreover, there is no requirement that the plaintiff be aware of the confinement. Finally, for an area to be "bounded," the plaintiff's freedom of movement must be limited in all directions. Merely blocking one of many exits is insufficient; and thus if there is a reasonable means of escape, which the plaintiff was aware of, the area is not bounded, and there is no tort liability.

Management Implications and Recommendations:

Employers and managers must be aware that regarding assault and battery claims that workplace violence rarely occurs without some type of warning. Consequently, England (2020) advises that employers develop strategies and tactics to ward off workplace violence and assault and battery lawsuits. As such, England (2020) recommends the following: the use of workplace training, mediators, facilitations, and team-building exercises; contacting and talking to an employee who shows signs of anger, irritation, and/or distress; establishing a reporting procedure for employees to use if they observe violence, fear potential violence, or feel threatened by violence; the use of professional third parties to meet individually with an employee or with groups of employees to try to resolve conflicts and defuse potentially violent situations; train managers, supervisors, and all personnel how to deal with violence and potential violence; and finally in a "worst case" violence scenario provide emergency preparedness training to stem the violence and ensue safety and security. Workplace violence and how to avoid it will also be covered in a discussion of workplace bullying and the tort of intentional infliction of emotional distress.

Managers also must be aware that one important business ramification of the assault, battery, and false imprisonment torts occurs in shoplifting cases where a merchant suspects a person of shoplifting, and then detains – physically or by threats - that person to make an investigation. What exactly is the merchant's liability for false imprisonment and these other torts? Under the common law as well as pursuant to several state statutes merchants have been accorded a "privilege" to detain a suspected shoplifter for an investigation. This privilege also extends to a merchant's security personnel. There typically are three basic elements to this merchant's or shopkeeper's privilege: 1) the merchant must have a reasonable belief as to the occurrence of a theft, which must be on store property; 2) the detention must be conducted in a reasonable manner, and concomitantly only non-deadly force can be used; 3) the detention must be for a reasonable period of time; and 4) only for the purposes of making an investigation as to the suspected theft (Carnegay v. Wal-Mart Stores, 2020, applying Georgia law). Typically, once a court determines that a detention has occurred, a jury then determines if the grounds for the detention and the manner of the detention were reasonable and if the purpose was proper (Carnegay v. Wal-Mart Stores, 2020, applying Georgia law). Under the common law, this privilege was referred to as the merchant's or shopkeeper's "shoplifter detention" privilege, but today pursuant to modern state statutes, the privilege is more euphemistically referred to as a "merchant's protection" privilege. Nevertheless, the merchant must be very careful in exercising this privilege because if abused the alleged shoplifter can sue for the intentional tort of false imprisonment as well as false arrest. Hamblen (2020) provides the following recommendations to properly use the protection afforded by the statute and thus to avoid liability, to wit: the merchant and/or its security personnel must witness the shoplifter select, conceal, or carry away merchandise; continual observance of the shoplifter must be maintained; the shoplifter must be observed not paying for the merchandise; the shoplifter must be detained in or near the store; reasonable non-deadly force can be used if the shoplifter resists detainment or attempts to flee, but the merchant should avoid detaining the shoplifter in a confined area; the investigation also should be conducted on or near the store; and, very importantly, the merchant must take utmost care to ensure that its security personnel are not engaging in racial profiling when they accuse a person of shoplifting.

Intentional Infliction of Emotional Distress

This section examines the common law tort of *intentional infliction of emotional distress* in the context of the modern-day employment relationship. The focus is to examine the efficaciousness of the tort as a cause of action by an employee, especially a discharged at-will employee, against his or her manager, colleagues, and/or employer, especially the latter. This section also examines the efficacy of the tort as a means of legal redress for employees who suffer "bullying" behavior in the workplace. "*Bullying*" can be viewed as repeated mistreatment, emotionally and/or physically, of one person by another (or others), including abusive, threatening, humiliating, and/or intimidating conduct, including verbal abuse, which prevents a person from performing at work. The tort of intentional infliction of emotional distress arises when the defendant purposefully acts in an extreme, outrageous, and atrocious manner and thereby causes the plaintiff to suffer severe emotional distress. The wrongful conduct must be conduct that goes beyond all bounds of decency tolerated by a civilized society. Such conduct is again measured by a "reasonableness" test. Mere indignities and annoyances are insufficient. However, if the defendant knows that the victim is more sensitive and thus more susceptible to emotional distress than an ordinary person, then the defendant's conduct will be measured by that "sensitivity" standard. Children and the elderly would be examples of usually more sensitive people. Although business examples of this intentional tort are rare, they do occur, usually in a situation where an employee is discharged in an abusive, threatening, humiliating, mocking, and disrespectful manner in full view of his or her co-workers. Although the employer may have the legal right to discharge, especially if the employee is an *employee at-will*, that is, one not contractually protected regarding discharge, the outrageous manner of the discharge may give rise to a separate independent tort.

In order to analyze the tort of intentional infliction of emotional distress in the employment sector, it is first necessary to set forth the elements of this cause of action. Although this body of law is state-specific, there are several components to the tort which the plaintiff bringing the lawsuit must establish to prevail: 1) the defendant intended to purposefully inflict emotional distress on a person; 2) the conduct of the defendant (the employer in the context herein) was extreme and outrageous; 3) the actions of the defendant caused the plaintiff to suffer emotional distress; and 4) the resulting emotional distress was severe (see, for example, *Kamdem-Ouaffo v. Balchem Corp.*, 2018, applying New York law). The burden of proof and persuasion is on the party bringing the lawsuit, the plaintiff employee in the principal context herein, to establish all the elements of the cause of action. The typical burden of proof in a civil case is the "preponderance of the evidence" standard; however, some courts for intentional infliction of emotional distress cases require that the plaintiff demonstrate the elements of the case by providing "substantial evidence."

It is also necessary to point out that the tort of intentional infliction of emotional distress often arises in the context of the employment at-will doctrine, specifically when an at-will employee is discharged for reasons that the terminated employee feels are unfair or unjust or when the employee believes that he or she was discharged in a coercive, abusive, or retaliatory manner. Pursuant to the *employment at-will* doctrine, which the vast majority of states in the United States adhere to, an employee at-will is an employee without a contract which limits the circumstances which he or she can be discharged, meaning that the at-will employee can be terminated at any time for no reason, any reason, even a morally bad one, without any explanation or justification, and without notice or warning; but the employee cannot be discharged for an illegal reason or in an illegal manner. Discharging the employee for an illegal reason, such as discrimination based on an impermissible category such as race or religion, or in an illegal manner, such as by the employer committing an independent tort, converts the legal but perhaps immoral discharge into a "wrongful discharge," that is, an illegal one, thereby affording the discharged employee a legal cause of action against his or her employer.

Accordingly, the discharged at-will employee will be looking to carve out some sort of "exception" to the employment at-will doctrine to secure legal redress against the employer, such as by presenting evidence that the manner of the discharge was extreme or outrageous. The tort of intentional infliction of emotional distress may provide the terminated employee with the legal means to contest the discharge. However, many states do not have a cause of action for the wrongful and/or abusive discharge of an at-will employee, and thus will be very reticent in the discharged employee attempting to supersede his or her at-will status by using the intentional tort of infliction of emotional distress to challenge a discharge (see, for example, *Kamdem-Ouaffo v. Balchem Corp.*, 2018, applying New York law). For example, terminating an at-will employee, a coach, because the coach did not meet the core beliefs, mission, and values of the school was "hardly extreme and outrageous conduct" (*Carrington v. Carolina Day Sch., Inc.*, 2020, applying North Carolina law).

Some states even maintain that discharging an employee based on racial or disability discrimination, though "insulting and humiliating" and at the "core of federal Civil Rights Acts," nonetheless is not insufficiently outrageous or extreme to convert a termination into the intentional infliction of emotional distress tort (see, for example, *Fisher v. Nissan N. Am., Inc.*, 2020, applying Tennessee law), although redress could be provided by the federal statutes. However, it also should be pointed out that the tort may be the means of legal redress for an employee who is subject to "bullying" behavior in the workplace. First, though, it is necessary to examine in detail the "elements," that is the components, to this common law tort.

The conduct necessary to support a cause of action of intentional infliction of emotional distress must be extreme and outrageous; consequently, the conduct must go beyond the bounds of decency recognized by a civil society; the conduct must be intolerable in a civilized society; it must be atrocious (*Thomas v. Hospital Board of Directors of Lee County*, 2010, applying Florida law). As such, verbal outbursts by a supervisor, raised voices, verbal alterations, calling an employee a "hell employee," telling him to take his belongings to human resources and to never to return again, and ultimately terminating him, did not rise to the level of extreme and outrageous conduct (*Kamdem-Ouaffo v. Balchem Corp*., 2018, applying New York law). In the context of an employment lawsuit, the defendant calling the plaintiff a "concubine" and a "mistress" was not sufficiently outrageous, extreme, or indecent to support the tort (*Ifantides v. Wisniewski*, 2020, applying New York law). Merely demoting an employee to clerical shredding and scanning duties in an office setting will not support a worker's intentional infliction of emotional distress claim against the employer even if the employee felt that the tasks were humiliating and caused the employee to be ostracized by fellow workers since such employer actions were not totally intolerable in a civilized society (*McMiller v. Precision Metal Products, Inc,* 2015, applying Connecticut law). Moreover, "narrowmindedness and meanspiritedness," criticism of job performance, conditional threats of termination, "calling names," insulting, derogatory remarks, and even taunting were not adjudged to be sufficiently atrocious and intolerable for tort liability (*Kamdem-Ouaffo v. Balchem Corp*., 2018, applying New York law). Similarly, mere verbal abuse, insults, indignities, annoyances, bad manners, rudeness, or insensitivity typically will not be sufficient to be deemed "extreme" and "outrageous" and thus support a cause of action for intentional infliction of emotional distress (*Koutsouradis v. Delta Airlines, Inc*., 2005, applying Florida law). To demonstrate how difficult it is to meet the outrageous standard for this tort, reference can be made to the Texas supreme court decision in *Creditwatch v. Jackson* (2005), where the court ruled that a supervisor's alleged sexual advances and retaliatory conduct towards a subordinate employee, though condemned as "callous, meddlesome, mean-spirited, officious, overbearing, and vindictive," were nonetheless neither sufficiently atrocious nor intolerable to sustain a cause of action of intentional infliction of emotional distress. Regrettably perhaps, at least pursuant to this tort, everyone must deal with certain slights, insults, and even misconduct at the workplace and otherwise.

Moreover, the test to determine if the misconduct is outrageous or atrocious is an objective, and not a subjective, one. That is, outrageousness is measured by the standard of a reasonable and prudent person and not the subjective feelings of the aggrieved party (*Liberty Mutual Insurance Company v. Steadman*, 2007, applying Florida law). For example, a Delaware court upheld a jury award in favor of a teenage worker for his intentional infliction of emotional distress claim. The Delaware Superior Court stated it was not surprised of the jury's $500,000 award because on multiple occasions the defendant business owners drugged and sexually assaulted him at their house over an eight-month period (*DeLucia v. Great Stuff, Inc.*, 2017). The teenager worker testified that he felt disgusted and in a state of turmoil, and he became resentful, confused, and more reclusive and hated himself because of the sexual assaults that occurred to him by his employer's principals, all of which the court held could be a reasonable basis by the jury to conclude the conduct was outrageous and atrocious (*DeLucia v. Great Stuff, Inc.*, 2017). In determining whether certain conduct is extreme and outrageous the courts will look at the totality of the circumstances involved, particularly if certain objectionable conduct is repeated, ongoing, and regular. As such, conduct which is isolated in the form of a single incident or standing alone may not be sufficient to establish a case but if the conduct is repetitive and forms a larger regular pattern of offensive conduct the actions in total could rise to the level of extreme and outrageous behavior. However, one single act could be so egregiously severe or objectionable that it could amount to extreme and outrageous conduct.

Since the context of this book is the workplace it is important to also point out that the fact that the offending or abusive party is a manager or supervisor of the employee or someone in a "position of power" over the employee may worsen the offensive nature of the actions to render them extreme and outrageous as well as exacerbate the severity of the emotional response. The federal Tenth Circuit Court of Appeals in *Hasen v. Skywest Airlines* (2016) recognized the Wyoming supreme court precedent specifically addressing the intentional infliction of emotional distress claims in the context of employer-employee relationships. The relationship between the parties is a significant factor in determining outrageousness; and it is only natural that an employer's position of power over an employee may enhance the employer's ability to do harm to the worker. In *Hansen*, the employee suffered from PTSD, and his fellow male supervisors and managers sexually harassed him in the workplace in the form of physical unwanted touching; rubbing and pressing their genitals against him when passing him; conditioning promotions based on sexual interactions with them; sending unsolicited explicit e-mails to him; engaging in ongoing graphic "sex" talk at work to him; solicitating sexual conduct from him on occasions during work periods; and retaliating when he would not share hotel rooms or a hot tub with them during travel periods for training. The federal court felt that these allegations were sufficient to allow a jury to decide his intentional infliction of emotional distress claim against his employer because reasonable persons could determine that the conduct was extreme and outrageous, compounded by the fact that the conduct was from those in a position of power and direct authority over the worker (*Hasen v. Skywest Airlines,* 2016). To further illustrate, an elementary teacher's allegations that her school's principal conduct rose to the level of "extreme and outrageous" to avoid dismissal of her complaint against her employer in the case of *Brown v. Kourentsos* (2016), applying Illinois law. In that federal trial court case, a principal continually mocked and berated the plaintiff for missing days off when she was recovering from a suicide attempt. The principal also accused her, in front of other educators, of stealing yarn from classroom supplies and smoking illegal substances on school premises, all of which were untrue. The principal continued the mistreatment of the teacher in front of her peers, making fun of her alleged inability to write, slamming a door near her after a meeting had ended nearly missing her, inappropriately conducting classroom observation visits, and mocking her for hiring an attorney to deal with this workplace mistreatment. The court held that these allegations were beyond the "garden variety" workplace complaints and unpleasantries typical in an employer/employee dispute, and the potential harm of the accusations against the teacher was considerable to her continued professional career (*Brown v. Kourentsos,* 2016).

As with any intentional tort cause of action, intent is required to sustain a lawsuit. That is, the defendant wrongdoer must have acted intentionally and purposefully to inflict emotional distress on the aggrieved plaintiff. The intent requirement is also satisfied when the evidence indicates that the defendant acted recklessly, that is, with a deliberate or conscious or reckless disregard or indifference that emotional distress would follow from certain conduct. In *McClean v. Pine Eagle School District No. 61* (2016), applying Oregon law, the defendant school conducted an announced "active shooter" drill in which the plaintiff teacher suffered mental anguish and suffering when masked gunmen actors roomed the school hallways, lighting firecrackers and firing starter pistols loaded with blanks at school employees including directly at the plaintiff. The school defended itself against the teacher's intentional infliction of emotional distress action by claiming they did not intend to inflict emotional distress on the plaintiff. The court rejected the school's summary judgment motion based on this rationale because the general intent of the exercise was to place the workers in a stressful situation or at least the employer knew with substantial certainty that its agent's conduct would cause such distress. Therefore, the court concluded that a reasonable jury also could find that defendants' actions were intended, extreme and outrageous (*McClean v. Pine Eagle School District No. 61,* 2016).

Causation is another element to the legal wrong of intentional infliction of emotional distress. That is, there must be a causal connection between the defendant's intentional conduct and the plaintiff's subsequent emotional distress. Causation can be found when the distress was the primary consequence of the intended actions, where there is a probability that the conduct would cause distress, or when the distress was a reasonably foreseeable consequence of the intentional conduct. In the Eleventh Circuit Court of Appeals case of *Malphurs v. Cooling Towers Systems, Inc.* (2017), applying Georgia law, the plaintiff worked for the employer for thirty days, and the jury found in favor of her intentional infliction of emotional distress claim against the company. In that case the jury believed the plaintiff's testimony that the company's owner constantly made comments about wanting to have sex with her and that he took her hand and forced it to touch his erect penis. She also testified that on "four or five" occasions he brushed his groin against her so that she would feel his erect penis on her shoulder. Further the plaintiff said that the company owner was always touching her butt, breasts, and inner thigh and shoulders, and he squeezed her nipple, and on two other occasions reached up beneath her shirt and touching her bare breast. The court upheld the jury finding in favor of the plaintiff's intentional infliction of emotional distress claim against the employer because a reasonable jury could, and did, conclude that the owner's actions caused the worker's emotional distress because such actions would naturally humiliate, embarrass, frighten, or outrage an employee in the workplace (*Malphurs v. Cooling Towers Systems, Inc.*, 2017).

The fact that the intentional extreme and outrageous conduct in fact caused emotional distress is thus an essential component to the legal wrong of intentional infliction of emotional distress. Emotional distress means that a person is harmed, injured, disturbed, or impaired in his or her tranquility. Moreover, the distress caused must be severe or serious; consequently, plaintiffs seeking to recover for emotional distress must show that their distress was particularly acute and more than being merely upset or angry. Many workplace actions can cause distress to the employee. However, a plaintiff employee must allege more than the fact that he or she was caused distress, even intentionally, by certain workplace conduct; rather, the plaintiff employee must demonstrate that the distress was in fact severe and that such distress would be considered severe to a reasonable person or a person of ordinary sensibilities. For example, in the federal district court case of *Dokes v. Safeway, Inc.* (2018), applying California law, the plaintiff employee, who was terminated for violating store alcohol sales rules, testified that as a result he was upset, angry, depressed, and worried about supporting his family; but the court ruled that such emotional distress was not sufficiently severe or serious to support a cause of action for intentional infliction of emotional distress. Similarly, the facts alleged by the plaintiff in *Grost M.D. vs. United States* (2015), a federal district court case applying Texas law, fell short in this regard when the court granted the employer's summary judgement against her intentional tort claim because the plaintiff failed to offer any proof regarding the severity of her alleged mental anguish beyond mere allegations that her workplace conditions caused her grief, severe disappointment, indignation, wounded pride, shame, despair and/or public humiliation.

Yet medical testimony or any expert testimony is not necessarily required for there to be a finding of severe distress. However, the problem is that stand-alone claims for emotional harm, i.e., claims unaccompanied by any physical injury, are difficult to win. Plaintiffs in these cases are typically required to prove that their emotional injury is severe and serious, that is, distress beyond that which a reasonable person would be expected to tolerate. As such, the conduct could be so outrageous and extreme so that it gives credence to the assertion that the plaintiff employee suffered severe distress. Of course, having an expert witness to testify as to the presence and severity of the distress will naturally help the aggrieved plaintiff employee to establish his or her case for intentional infliction of emotional distress. However, evidence of any physical impact or harm is not required to sustain a lawsuit for intentional infliction of emotional distress, as opposed to a lawsuit for negligent infliction of emotional distress, as will be seen. However, if there is evidence of objective manifestations of physical harm, such as shock or illness, then naturally such evidence will make it easier for the plaintiff employee to prove that the distress caused was severe.

Nevertheless, even if the plaintiff employee can show that his or her distress was severe, he or she still must demonstrate that the distress would be construed as severe to a reasonable person, that is, a reasonable employee in the same or similar circumstances. In the case of *Cruz v. English Nanny & Governess School, Inc.,* 2017), an Ohio appeals court case, the plaintiff was attending courses at a prestigious trade school which was teaching students how to be professional nannies and governesses. Upon graduation, she was placed by the school's employment agency at a residential site for a weekend. While working at the site, she observed a father sexually abusing one of his young daughters which she reported to the school upon her return. The school authorities put tremendous pressure upon her not to report the child sexual abuse allegations to authorities and tried to convince her she did not really see what she thought she saw. The school officials also "black-balled" her and placed undue influence over her in order to force her to participate in an alleged cover-up of the sexual child abuse she had personally observed. The plaintiff sued the school and its work placement agency for emotional distress; and the jury awarded her considerable damages, which were ultimately reduced to about $194,000.00 plus recovery of an additional $125,500.00 in attorneys' fees and costs. The court upheld the jury award since the plaintiff established that she suffered anxiety, low self-esteem, and sleepiness (*Cruz vs. English Nanny & Governess School, Inc.,* 2017). The appeals court felt that the jury could rightfully conclude she suffered distress after hearing from a medical expert supporting her claim of distress and her direct testimony that the defendant's actions caused her to feel that she was "going crazy." Finally, a legal and practical problem arises in intentional infliction of emotional distress law when the aggrieved party is a person of sensitivity or susceptibility to mental anguish. According to an old common law maxim, "the plaintiff takes the defendant as it finds him or her," and thus the plaintiff may be liable to the distress caused to a person who is emotionally vulnerable. However, the aggrieved party bringing the lawsuit still must show that the severe distress caused would be reasonable to a person with that same special sensitivity and susceptibility.

Various tort damages are available for the intentional tort of infliction of emotional distress. Compensatory damages are available to the aggrieved plaintiff pursuant to the tort of intentional infliction of emotional distress. Compensatory damages are broadly construed and thus can encompass pecuniary awards for mental and emotional pain and anguish, humiliation, ridicule, indignation, shock, grief, rage, shame, fright, despair, anxiety, stress, depression, as well as for any physical harm caused by the defendant's extreme and outrageous conduct. The practical problem, however, is that most of the aforementioned harms are difficult to estimate and to prove. Damages, moreover, can include medical expenses, economic losses, lost income or wages, lessening of earning capacity or future profits, as well as loss of consortium. However, additional damages in the form of punitive damages generally cannot be recovered since the outrageous action itself forms the basis for the cause of action, and consequently an award of compensatory damages is deemed to be sufficiently punitive and deterrent.

The jury's role in emotional distress cases is another problematic issue in this type of lawsuit. In some states the issue of whether conduct is sufficiently "outrageous" is a question of fact for the jury to determine, whereas in other states the issue is deemed to be a question of law for the judge to determine (see, e.g., *De La Campa v. Grifols America, Inc*., 2002, applying Florida law). In *Grost M.D. v. United States* (2015), the federal district court, applying Texas law, held that even though the employee's supervisor refused on one occasion to shake her hand at work, failed to include her in social gatherings outside of work, and at one time called her "neurotic," and twice yelled at her in the workplace, and listed her deficiencies to other fellow doctors, these occurrences, though rude and insulting, did not raise a genuine issue of fact as to whether the supervisor engaged in the level of "terrorizing, threatening, and assaultive conduct" necessary to elevate those employer actions outside the context of an ordinary employment dispute. Thus, the court granted summary judgment against the plaintiff on her intentional infliction of emotional distress claim before it reached a jury (*Grost M.D. vs. United States*, 2015). However, in other states the court first makes a determination as to whether the conduct is outrageous; and if there is a judicial determination that reasonable minds could disagree as to the outrageous nature of the defendant's conduct, the issue becomes one for the jury to resolve. In *Gillespie v. City of Battle Creek* (2015), the federal district court, applying Michigan law, refused to dismiss the emotional distress claims against a city police force that installed a video recorder in the female locker room that recorded a partially nude female plaintiff police officer. The female officer sued; and the court held that "reasonable minds could differ" as to whether recording and playing the video during an investigation conducted by male colleagues was sufficiently extreme and outrageous to result in liability. This was the same result reached in the federal district court case of *Kubler v. Heritage Automotive Group, Inc.* (2017), applying Vermont law, where a male coworker routinely assaulted a female worker and who would "stomp his foot at her," and would lean into her while simultaneously telling her to “get the ____ out of his way" and consequently causing her to continually shake with fear in the workplace. The court concluded that a reasonable jury could find this conduct sufficiently extreme and outrageous and that this behavior easily transcended the normal ignoble unpleasant workplace conduct. To compare, in *Guobadia v. Irowa*, (2015), the federal district court, applying New York law, rejected the defendant employer’s summary judgment motion for dismissal of the plaintiff's emotional distress claim because, there was evidence that the live-in domestic worker was physically abused by the employer who kept her isolated from others and who threatened to have her arrested or deported if she spoke to people outside the home. This situation created a genuine issue of fact for the jury to decide if the employer’s actions were extreme and outrageous. In another case, *McManus v. Auchincloss* (2015), an Oregon appeals court case, the plaintiff was a full-time, live-in, house personal assistant whose job duties included cooking, serving meals, housecleaning, laundry, pet care, yard work, grocery shopping, and organizing defendant's personal affairs. Throughout the employment the home-owner employer constantly exposed the worker to his viewing of child pornography, and when the worker cooperated with the police for the home-owner’s arrest, the worker was fired and barred from retrieving his belongings from the house. The appeals court reversed the trial court’s granting the defendant’s motion for summary judgment for dismissal of the employee’s intentional infliction of emotional distress claim. In doing so, the appeals court held that the plaintiff made a *prima facie* case of intentional infliction of emotional distress, and that a reasonable jury could find that defendant's actions violated social norms in the workplace beyond all tolerable bounds of civilized behavior (*McManus v. Auchincloss*, 2015). Although not an employer-employee case *per se*, mention should be made of a very tragic 2018 case where a family is suing Royal Caribbean cruise lines for negligently causing the death of their son, who fell overboard, by providing him with too much alcohol. The family is also suing for the intentional infliction of emotional distress, contending that their distress was caused by the cruise line telling the ship and media that their son had intentionally fallen overboard, thereby causing the family to believe he had committed suicide, although many witnesses told ship officials that their son slipped from a handrail while pretending to go overboard in response to a joking suggestion by another passenger (Hurtibise, 2018).

Regarding the defenses to this tort, it first must be noted that there are no specific affirmative defenses to the tort of intentional infliction of emotional distress, though the traditional general tort defenses to intentional torts – consent and self-defense – could be applicable. Moreover, the intentional infliction of emotional distress cause of action could be preempted by a statute, for example, by means of the exclusivity provisions of state Workers' Compensation acts if the conduct in question is a normal aspect of the employer relationship, as explained in *Thomas vs. Starz Entertainment LLC* (2016). In the *Thomas* case, the plaintiff's intentional infliction of emotional distress claim was preempted by the California's Workers Compensation statute even though the actions by the employer allegedly caused the worker to feel ridiculed and caused him to suffer depression and anxiety because of the work environment. The same result was reached in the case of *Van v. Language Line Services, Inc* (2016), a federal district court case applying California law, where the employee attempted to recover damages for emotional distress by way of filing an intentional infliction of emotional distress claim against the employer for failure to pay overtime, provide breaks and meal periods, and provide accurate itemized wage statements. That court held that the plaintiff's claims all fell within the exclusivity provisions of the California's Workers Compensation statute and thus were preempted. However, if the employer's actions fall outside the confines of a state's workers compensation statutes, intentional infliction of emotional distress claims are viable against an employer. To illustrate, in the case of *Lee v. West Kern Water Dist.* (2016), the California appeals court upheld the jury verdict in the amount of $360,000.00 against the employer based on several of the worker's causes of action, including intentional infliction of emotional distress, stemming from an unannounced "mock" robbery of the business conducted by the manager. The plaintiff clerk, who had a gun pointed at her, and who was demanded money, was terrified, thinking it was a real robbery, and consequently gave the "robber" the money. After the event was concluded, the plaintiff left work early, crying, and suffered from fears, depression, nightmares, headaches, loss of appetite, and ongoing nausea. She sought psychological treatment and had to use all her accrued sick leave and vacation time during her extended absence from work (*Lee v. West Kern Water Dist.*, 2016). The court held that such workplace trauma was not related to an "industrial causation," and thus was not preempted by the state of California Worker's Compensation statute.

Management Implications and Recommendations:

Although "bullying" in the workplace or otherwise is not recognized as an independent legal wrong in the United States, nonetheless bullying-like conduct can rise to the level of the tort of intentional infliction of emotional distress if the conduct is atrocious as well as a battery (assuming physical contact which is harmful and/or offensive). As such, managers and organizational leaders must be prepared to effectively train employees and managers on the form, implications, and consequences of bullying and other unprofessional or stressful behaviors. A principal goal of this part to the book has been to make employers and managers aware of the potential efficacy of the common law tort of intentional infliction of emotional distress in the context of the modern employment relationship. Two important areas have been emphasized; first, the application of the tort to the discharge of at-will employees and thereby the creation of a wrongful discharge situation; and second, the efficacy of the tort in redressing bullying behavior at work. The courts have been reluctant to recognize a cause of action for intentional infliction of emotional distress in the employment context for what the courts deem to be normal and ordinary employment activities or disputes. An "ordinary" dispute, legally at least, would be the discharge of an at-will employee. Thus, the courts have been reluctant to convert the discharge of an at-will employee into a "wrongful," i.e., illegal, discharge, absent evidence of extreme and outrageous conduct in the manner of the discharge. Moreover, the cases indicate that "normal" workplace activities, disputes, or discharges must go way beyond these aforementioned actions, and rather be disrespectful, degrading, demeaning, and/or humiliating in order to rise to the level of "extreme" and "outrageous." As such, one can sense that the courts are attempting to delimit the scope of this tort by requiring extreme and outrageous conduct as well as severe distress.

However, employers and managers must be cognizant of the fact that certain employment actions, such as supervising or investigating, increasing workload or hours, criticizing or reprimanding, transferring or not transferring, not promoting or demoting, suspending or otherwise disciplining, and (surely) discharging employees can and likely will cause stress and mental anguish. Moreover, many employees may feel that these actions are "outrageous" in-and-of themselves. Consequently, the employer must be keenly aware that unfavorable employment actions will probably cause some employees to suffer emotional distress. As such, there is even more reason for the employer to conduct these activities and to resolve employment disputes in a respectful, fair, and ethical manner. Nevertheless, when workplace behavior or actions, whether characterized as bullying or otherwise, degenerate into conduct that a reasonable person would find abusive and demeaning, based on the nature and severity and frequency of the behavior, thereby resulting in emotional, psychological, and/or physical harm, the victimized employee may have legal recourse pursuant to the intentional infliction of emotional distress tort. For example, laughing at and mocking discharged employees, humiliating them, and making a "spectacle" out of their termination are actions not right morally and not right legally as such atrocious conduct likely will give the discharged employee the grounds for a lawsuit for intentional infliction of emotional distress even if the discharge itself was permissible under the employment at-will doctrine.

Another problem with bullying in the workplace is the difficulty of precisely defining the term as well as the concomitant challenge of ascertaining what type and level of bullying conduct will rise to the level of the intentional tort of emotional distress examined herein. Another major problem with this tort in the employment context and otherwise is that the key terms "extreme" and "outrageous" are determined by a discrete body of state law and thus, even on an individual state level, there are no specific definitions of these critical terms. Due to the lack of clarity in the meaning of these terms, employers, managers, and their attorneys may be forced to speculate as to what conduct in the workplace is sufficiently egregious to be "extreme" and "outrageous." Another problematic result is a body of law with inconsistent decisions among the states and even among the courts within a state. Due to the aforementioned legal and practical problems, the employer in order to avoid legal difficulties must attempt to create a proper corporate culture premised on the values of legality and morality; and thus a culture that will proscribe, prohibit, prevent, and punish abusive, demeaning, and bullying conduct in the workplace.

The objective for the employer is to create a corporate culture of dignity and respect, ethics and integrity, fairness and justice, and one which values diversity and inclusion. The employer certainly has an egoistic reason to do so since such a culture will prevent bullying behavior as well as discrimination, harassment, and retaliation in the workplace. As such, lawsuits will be minimized and hopefully eliminated, employee turnover should decrease, both of which are costly to the employer, and productivity should be increased too. Corporate culture is a critical factor in "bully-proofing" the organization and preventing legal liability. Culture serves here to define the necessary way to behave within an organization consisting of shared beliefs and values established by leaders cascaded through communication and inculcated using various methods to shape and reinforce employee perceptions, behaviors, and understanding regarding a zero tolerance for workplace bullying. Business leadership and management set the cultural climate for actions fostering worker dignity, respect, and civility in the work environment. To formulate such a cultural climate, organizations must design and create internal policies that promote these desired goals. Places of employment should aim to have annual training on workplace bullying, its impact, and the potential consequences for bullies and their targets through the human resources and/or legal departments. Cross-cultural considerations, education, and training will ensure cultural awareness and accordingly will help to create a corporate culture of dignity and respect.

Therefore, the legal, moral, as well as ethically egoistic company or organization must raise awareness within the entity about the nature and stages of abuse and harassment, train how to identify them by recognizing the signs in both victims and perpetrators, and then implement appropriate measures for each stage to prevent and redress bullying conduct. Effectively managing and establishing an anti-bullying corporate culture that values respect, equality, diversity, and inclusion certainly is in the best interest of the employer and its stakeholders. Such an appropriate culture will lessen turnover, enhance productivity, and reduce and ideally eliminate lawsuits for abusive behavior in the workplace, and not "merely" lawsuits for intentional infliction of emotional distress, but also for other legal wrongs premised on "bad" behavior, such as common law wrongs for assault and battery and defamation as well as statutory civil rights wrongs for discrimination, harassment, and retaliation.

The authors now will supply additional specific recommendations to employers and managers regarding the tort of intentional infliction of emotional distress in the context of workplace bullying as well as the wrongful discharge of employees. Employers must create a corporate culture of ethics, integrity, diversity, inclusion, and respect, where the employees are valued and treated as worthwhile human beings deserving of dignity and respect. Employers must have a "zero-tolerance" policy when it comes to bullying in the workplace. Employers should never conduct unannounced "mock" robberies, active shooter, or other similar live-action scenario training in the workplace without prior notification to the employees, so they do not undergo emotional trauma thinking the event is real. Employers, furthermore, must promulgate codes of ethics and codes of conduct that prohibit bullying and other forms of abusive conduct as well as disrespectful, demeaning, discriminatory, harassing, or retaliatory conduct in the workplace. The employer must make it clear that these codes and the prohibitions therein apply to all the employees and not just those employees who are protected by civil rights laws. Employers must communicate such codes, train all employees as to their rights and responsibilities pursuant to the codes, "police" the application of the codes, and enforce them. The employer, moreover, should have a fair and objective investigative process to investigate complaints of bullying in the workplace. Similarly, employers must establish "whistleblowing" and other channels of communication for the employees to report bullying and abusive conduct in the workplace; and employers must make it very clear that no reprisals will be taken against the employees making such disclosures. Employers must train managers and supervisors as to appropriate vs. inappropriate conduct in the workplace. Specifically, employers should instruct managers and supervisors to avoid excessively harsh or "stinging" criticism, as well as yelling, verbal abuse, and laughing at and belittling employees, especially in front of others, as such conduct could be construed as bullying conduct which could rise to the level of the intentional infliction of emotional distress tort. However, if there is bullying or abusive conduct by a manager or supervisor the employer should seek evidence that the perpetrator acted out of personal motives and was not attempting, even if in a misguided manner, to do his or her job duties or functions. Perpetrators of bullying behavior should initially be coached as to the wrongfulness of their bullying behavior and progressively disciplined depending on the severity of the bullying action. These recommendations, the authors trust, will help employers and managers to further reduce and eliminate abusive and bullying conduct in the workplace and thus to avoid legal liability, particularly pursuant to the intentional tort of infliction of emotional distress.

Invasion of Privacy

This section of the book will examine the intentional tort of *invasion of privacy,* which protects the right to maintain one's private life free from unwanted intrusion and unwarranted publicity. Invasion of privacy is a broad legal doctrine as it consists of not one, but rather four distinct invasions of a person's privacy and personality. The four "privacy" torts succinctly stated are: 1) appropriation, 2) intrusion, 3) "false light," and 4) public disclosure.

The "appropriation" tort occurs when the defendant appropriates without permission the plaintiff's name or picture for the defendant's commercial advantage, typically for the advertisement, marketing, and promotion of the defendant's products or services.

"Intrusion" occurs when the defendant intrudes on the plaintiff's private life, private affairs, or seclusion. It is absolutely essential for "intrusion" tort liability that the intrusion invades a person's private domain, and not a public domain. For example, taking a picture of a celebrity in a public place is not legally actionable. Moreover, the aggrieved party is held to a reasonableness standard; that is, only a reasonable expectation of privacy is protected by the tort. Also actionable as a privacy tort is the publication of facts by the defendant which places the plaintiff in a "false light." "False light" means the public disclosure attributing to a person a view or opinion which he or she does not possess or actions which he or she did not take. Finally, public disclosure of private facts about the plaintiff by the defendant is actionable as a privacy tort. Of course, the facts must be private and not in the public record. It must be emphasized that even if the facts about a person are true, the tort may still lie.

Invasion of privacy is an intentional tort; as such, there is no such legal concept as a careless or negligent invasion of privacy as opposed to a negligent infliction of emotional distress tort lawsuit. The intent to invade, that is, to do a purposeful intrusive act, is an indispensable element of the tort. Actually, "intentionally" means that a person desires to cause the consequences of his or her act or one believes that the consequences are substantially certain to result from the act. The requisite intent, it must be emphasized, is not necessarily to cause the harm produced, but rather the intent that will cause the means and the ends of invading the privacy interests of another in a manner that the law forbids.

The *intrusion* component to the intentional tort of invasion of privacy is based on an impermissible intrusion into a person's solitude, seclusion, or private sphere or place or into one's private place, affairs, or concerns wherein one has a reasonable expectation of privacy and which intrusion is regarded as highly offensive to a reasonable person (*Brad Newkirk v. GKN Armstrong Wheels, Inc., 2016,* applying Iowa law; *Armstrong v. H & C Communications, Inc.*, 1991, applying Florida law). According to Jones (2020), pursuant to Texas law the intrusion must be "unreasonable, unjustified, or unwarranted." The intrusion can be physical means or electronically (*Agency for Health Care Administration v. Associated Industries of Florida, Inc.*, 1996, applying

Florida law). Accordingly, a legally actionable intrusion must invade a private sphere, place, or concern where a person has a reasonable expectation of privacy. This protected "zone of privacy" also encompasses information which a person would reasonably expect to be and to remain private. According to Jones (2020), examining Texas case law, the reasonableness of the expectation of privacy is ascertained by the employer's interest in the monitoring or surveillance, the means used, and whether notice to the employees was provided. Accordingly, if one is in an area or place deemed "public," or if information is deemed "public," there generally will not be a reasonable expectation of privacy; and thus no liability for any subjectively perceived "invasion" (*Allstate Insurance Co. v. Ginsburg*, 2003, applying Florida law). For example, in one leading case, *I.C.U. Investigations, Inc. v. Jones* (2000), applying Alabama law, the employer as part of a workers' compensation investigation hired an investigator who conducted surveillance of the employee, videotaping the employee from roadways near his home and using a telescopic lens. The videotaping, which was turned over to the employer, included the employee urinating four times in his front yard. The employee then sued his employer and the investigative firm, though the trial proceeded only against the latter. Although the jury found for the employee, assessing $100,100 in damages, the state supreme court reversed the decision, explaining that the investigation had a legitimate purpose and that the activities carried on in his front yard could have been observed by any person passing by; and thus the intrusion was not legally actionable as an invasion of privacy tort (*I.C.U. Investigations, Inc. v. Jones*, 2000).

Certain key privacy questions, therefore, emerge in these intrusions into private place, sphere, or concern cases: first, is the activity truly private; second, whether there is a reasonable expectation of privacy, particularly in the workplace setting; and, third, if so, what is the extent of that expectation. To illustrate, in one older but leading federal appeals court case, the Third Circuit Court of Appeals held that a corporate officer reading an employee's mail, which was marked personal, but delivered to the corporate offices, would constitute an invasion of privacy based on a highly offensive intrusion into the employee's seclusion because an employee would have a reasonable expectation of privacy in one's personal mail even in the workplace (*Vernars v. Young*, 1976). Private places would be areas where employees primarily engage in personal activities, such as locker rooms and lounges, and accordingly the employees would have a reasonable expectation of privacy. To search or conduct surveillance of such private places absent a very compelling reason would likely bring about tort liability. Searching offices, desks, files, and briefcases can also be problematic for the employer because they may be considered private areas by the employees, though there may be a diminished expectation of privacy if the office is shared office space (*Diana Retuerto v. Berea Moving Storage and Logistics*, 2015, applying Ohio law). Yet if the search is limited, not overly intrusive, motivated by legitimate reasons, based on reasonable suspicion, and conducted in a narrow and specific manner by proper personnel, the employer may be able to conduct the search without adverse legal consequences. To illustrate, in one Texas appeals court case the court found that the employee had a reasonable expectation of privacy regarding her locker, even though it was provided by the employer, because the contents of the locker were secured by the employee's own lock (*K-Mart Corporation v. Trotti*, 1984). To compare, in the federal district court case of *Marrs v. Marriot Corp.* (1992), applying Maryland law, the employer monitored the office and desk of an employee security investigator with his permission as he believed that someone was wrongfully accessing his files. The employer then observed another employee attempting to pick the lock of a desk drawer with a paper clip. The employee was fired and sued for invasion of privacy; but the court denied the claim ruling that the plaintiff employee did not have a reasonable expectation of privacy in an open office.

Other examples of clearly private activities are bathroom activities and bodily functions and fluids, medical examinations, and dressing and undressing. To illustrate, in one case from the federal First Circuit Court of Appeals, a drilling rig employee who was discharged after testing positive for marijuana was awarded damages for invasion of privacy, including emotional distress damages, based on the fact that the employee was observed urinating by the employer's representative (*Kelley v. Schlumberger Tech. Corp.*, 1988, applying Massachusetts law). However, the courts have upheld private sector drug testing when the employees have been given advance notice of the testing and the employer had legitimate reasons, obviously maintaining safety in the workplace, and thus to be sure the employees are free from illegal drugs (*Fry v. IBP, Inc*., 1998, applying Kansas law). Even suspicion-less urine drug testing has been upheld when the employer made drug testing a condition of employment and the employer had very good reasons for the drug testing, for example, a report from an undercover agent that about 60% of the employer's workforce were using illegal drugs (*Baggs, v. Eagle-Picher Industries*, Inc., 1992, applying Michigan law). The courts have even upheld private sector random drug testing conducted on all employees despite the fact of statements in company policy manuals that the employer would respect the personal lives of employees (*Gilmore v. Enogex, Inc*., 1994, applying Oklahoma law). The preceding cases dealt with a private sector employer; consequently, there would be no federal constitutional issues. Pursuant to the U.S. Constitution Fourth Amendment "search and seizure" issues, where a government employer would be doing the testing or searching, could arise in the context of an "unreasonable" search by government; but this area of constitutional law is beyond the purview of this book.

Some sexually oriented actions also may be construed as clearly blatant physical intrusions into private spheres where one clearly has an expectation of privacy; consequently, such an intrusion will lead to tort liability. For example, an invasion of privacy occurs when one looks up a woman's skirt (*Michael Stancombe v. New Process Steel LP*, 2016, applying Alabama law) or when a co-worker picks up a woman's legs while she is sitting on a chair so as to look under her skirt (*Vernon v. Medical Management Associates of Margate, Inc.*, 1996, applying Florida law). Similarly, a woman has an obvious expectation of privacy in a ladies bathroom and thus a cause of action existed when a male employee entered the ladies room and observed a female changing clothes (*Stockett v. Tolin*, 1992, applying Florida law) as well as when a male "Peeping Tom" employee secretly videotaped female employees and performers in their dressing room at Disney World (*Liberti v. Walt Disney World*, 1995, applying Florida law). However, unwelcome sexual advances, unwelcome sexual touching, patting or grabbing, sexual gestures or jokes, as well as sexually offensive comments may not constitute a cause of action for invasion of privacy (*Carly Singer v. Colony Insurance Company*, 2015, applying Florida law; *Topolski v. Chris Leef General Agency*, 2012, applying Kansas law; *Allstate Insurance Co. v. Ginsburg*, 2003, applying Florida law), though any physical touching can be grounds for the intentional tort of battery, and all can be grounds for a lawsuit for sexual harassment premised on civil rights laws. Yet one federal appeals court, the Eleventh Circuit, citing Alabama precedent, stated that inquiries into one's sex life may be grounds for an invasion of privacy lawsuit but only if the inquiries are "extensive" (*Michael Stancombe v. New Process Steel LP*, 2016). Similarly, a federal district court, also applying Alabama law, said that sexual harassment has to be "severe" and of a "prying nature" to constitute invasion of privacy; and as such asking an employee for a date or even making sexual propositions usually will not constitute an invasion of privacy (*Tison v. Alachua Straw Co. LLC*, 2020). Of course, the aforementioned sexual conduct also could very well constitute a civil rights violation under Title VII.

As a general rule, most work-related activities will not be considered "private" as far as the employer and the courts are concerned; as such, generally there will be no liability for any employer perceived intrusions (*Acosta v. Scott Labor LLC*, 2005, applying Florida law). Nevertheless, there will be some activities that are work-related that still will be viewed as private, for example, changing uniforms at work. To illustrate, in *Doe v. B.P.S. Guard Services, Inc.* (1991), the Eighth Circuit Court of Appeals, applying Missouri law, held that fashion models could pursue an invasion of privacy claim against the employer of security guards when the guards videotaped the models in a dressing room, even though some of the models could not demonstrate that they were videotaped in a state of undress. To compare, in the federal district court case of *Thompson v. Johnson County Community College* (1996), applying Kansas law, there was no liability even though the employer videotaped the changing and locker rooms of security guards as part of a workplace investigation of theft because the area was not enclosed and anyone could walk into and through the area.

The employer's surveillance, monitoring, and searching may extend beyond the workplace. Yet the employees likely will have expectations of privacy regarding their off-the-job activities. As such, the employer must have legitimate business reasons for such conduct. Consequently, these employer actions can give rise to lawsuits for invasion of privacy if the employer lacks a strong reason and the methods are unreasonable and offensive. Yet if the surveillance or monitoring is in a public place there should be no liability because the employee will not have a reasonable expectation of privacy. When the surveillance is of the employee inside of his or her home the legal situation becomes even more problematic, particularly if vision-enhancing equipment is used. Compare the federal district court case of *Salazar v. Golden State Warriors* (2000), applying California law, where the court rejected an invasion of privacy claim even though the employer's investigator used a high-powered, infrared, night-vision, telescoping device to take footage of an employee using drugs in his sports utility vehicle in a dark parking lot, with the Michigan court of appeals case of *Saldana v. Kelsey-Hayes Company* (1989), where the court said that the use of such a comparable device to view an employee, suspected of malingering, in the interior of his home could be objectionable on privacy grounds. Nevertheless a very strong and legitimate business reason may legitimize an intrusion into the employee's home.

The prevalence today of social media presents another challenge to the law. Now, one would think that an employee might consider his or her social media postings as private. Yet, two federal district court cases are most instructive; thus, they can serve as valuable counsel to the employer as well as a warning to employees. In one federal case, the former employer accessed and used the employee's personal Twitter and Facebook accounts without the employee's authorization; but the court dismissed the employee's invasion of privacy claim explaining that matters discussed on these social media accounts were not private (*Maremont v. Fredman Design Group, Ltd.*, 2011, applying Illinois law). In the other federal case, the plaintiff employees contended that their manager accessed a secure password protected chat room on Myspace where the employees were complaining about their employer; but a jury ruled against the plaintiff employees on their invasion of privacy claim because the jury determined that regardless of the unauthorized access the plaintiffs did not have a reasonable expectation of privacy for their chat room communications (*Pietrylo v. Hillstonne Restaurant Group*, 2009, applying New Jersey law). These cases clearly underscore the maxim that nothing on social media is truly private. Yet as a result of these cases several states have promulgated statutes that prohibit employers from requesting social media passwords from applicants and potential employees. Of course, these laws may not protect current employees or prohibit the employer from obtaining social media information from a third party with access or knowledge of access. Moreover, many companies have promulgated policies that directly prohibit the use of social media during working hours; consequently, these employment policies would materially lessen the expectation of privacy of employees regarding social media and email use. The personnel information and records that the employer obtains and maintains as part of its human resources function, including medical records of the employees, will usually not be considered private for the intrusion aspect of the invasion of privacy tort so long as the information relates to the employer's management of the workplace or is otherwise public information, for example arrest and conviction records. However, the information may be deemed private regarding others; thus, its disclosure could trigger the disclosure of private facts component to the invasion of privacy tort.

Another factor in determining liability for surveillance is the place of surveillance. Accordingly, this key fact is whether the employer conducted the viewing, monitoring, or surveillance from a proper observational location. Consequently, watching or photographing a person through the windows of his or her residence could be an impermissible intrusion as well as a possible trespass (*Diana Retuerto v. Bera Moving Storage and Logistics*, 2015, applying Ohio law). Even if the surveillance is conducted by means of telescopic or image-enhancing equipment, and even if the employer had a good reason for the surveillance, if the employer was in place that the employer did not have a right to be then the courts may find the employer liable for invasion of privacy. For example, if a manager or supervisor enters the employee's trailer home without permission, even for a good reason, such as to see if the employee had a drinking problem and thus was not suitable for a supervisory position (*Love v. Southern*

Bell Telephone & Telegraph Co., 1972, applying Louisiana law), or if there was a trespass and the employee was watched in his home by investigators using binoculars who also eavesdropped on the employee and his wife (*Souder v. Pendleton Detectives, Inc.*, 1956, applying Louisiana law), there would be legal violations.

The employer must also have a legitimate job-related reason for the surveillance or monitoring. For example, the supervisor of an employee who tries to obtain her medical records to discredit her and to spread rumors that she is a lesbian because she rebuffed the supervisor's sexual advances is clearly not a legitimate business reason (*Lankford v. City of Hobart*, 1994). As noted, many valid reasons can be offered as "legitimate" ones for surveillance and monitoring, such as promoting productivity and efficiency at work (*Thomas v. General Electric Company*, 1962, applying Kentucky law); and these legitimate reasons can even encompass off-the-job surveillance of employees, for example, investigating wrongdoing by employees (*DeLury v. Kretchner*, 1971, applying New York law) or defending a legal claim asserted by an employee (*Ellenberg v. Pinkerton's, Inc*., 1973, applying Georgia law). However, even if the employer has such a legitimate reason, the employer still must be careful that the means of surveillance, monitoring, and searching are not highly offensive to the reasonable person. Consequently, even if the employer has a legitimate reason for the surveillance the means involved may go beyond the bounds of decency and thus trigger tort liability. For example, in the federal district court case of *Acuff v. IBP, Inc.* (1999), applying Illinois law, the employer as part of a workplace investigation as to theft installed a camera in the ceiling tiles of the nurse manager's office because certain items were disappearing from the office. That investigatory rationale for the surveillance could be construed as a legitimate one. However, the office was also used for employee medical examinations, which the nurse manager and the employee who viewed the videotapes were aware of, and this knowledge was imputed to the employer, thereby resulting in liability for invasion of privacy for the surreptitious surveillance (*Acuff v. IBP, Inc.*, 1999). To compare, in one federal district court case, *Corian Branyan v. Southwest Airlines Co*. (2015), applying Massachusetts law, the employer, an airline company, was attempting to contact an employee, a flight attendant on paid-leave with a wrist injury, to determine her status and availability for work. The employer attempted to contact her 25 times to no avail. As a result, the employer contacted the local police to find her, providing to the police her name, home address, and employment status. The employee sued for invasion of privacy contending that such an unfair intrusion led to the police coming to her residence. The court, however, denied her claim, stating that those allegations were insufficient to constitute an actionable invasion of privacy claim. A person's name, home address, and employer are not facts of a highly personal or intimate nature. Moreover, the court stated that a brief home visit from a police officer could not be properly be characterized as an unreasonable, substantial, or serious invasion of the plaintiff's privacy (*Corian Branyan v. Southwest Airlines Co.*, 2015). The court, finally, pointed out that there existed legitimate business reasons for the reasonable collection or dissemination of the private employee information, and thus the lawsuit was not actionable (*Corian Branyan v. Southwest Airlines Co.*, 2015). Therefore, in the employment sector or otherwise there are many factors to consider; and consequently, the entire facts and circumstances of the situation must be considered. A key factor to determining the "offensiveness" is whether the employer's legitimate business interest supersedes the employee's privacy interest. A jury, therefore, may be necessary in order to determine the application of this objective "reasonable person" test; that is, the jury as trier of fact must decide if such a hypothetical reasonable person would be highly offended and outraged by the intrusion or disclosure even though the employer may have had a good reason to obtain or disclose certain information.

Another challenging aspect of this area of the law is the application of the tort of invasion of privacy to the electronic monitoring of employees. The maxim is that "the law is always trying to catch up to technology." And this maxim has never been more true than today, when the old English, common law tort of invasion of privacy is applied to modern electronic monitoring, particularly in the workplace. Employers today in the global "virtual" economy routinely provide to their employees "smart phones," Internet access, email and other forms of electronic communication and access. Employers have the technical ability to electronically monitor these modalities as well as phone calls and text messages. However, employers contemplating the use of this new technology should take heed of an older case where the court, the Eleventh Circuit of Appeals, held that the employer violated a precursor to the Electronic Communications Privacy Act when the employer allowed employees to use phones for personal calls as well as for work, stated that monitoring would occur but assured the employees that their calls would be monitored only to determine if they were for business purposes; yet nonetheless a supervisor listened in to a personal call between an employee and a friend (*Watkins v. L.M. Berry Co*., 1983).

Employers also have legitimate reasons for engaging in electronic monitoring as well as the surveillance of employees. As emphasized, employers have a duty to protect confidential information and trade secrets and to prevent defamation, cyber-bullying, discrimination, and harassment in the workplace. An interesting and instructive case dealing with alleged misappropriation of trade secrets by a former employee is the federal district court case of *Sunbelt Rentals, Inc. v. Santiago Victor* (2014), applying California law. As part of its investigation into misappropriation the employer reviewed the former employee's text messages on the iPhone which the employer had previously issued to the employee. The former employee sued for invasion of privacy for the allegedly impermissible intrusion, claiming that he had a reasonable expectation of privacy in the text messages. However, the court denied his claim, stating firstly that the device belonged to the employer; and secondly that while he may have had a subjective expectation of privacy it was not a reasonable one because the employee personally caused the transmission of his text messages to the iPhone by "syncing" his new devices to his Apple account without first linking his former employer's iPhone (*Sunbelt Rentals, Inc. v. Santiago Victor*, 2014). The court further explained that even if the employee had *subjectively* harbored an expectation of privacy in his text messages, such expectation could not be characterized as *objectively* reasonable, since it was the employee's conduct that directly caused the transmission of the text messages to the employer initially (*Sunbelt Rentals, Inc. v. Santiago Victor*, 2014). In addition to underscoring the critical distinction between a subjective and an objective expectation of privacy, the case also serves as a reminder of the "perils and pitfalls" of technology on privacy. Employers who wish to monitor the text messages of their employees must be careful too. Since employees may have a reasonable expectation of privacy regarding their text messages (*Quon v. Arch Wireless Operating Company,* 2008), employers should clearly notify the employees that their text messages will be monitored and also obtain an express acknowledgement from the employees as to the monitoring.

Employers are also very concerned about their reputations – "virtually" and otherwise. And the advent and extent of social media sites and networks provide the means for employers to monitor employees' online statements and activities. Consequently, employers rightfully contend that they have legal, ethical, and practical reasons to monitor their employees' electronic communications as well as social media sites. Yet, naturally, employers want to avoid liability for invasion of privacy. The Electronic Communications Privacy Act (ECPA) of 1986 affords the employer a great deal of protection since the employer can access and retrieve information on its computer systems or the employee otherwise gives consent to access. Accordingly, managers should be aware that there is this federal statute which allows the employer to monitor the employee's use of the employer's email system. The federal Electronic Communications Privacy Act regulates electronic forms of communication, including emails and cell-phone use. Pertinent to the privacy examination herein is the "business-extension exception" to the Act, which permits employers to monitor the employees' electronic communications in the ordinary course of business. The ECPA, however, does not allow an employer to monitor the employees' personal communications unless the employees have consented to having their communications monitored by the employer (Electronic Communications Privacy Act, 1986). Since statutes supersede the common law, so long as an employer is acting within the confines of a statute – federal or state – in monitoring or testing employees, the employer will be protected from common law tort liability.

The fact that the employer provided the email system to the employees emerges as another critical factor in determining liability. For example, the courts have held that an employee has no reasonable expectation of privacy in email communications that the employee voluntarily made on the company's email system (*Symth v. Pillsbury Co.*, 1996, applying Pennsylvania law), even when messages are stored in a password-protected location on the employees' computers at work (*McLaren v. Microsoft*, 1999, applying Texas law). The courts have even held that an employer can monitor its independent contractors, holding that the fact that the person was not technically an "employee" was irrelevant; and thus again the key fact is that the employer provided the email system to the independent contractor (*Fraser v. Nationwide Mutual Insurance Co.*, 2004, applying Pennsylvania law). However, to compare, in the federal district court case of *Ali v. Douglas Cable Communications* (1996), applying Kansas law, the court drew a distinction between the employer's monitoring of its customer-service employees' work-related calls for supervision and training purposes, which were deemed permissible intrusions, versus the employer's monitoring and recording of the employees' personal calls without prompt notification, which actions were held to violate their right to privacy since their expectation that the personal calls would remain private was a reasonable one.

Yet another complicating factor arises when employees are permitted to work at home, that is, they are "telecommuting" employees. As a result of new technologies, as well as the Covid-19 coronavirus and required quarantines, a growing number of employees now work in the virtual workplace – not in the office, but sometimes on-the-road or at home. Since there is less face-to-face interaction among workers, there is a greater reliance on electronic communications. Further complications arise when the employee is not technically a "telecommuting," one but rather the employer has given the employee a computer for home use so the employee can conduct some of the employer's business from home. The employee of course will have access to the employer's business systems, but he or she may use this home computer provided by the employer for personal use, thereby raising privacy questions. Key factors, therefore, in the legal analysis would be whether the employee had a reasonable expectation of privacy regarding the online information, the legitimacy and strength of the reason by the employer to obtain the information, the means used by the employer to access the information, and whether the employer's business need superseded the employee's privacy interest.

Moreover, employers today can even monitor the physical movements of their employees by means of Global Positioning System (GPS) technology. Privacy issues can arise when the employer used GPS systems to keep track of employees, vehicles, and equipment; but the employer may have legitimate reasons to do so. One leading GPS decision is the federal district court case of *Elgin v. St. Louis Coca Cola Bottling Co.* (2005), applying Missouri law, where the court held that the employer did not commit an invasion of privacy intrusion tort by engaging in the GPS monitoring of an employee in a company-owned vehicle even on the employee's personal time. However, to compare, the Oregon court of appeals in *Reed v. Toyota Motor Credit Corp.* (2020) ruled that it was for a jury to decide if an invasion of privacy occurred when the defendant Toyota, as part of a separation agreement, allowed the plaintiff former employee to continue exclusive use of a truck, but without telling him that the company had secretly installed a GPS device on the truck. The company argued that the system was a "passive" system; and as such the system was neither accessed nor monitored, nor was any data collected. Nevertheless, the appeals court, overruling the trial court, ruled that it was for the jury to decide whether merely the obtaining of the unwanted and covert access by means of the GPS device, and not whether data was ever collected or disclosed, was sufficiently intrusive into the plaintiff's seclusion to constitute a tortious invasion of privacy (*Reed v. Toyota Motor Credit Corp.*, 2020). Note that the preceding cases are private sector ones; thus, the result may be different when the government as employer or otherwise engages in GPS tracking due to Fourth Amendment constitutional concerns. Monitoring, therefore, involves a consideration of the means of the monitoring and the employer's interest in doing the monitoring as well as the relevance of the information received to the employer's interest. If the monitoring is aimed at the employee's private or personal information the likelihood increases that the monitoring will be an illegal intrusion unless the employer has a very compelling reason for the monitoring.

The public disclosure component of the invasion of privacy tort is based on the unauthorized public disclosure by a person of private facts regarding an individual that a reasonable person would find highly offensive, objectionable, or embarrassing and the matter is not of legitimate public concern (*Jane Doe v. Bernabei & Wachtel, PLLC*, 2015, applying District of Columbia law). It is important to note that this legal wrong is different from defamation where the negative material about a person must be false; rather, with public disclosure there may be liability pursuant to this privacy tort even if the information is true, because the information is private and not a matter of public concern. A key question here, as with the intrusion aspect of the tort, is whether the information disclosed was highly offensive to a reasonable person. For example, in the federal district court case of *Jennifer Pwlaczyk v. Besser Credit Union* (2014), applying Michigan law, when the vice-president of a credit union was discharged, the CEO of the credit union emailed other credit union CEOs to inform them that the VP was no longer employed at the company. The former VP then sued pursuant to the public disclosure of private facts component to the tort of invasion of privacy. The court, however, denied the VP's claim for the following reasons: only a small group of CEOs was contacted; there was no evidence that the information would become public knowledge; there was no evidence that the VP would not be able to find suitable employment in her field; and, most importantly the CEO just said that the VP was no longer employed at the company; and the communication by the CEO did not disclose the nature of the separation or any reasons for it (*Jennifer Pwlaczyk v. Besser Credit Union* (2014). Another key question is whether the private information was sufficiently disclosed to rise to the level of a "public disclosure." As such, disclosure to a single person or even a small group of people will not be adequately "public," for example, when a company's human resources department disclosed the personal bank account information of an employee, who was having a pay dispute with his company, to his supervisor (*Anand Venkatrman v. Allegis Group, Inc.*, 2015, applying Maryland law).

If information is deemed to be public or in the public record then one can examine and transmit such information without violating tort law (*Markovitch v. Panther Valley School District*, 2014, applying Pennsylvania law). Yet if information about a person is deemed to be "private" tort liability for invasion of privacy may ensue. Yet, particularly in the employment context, ascertaining whether certain information is private or public information is a difficult task indeed, especially with the advent of highly developed technologies. One of the first public disclosure of private facts employment cases is the 1990 decision by the Illinois court of appeals in *Miller v. Motorola* (1990), where the employer revealed to many co-workers that the plaintiff employee had a mastectomy, thereby resulting in tort liability for invasion of privacy. Another leading case is the Colorado supreme court case in *Ozer v. Borquez* (1997), where tort liability was premised on a law firm partner's telling other employees that a law associate was homosexual, that his domestic partner had been diagnosed with AIDS, and that he needed to get tested to determine if he was HIV positive. Other examples would be disclosure of details of sexual relations and intimate private conduct. The aforementioned examples would be highly offensive to the reasonable person. Finally, it should be pointed out that the public disclosure tort requires that the private information be made public, but the intrusion aspect of invasion of privacy is not based upon any publicity given to the person whose interest is invaded or to his or her affairs (*Dawn Hahn v. Cynthia Loch, L.P.N., Lehigh Family Practice Associates, LLC, and Leroy Hahn*, 2016, applying Pennsylvania law).

As with any intentional tort there are a wide variety of damages that the aggrieved party can recover from the defendant wrongdoer for an invasion of privacy. These damages include nominal damages, actual compensatory damages (past and future so long as the latter are not "speculative"), mental anguish and emotional pain and suffering damages; and, since this legal wrong is a purposeful one, punitive damages (that is, additional damages to act as a punishment and a deterrent). For example, in one case, a California appeals court held that even though the employer had the right to inspect the employee's office, desk, and computer, the rifling through the employee's purse was an invasion of privacy that could support a punitive damage award because the employee had a reasonable expectation of privacy regarding her personal property and the rifling was highly offensive (*Greenberg v. Alta Healthcare System, LLC*, 2004). Damages can be recovered for the outrage and mental suffering caused by the invasion as well as for the shame and humiliation that a person of ordinary sensibilities would suffer. Malice is not required for ordinary compensatory damages. However, in order to sustain a recovery of additional punitive damages a showing of malice, spite, hatred, or outrageousness is required. Moreover, the standard to recover mental anguish damages for this tort (as well as the tort of intentional infliction of emotional distress) is based on a person of ordinary and reasonable sensibilities and not a hypersensitive or overly sensitive person (unless the wrongdoer knows of the sensitive nature of the victim) (*State Farm Fire & Casualty Co. v. Compupay*, 1995, applying Florida law). However, for any type of the aforementioned damages for this invasion of privacy tort (as well as for the tort of intentional infliction of emotional distress) it is not necessary for the aggrieved party to show any physical impact by the wrongdoer (as would be the case in a negligent infliction of emotional distress lawsuit, as will be seen) (*Kush v. Lloyd*, 1992, applying Florida law; *Gracey v. Eaker*, 1999, applying Florida law).

Consent is a complete defense to an intentional tort, assuming the consent is a knowing and voluntary one. Accordingly, if an employee consents to being watched, searched, monitored, or contacted, he or she will forego the right to sue for invasion of privacy. *Waiver,* that is, the knowing and voluntary giving-up of legal right, can also be a defense. Moreover, consent as well as waiver may be inferred from the surrounding circumstances. For example, consent to a drug test may be inferred when the employee provides a urine sample. As such, in one state appeals case the employee truck driver consented to take a random drug and alcohol test and to have the results and concomitant report sent to prospective employers, thereby vitiating his invasion of privacy lawsuit (*George H. Larson v. United Natural Foods West Inc*., 2014, applying Arizona law).To further illustrate, in the federal district court case of *Curtwright v. Ray* (1991), applying Kansas law, the court held that there was no invasion of privacy seclusion claim when the board of directors of a company initiated an investigation as to whether the company's president's alcohol use was affecting his performance because the president had agreed to the inspection and the company had a legitimate reason for the investigation. Assuming there are no defenses the next step in the analysis herein is to examine some of the key elements and factors with the invasion of privacy tort that can lead to legal liability. Since there are so many aspects to the tort of intentional invasion of privacy as well as factors that can affect liability, it is essential for managers and employers to be proactive in seeking to avoid liability for this tort.

Management Implications and Recommendations:

A major legal, ethical, and practical area of employer and management concern is the extent to which the employees' right to privacy is protected in the workplace. An employer can have many reasons for conducting surveillance and monitoring of its employees – in the workplace and off-the-job – and by physical and electronic means. The employer may want to investigate performance issues, particularly the lack thereof, as well as to try to improve safety, performance, efficiency, and productivity. Management, supervision, and training are proper reasons for surveillance, searching, or monitoring, for example, of the employees' work-related phone calls, including the recording of interactions with customers or clients. The employer, moreover, may want to determine if the employees are engaged in theft of property, misappropriation and/or disclosure of confidential information and trade secrets, as well as violations of other company policies and procedures. The employer, moreover, may be concerned with the employees contracting computer viruses by downloading email attachments. The employer may wish to discover if the employee is engaging in other illegal, fraudulent, or malingering misconduct, perhaps as a part of a workers' compensation investigation. The employer also may want to discover if the employee is engaged in illegal activities, such as using illegal drugs, or even if excessive alcohol use is adversely affecting a supervisor's judgment. Surveillance, searching, and monitoring may provide the employer with concrete factual information that the employee has violated some law, company policy, or work rule so as to discipline or discharge an employee without legal liability, or for the employer to defend itself from lawsuits by employees, especially wrongful discharge and retaliation ones.

Employers, moreover, have a legal duty pursuant to the law of negligence to carefully supervise their employees; and the failure to do so in a reasonable manner may lead to liability for the tort of negligent supervision and/or retention. That is, once private online content is available to the employer, a jury could infer that it would be negligent for a current or prospective employer to have failed to examine the material and take appropriate action based on the information. Consequently, it could be deemed irresponsible – legally and ethically - for the employer not to monitor computer use due to the prevalence, access, and abuse of workplace computers. Therefore, careful though reasonable supervision may have to encompass the surveillance, searching, and monitoring of the employees at times. Therefore, such supervisory actions and the resultant obtaining of appropriate information in a proper manner should reduce the risks of lawsuits and defending lawsuits. Thus, proper surveillance will save the employer time, effort, and money in the long-term.

Accordingly, the employer's ability to demonstrate to the court one of the aforementioned legitimate reasons for the monitoring, searching, or surveillance of its employees is an important factor in avoiding liability. Yet, as indicated and underscored, even if there is a good reason for the employer's actions, any surveillance, searching, and monitoring must be done in a suitably non-invasive, non-intrusive manner, and non-offensive manner. In an employment setting, managers must be careful when conducting surveillance of employees, monitoring employees, and searching employees, even in the workplace as the employee is still entitled to some "private space" therein. Moreover, when conducting surveillance off-the-job, for example, to enforce an employer's "office romance" policies of no-dating of co-workers or no-smoking at all, the employer must be extremely careful not to contravene the employee's privacy rights protected by the "intrusion" tort. Of course, an astute employer will give the employee notice that certain types of surveillance, monitoring, and searches will be conducted, since it will be more difficult for an employee to claim a reasonable expectation of privacy if he or she is informed that an intrusion therein, for example, for drug-testing, will be conducted under certain circumstances.

The authors wish to emphasize that first, not all surveillance, searching, and monitoring are legally actionable; and second, invasion of privacy cases – in employment and otherwise – are very fact-specific types of cases; and thus the result depends on the circumstances in the individual case. The courts seek to balance the legitimate interests of the employer with the employee's right to privacy. That is, the employer's legitimate interest in determining the employee's effectiveness in his or her job needs to be balanced against the seriousness of the intrusion on the employee's privacy. Similarly, in an employment relationship, courts will balance the legitimacy of the employer's need to obtain personal information against the seriousness of the intrusion into the employee's privacy. A key question, therefore, is whether the employer's legitimate need for certain work-related information outweighs the employee's interest in privacy.

As emphasized, most work-related activities will not be deemed to be sufficiently "private" as far as the employer is concerned, thus obviating tort liability. Generally, therefore, employees do not have the right to be free from surveillance in the workplace – surreptitious or otherwise. Employers typically own, control, and manage the workplace; consequently, employers are to some level responsible for the conduct that occurs in the workplace. Employers must be able to manage and control their property and thus need to monitor their employees to ensure they perform their jobs in a satisfactory, efficient, effective, and safe manner. For example, since employers typically own their computer systems it will be very difficult for an employee to successfully claim that he or she has a reasonable expectation of privacy regarding such computer use. Moreover, employees would not have a right to privacy in offices, even if "their" offices, since the offices belong to the employer and can be accessed by the employer's managers and supervisors, even if the access is accomplished by video surveillance.

Nonetheless, even in the workplace and during the work relationship employees are accorded a protected sphere of privacy and seclusion. Some areas of the workplace are private; accordingly, the employees can have a reasonable expectation of privacy, for example, as pointed out, going to the bathroom, dressing and undressing at work, and regarding personal items contained in their purses, backpacks, briefcases, desks, and lockers As such, to impermissibly intrude into this private sphere without a very strong countervailing reason can bring legal liability on the employer in the form of an intentional tort invasion of privacy lawsuit as well as other legal actions by the aggrieved employees.

However, for there to be an illegal invasion the employee, as any person, must have a reasonable expectation of privacy. As such, in order for the employee to prevail on an invasion of privacy lawsuit based on the employer's allegedly intrusive actions the employee must be able to show that he or she had a reasonable expectation of privacy. "Reasonable," as emphasized, is measured by an objective – "reasonable person" standard and not by the employee's subjective feelings. Accordingly, if the employee is in a public place and can be viewed from such a location there typically will not be an invasion of privacy, even if the employee is photographed or videotaped. Moreover, if an employee is informed by management that he or she will be watched, searched, subject to surveillance, or monitored – physically or "virtually" – it will be very difficult for the employee to claim that his or her expectation of privacy was a "reasonable" one – whether on- or off-the-job, thereby typically obviating tort liability on the part of the employer for any perceived "invasion." Conversely, if the employee is not notified by management of certain monitoring or surveillance it is more likely that the employee will be able to sustain an invasion of privacy lawsuit based on intrusion. A notification policy must be thorough, clear, and specific as well as communicated to the employees. Moreover, it should emphasize that even certain activities which might be considered "private" can and will be viewed by the employer. Furthermore, the notice policy should be part of the employee's handbook or manual. Ideally, consent and waiver forms by the employees should be obtained. When the line between the employee's work life versus personal life is "blurred," for example off-site monitoring or when the employee is allowed to bring his or her own computer to work, Jones (2020) advises that the employer should then very carefully consider whether and how to conduct monitoring or surveillance. For internet use, Jones (2020) suggests that a less intrusive alternative to monitoring, for example, blocking, should be considered.

Allegations of invasion of privacy can also arise during the application, screening, interviewing, and testing process of the employment relationship. Employers, therefore, must be careful as to what questions they can ask so as not to be perceived as intruding on a job applicant's private sphere. For example, asking about an applicant's sexual orientation, political affiliations, or religious beliefs might well be construed as improper questions, particularly if asked in a selective manner. Consequently, any and all questions and testing must have a reasonable connection to the job or position and must be asked in a non-discriminatory manner. The employee's expectation of privacy and whether such an expectation is reasonable are seminal issues in invasion of privacy cases. Accordingly, the key to avoiding liability for invasion of privacy is for the employer to be aware of its employees' expectations of privacy and to guide those expectations in a proper manner for workplace behavior. An important factor is to educate the employees. In particular, the employer must explain to them the reasons for surveillance, monitoring, and searching.

Another challenging employment issue with privacy concerns arises with the use of Smart Phones, particularly when employers require employees to install GPS or other tracking type devices on their Smart Phones and/or other technology so that the employers can monitor their communications and movements while on- and off-duty, especially when employees spend a great deal of time on-the-road. Many companies sending employees out on service calls track their movements using mobile applications. Tracking movements can help employers plot better delivery routes and thus save on fuel costs, as well as helping employers to know when employees are "goofing off." Yet some employees are tracking employees on a continual basis, thus triggering privacy concerns – legal and ethical. Under the common law tort of invasion of privacy, employees are entitled to a reasonable expectation of privacy on- and off-duty. Moreover, to be legally actionable the invasion of privacy must be outrageous, say the courts. Of course, if an employer has a legitimate business reason for monitoring employees and tells the employee that he or she will be monitored, and why, it will be a challenge indeed to prevail on an invasion of privacy lawsuit. Some states, such as California, have in their state constitutions privacy protections that protect private sector employees from having their private life intruded on by their employers; but the employer's conduct nevertheless must be an unreasonable invasion of privacy. The problem that is emerging is that today technology has blurred the lines, both legally and ethically, between what is on-and off-duty work as well as what is in one's work life as opposed to what is in one's personal and private life.

The authors will now offer the following concrete suggestions to management to help manage the employees' expectations of privacy; and thus to avoid liability for invasion of privacy lawsuits: Management must develop surveillance and monitoring policies that are clear and definite as well as surveillance and monitoring policies that are fair and dignified and respectful to the employees. Accordingly, management must establish a precise privacy policy that clearly, thoroughly, explicitly, and specifically notifies the employees how, when, and what will be watched, monitored, tested, searched, or subject to surveillance, especially regarding activities and/or areas that could be deemed to be "private." It is critical, therefore, for the employer to consult with legal experts, human resource professionals, and information security personnel before developing monitoring and surveillance policies. Training, of course, is critical, and as such managers, supervisors, and employees must be educated as to the company's privacy policies. Furthermore, it is necessary to publish these policies in employee handbooks and codes of conduct. Require employees to sign waiver or consent forms as to surveillance and monitoring as conditions of employment. In addition, obtain a receipt from the employee that he or she has read and understands the surveillance and monitoring policy. It is very important to clearly let the employees know that not only emails but also text messages may be monitored. Moreover, inform the employees that the email system is the sole property of the employer and is to be used only for business purposes. Also, inform the employees not to expect email on their office computers to be considered as private communications. Tell the employees to make personal calls from their personal cell phones and not the employer's office phones. Also, tell the employees not to conduct personal activities on the company's computer network. Inform the employee that if he or she brings a personal laptop to work, which is then connected to the employer's system, that such use may be monitored by the employer. Managers also should inform the employees that they should tell their family members, friends, and co-workers not to send any personal emails or make any personal calls to the employee's office computer and/or phone. Management must be certain that the company has a clear, strong, legitimate, and demonstrable reasons for any surveillance, searching, testing, and monitoring of employees. If the surveillance or monitoring is to take place off-site the business reason must be not only legitimate but also substantial, for example, an employee activity that will put the company in legal or financial jeopardy. If it is necessary to search, only search an employee's office or desk for a legitimate work-related reason, such as to find a necessary file or materials pertinent to work, or when there are reasonable grounds to suspect that the employee is involved in some type of work-related misconduct. Do not engage in any overbroad, unnecessary, irrelevant, or unsupervised searches, for example, into the employee's personal property, such as a purse or jacket pocket, or by conducting an investigation of the employee's sexual practices.

Regarding private information, limit disclosure of private information concerning employees only to managers, supervisors, and others who have a business reason to know of such confidential information. Accordingly, inform managers, supervisors, and employees who deal with confidential information that any improper disclosure of private information concerning the employees will subject them as well as the company to potential invasion of privacy lawsuits. Managers, finally, must remember that the employee does not have to be terminated in order for the employee to institute a lawsuit against the employer for violating the employee's right to privacy. The authors trust that these recommendations and suggestions will help managers to avoid liability for the intentional tort of invasion of privacy.

Intentional Interference with Contract or Business Relations

The next intentional tort, which also has significant business ramifications, is the tort of *intentional interference with contractual or business relations*. This tort requires the presence of a contact, a business relationship, or the expectancy or the potential of a business relationship, which the defendant is aware of, and the defendant intentionally induces a breach of contract or interferes with or disrupts the business relationship or expectancy by improper means in order to advance his, her, or its own personal or business interests. A good example is the California appeals court case *Redfearn v. Trader Joe's*

Inc. (2018), where a defendant company made false statements to the clients of a food broker designed to harm the broker's professional reputation, thereby causing the broker's clients to terminate their contracts with the broker and to sell their products to the defendant company. A similar example would be one where a restaurant posts information on Facebook that a local competing restaurant has been cited for health code violations (Campbell, 2019). Another example would arise when one competing company wrongfully induces a key employee at another firm to break one's contract with his or her employer and to work for the competitor. Intent is required, of course; and as a result sufficient evidence is necessary that the defendant intentionally induced the former employee to break his or her contract with the former employer, not merely that the employee breached it, and then went to work for the defendant competitor.

This tort, therefore, is a very complicated one, whose full explication is beyond the purposes of this type of handbook. However, suffice to say, there must be some type of relationship to be interfered with, which can be either established by a contract or an advantageous business relationship – actual or potential. A business relationship is much more difficult to define but, for example, can be the relationship existing between a sales representative and a customer or a vendor (Campbell, 2019). Another major problem with this tort is that the laws governing the wrongful interference tort are not clear as to what conduct will be deemed to be improper interference. Clearly, a means that is contrary to the law – constitutions, statutes, administrative rules and regulations, and/or the common law – will be deemed "improper" (*C.R. Eng. V. Swift Transp. Co*., 2019, applying Utah law). For example, spreading "specious and salacious accusations" and rumors of a sexual nature about a distributor which caused her to lose a product distribution contract with a store could be construed as a violation of tortious interference with contract because of the defamatory nature of the statements (*Carr v. Wegmans Food Mkts, Inc*., 2020, applying New York law). Moreover, in some states, an improper means can be established by the violation of an objective, established, widespread, standard of a trade, industry, or profession (*C.R. Eng. V. Swift Transp. Co*., 2019, applying Utah law). However, as one legal commentator noted, the interference cannot be merely "garden-variety" interference, but rather interference that is intentional and "unjust" (Campbell, 2019). Accordingly, what exactly will be construed as legitimate and proper competitive actions in seeking new personnel and new business, as opposed to illegal, wrongful, "pirating," predatory, abusive, unjust, and malicious interference tactics? The line between illegal predatory and abusive competition and "merely" aggressive, "tough," "hard-hitting," but legal competition is not an easy one to draw, and not only for this intentional tort but also under antitrust law.

Nonetheless, the independent tort of intentional interference with contract or business relations can arise in a disloyal employee situation. This tort requires the existence of a contract or a business relationship which the defendant purposefully interferes with by improper means, for example, by improper solicitation of the employer's customers. Some courts require the existence of a valid and enforceable contract and not a mere business relationship for there to be a violation. However, it is a basic principle of law that merely hiring the employees of one's competitor is not sufficient for a claim of tortious interference with contract or other legal wrong (assuming, of course, that no covenant-not-to-compete is breached and no trade secrets are misappropriated). Rather, to sustain this tort, evidence will be required that the defendant employee intentionally induced a co-worker by improper means to break a contract with the employer and then work for the defendant former employee. Moreover, the fact that a person is an employee at-will does not preclude him or her for bringing a lawsuit for the tort of intentional interference with contract or business relations. For example, in the New York appeals case of *Conklin v. Laxen* (2020) the plaintiff, the director of an animal shelter and an at-will employee, was able to sustain an initial case against a veterinarian who communicated to the board of directors that the plaintiff had euthanized several cats who had ringworm without the approval of a veterinarian. The board of directors then terminated the plaintiff director's employment. The appeals court stated that fact that the director was an at-will employee did not preclude her from bringing the lawsuit and that the defendant veterinarian improperly interfered with her employment and business relationship. Critical to the case was the fact that the improper means of interference was the allegedly defamatory statement by the veterinarian about the plaintiff to the board of directors (*Conklin v. Laxen,* 2020).

Management Implications and Recommendations:

Managers must be aware that solicitation of one's co-workers to leave their employment and work for a new firm, especially one to be established by a fellow employee, is a very problematic area legally. In particular, this tort of intentional interference of contract can arise when an employee of a firm plans to leave and start his or her own business and then commences to solicit key employees of the employer during or after employment. If such solicitation occurs during current employment, particularly when the employee has an employment contract for a certain term, the prospective entrepreneur risks a lawsuit based on the old common law's duty of loyalty to one's employer, as will be seen. And in either case, the entrepreneur risks a tort lawsuit for the intentional interference of contract. Both can result in an injunction and the latter can result in tort damages. So, to be safe, the entrepreneurial employee should merely tell his or her co-workers that he or she is leaving or has left, and then if the employees ask why, the entrepreneur can state that he or she plans to, or has started, a new business, and then give them a phone number and email where the entrepreneur can be reached. Telling one's co-workers about your future plans is permissible, but "raiding" co-workers may be a violation of tort and contract law, if for the latter there is an "anti-piracy" clause in a contract.

Defamation

A major intentional tort with widespread business ramifications is *defamation*. The legal wrong of defamation, also called defamation of character, occurs when a person makes a false statement that harms the reputation of another person. The tort of defamation can arise in the employment context when the employer makes an intentionally false statement that harms the employee's character, reputation, and/or career. An oral defamatory statement is called "*slander*"; whereas a written defamatory statement is called "*libel.*" Libel also includes statements in other permanent forms, such as statements made on television or the radio.

The elements to a cause of action for defamation that the plaintiff must prove (in the employment context herein) are as follows: 1) false and defamatory language by the defendant; 2) "of or concerning" the plaintiff, that is, identifying the plaintiff to a reasonable reader, listener, or viewer; 3) "publication" of the defamatory language to a third party; 4) resulting injury to the reputation of the plaintiff; and 5) "fault," but in the sense that the employer knew that the statement was false, or acted in reckless disregard of its truth or falsity, or the employer should have known that the statement was false (that is, negligence in the latter case); 6) the absence of any privilege or defense; and 7) harm and damages to the reputation of the aggrieved party. An example of an employer acting in reckless disregard of truth or falsity could be when the employer repeats a harmful, damaging, and unsubstantiated rumor about an employee without checking into the facts (Guerin, 2020).

Moreover, there must be evidence as to who exactly made the defamatory statement and what exactly was said. For example, the fact that statements regarding an employee's poor performance were just part of the company "rumor mill" without evidence as to who made the assertion was "fatal" to the employee's defamation claim, ruled the federal district court in the case of *Wheeler v. Home Depot U.S.A.* (2017), applying District of Columbia law. To further illustrate, in the New York court of appeals case of *Wideberg v. Tiffany & Co.* (1992), the pleading by the plaintiff that he was defamed by the defendant making slanderous and defamatory remarks on several occasions was held to be insufficient to meet specific pleading requirements for defamation lawsuits. Finally, depending on the state, there typically is a two-year Statute of Limitations for the legal wrong of defamation; that is, the aggrieved party has two years to bring a lawsuit from the date the allegedly defamatory comments were published, or else the lawsuit is barred by the statute, which was the holding in the federal district court case of *Holliday v. Fairbanks*, 2017, applying New Hampshire law). Note, though, that some states only have a one-year limitations period (see, for example, *Meyer v. Shearson Lehman Bros*., 1995, applying New York law; *Smith v. Datla*, 2017, applying New

Jersey law; and *Gonalez v. City of Chicago*, 2018, applying Illinois law).

When defamation is committed the law provides a legal remedy – the legal cause of action for the tort of defamation – which can provide compensation for the harm caused by the false and defamatory statement. Damages for committing the tort of defamation can include nominal damages, actual damages (past and future), compensatory damages (past and future), including monetary loss (direct or indirect), for example, loss of employment income, mental anguish and emotional pain and suffering, and injury to one's reputation or loss in standing in the community. Punitive damages may also be awarded if the defendant knew the statements were false or had serious doubts about their truth and the defendant's primary intent on making the statements was to express ill will, hatred, malice, or harm. Juries, moreover, typically have a great deal of discretion in awarding damages, including punitive damages if malice or the equivalent is found. Defamation claims, furthermore, are not preempted by state Workers' Compensation statutes because a defamation lawsuit is more akin to an intentional tort and not a negligent personal injury type of claim which would be the basis of recovery for a physically injured worker. However, defamation lawsuits may be preempted by federal statutes, for example, the National Labor Relations Act (*Duane Reade, Inc. v. Local 338 Retail, Wholesale Department Store Union*, 2003) and the Railway Labor Act (*Harris v. Hirsh*, 1994).

Defamation is premised on false statements of fact. A "fact" thus is a necessary predicate to a lawsuit; and as such mere opinions are not actionable pursuant to defamation law (Cavico, 1999). Even harsh opinions and abusive words are not actionable since they are not "facts." For example, calling a person a "scumbag" is merely an opinion (*Carrington v. Carolina Day Sch., Inc.*, 2020, applying North Carolina law). Also, a statement by a manager that an employee has a "negative attitude" typically cannot form the basis of a defamation cause of action because the statement is too opinionated (Guerin, 2020). Similarly, in the federal district court case of *Prostrollo v. Scottsdale Healthcare Hosps.* (2018), applying Arizona law, a manager made a statement that the employee had witnessed and had been part of conduct that was unethical. Despite the implication (at the least) that the employee was unethical, the court ruled that the statement was too opinionated, too general, lacking specific standards that would assess what being "unethical" means; and that moral, ethical, and professional standards differ among persons, companies, industries, societies, and religions; and thus the statement at issue could not be objectively proven as factual (*Prostrollo v. Scottsdale Healthcare Hosps.*, 2018).

However, a problem in the law regarding the non-liability of mere "opinions," and not just in defamation law but also fraud and warranty law, is that opinions are not made in a vacuum; that is, there typically are some facts upon which the opinion is based; and as such the question arises as to how many specific facts are there in an opinion to "push" the "opinion" into the "fact" category for potential legal liability. To illustrate this dichotomy, a manager giving his or her opinion that an employee should not be trusted to handle large sums of cash could be construed as a mere opinion but also as "fact" if there are sufficient facts behind the opinion. Is calling an employee "uncooperative" merely an opinion; but calling him or her "insubordinate" factual? Is saying an employee is not "fit" for a job merely an opinion, but saying that he or she had "poor" job performance factual? To further illustrate, a Maryland appeals court ruled that the asserted "opinion" that a community college vice-president was discharged for poor or inferior performance on-the-job could be construed as factual because the statement indicated that it was based on the fact that the plaintiff, vice-president, was incapable or unqualified to fulfill the duties of a senior administrator at a community college (*Frank Samuels v. James D. Tschechtelin*, 2000). Similarly, one federal court of appeals, applying Maryland law, ruled that the statement that a union organizer was not a good organizer was factual though asserted initially as a mere opinion because the statement contained an underlying objective fact that the employee failed to fulfill the duties of his position as a union organizer (*Daniel C. Murray v. United Food and Commercial Workers International Union*, 2002, applying Maryland law).

To resolve this "fact" vs. "opinion" issue, some courts use a "totality of the circumstances" test to distinguish fact from opinion, encompassing such criteria as the context the statement was made, the exact words used, whether words or phrases were taken out of context, the means of communication used, and the audience. Innuendo, moreover, can be used to find a factual assertion. For example, in the federal district court case of *Soni v. Wespiser* (2017), applying Massachusetts law, the court stated that a comment that the employee, a doctor, was "trouble" was deemed to be "purely opinion," but another statement that the doctor was involved in prior lawsuits was true; nevertheless, the court explained that the word "trouble' and the statement that the doctor filed prior lawsuits could not be read in a vacuum. When taken together when they were uttered, the implication was that the doctor was litigious and had the propensity to file frivolous lawsuits. Consequently, the court ruled that the statements were statements of fact. To compare, one New York court held that an unfavorable assessment of work performance in "memos to a file" was a mere expression of opinion (*Corns v. Good Samaritan Hosp. Med. Ctr.*, 2014). The federal district court in *Pace v. Baker-White* (2020), applying Pennsylvania law, provided further guidance on the fact vs. opinion question. The *Pace* court said to look for "hedging language," such as "could" or "believe," as well as "equivocal language," such as "appears," "may," or "might have," since such language merely offers a subjective view, an interpretation, a theory, or conjecture, and not objective verifiable facts, and thus such language is merely non-actionable opinion. An "opinion" example would be a statement that a person failed to pay his taxes, which money he "seemingly" misappropriated from his employer (*Pace v. Baker-White*, 2020). Yet, to fully explicate this difficult "opinion" v. "fact" issue is a challenging task indeed, and thus beyond the purposes of this "handbook"; but one point is clear: statements combining facts and opinion will have to be examined very closely to see which predominates.

Moreover, if a "fact," the statement of fact must be, in fact, false. However, some courts hold that a statement does not have to be perfectly true or absolutely accurate; rather, it will be sufficiently false if the main aspect of the statement is false and defamatory (*Cape Publications, Inc. v. Reakes*, 2003, applying Florida law). It typically is the function of the jury to determine if a statement of fact is false or sufficiently false (*Cynthia Hyland v. Ratheon Technical Services Company*, 2009; *Frank Samuels v. James D. Tschechtelin*, 2000). However, the determination as to whether a statement is in fact a "fact" as opposed to a mere opinion is typically a question of law for a judge to decide (*Cynthia Hyland v. Raytheon Technical Services Company*, 2009, applying Virgina law; *Frank Samuels v. James D. Tschechtelin*, 2000, applying Maryland law).

As a basic component to the tort, the false statements must be defamatory; that is, the defendant's language must adversely affect the victim's reputation in the community; one's honesty, integrity, or virtue must be impugned or assailed. Declaring to a discharged employee that he or she is a criminal, a thief, a cheat, and a liar would suffice. Defamation is premised on culpability, that is, fault on the part of the defamer, the employer in the context herein. Fault can be intentional wrongdoing, that is, the employer knew that a statement was false or acted in reckless disregard of truth or falsity and nonetheless communicated the defamatory statement. Moreover, if the aggrieved party is a private person (as opposed to a public figure) he or she only needs to show negligence in the publication of the defamatory statement (*Frank Samuels v. James D. Tschechtelin*, 2000). Thus, in the context herein, as a general rule fault can be negligent wrongdoing, that is, the employer should have known that the statement was false before communicating it, for example, by not thoroughly checking out a disparaging but unsubstantiated office rumor before repeating it and communicating it to others. However, in a few states in the employer-employee context the requisite fault on the part of the employer must be that the statement by the employer was made with knowledge of the falsity or in reckless disregard of its truth or falsity; a showing of negligence is insufficient, for example, as stated by the federal district court case of *Trahanas v. Northwestern University* (2017), applying Illinois law. Accordingly, and most importantly, for the employer, if it honestly and in good faith believed a statement to be true and did not act recklessly or negligently in communicating it then there is no fault, no culpability, and no liability for defamation. The "of or concerning" the plaintiff requirement simply means that a reasonably prudent person would understand that the defamatory statement referred to the plaintiff.

The "publication" requirement mandates the defamatory statement must be communicated to a third party who understands it as such. So, for example, if the employer made such defamatory accusations of criminality and immorality but only to the employee, with no one else present, then publication is lacking. Similarly, if the defamatory statement is made in a letter, memo, or email which only the employee sees, then there is no publication. Conversely, if the employer makes the false accusations of employee criminality publicly, on a loudspeaker, employee bulletin board or "virtual" discussion board, or in a "global" email, then there is publication. To illustrate, in the federal district court case of *Doe v. Yackulic* (2019), applying Texas law, the court ruled that the essential publication requirement was missing, and thus the defamation case failed, because the plaintiff's false medical diagnosis was communicated only to the plaintiff and "pertinent medical staff" at the place of plaintiff's employment and not to "independent third parties." It is also necessary to point out that some states recognize a "self-publication" doctrine, where the employer makes a false statement directly to the employee, who is then compelled to repeat it to others, typically to a prospective employer who asks why the employee was terminated from his or her position (Guerin, 2020).

Regarding the intent requirement, defamation is at times called a "quasi-intentional tort" because even though intent is required, it is merely the intent to publish, and not the intent to defame. As such, once a purposeful publication is established, it is no defense that the defendant did not know that the statements were defamatory; and also it is no defense that the defendant did not intend to defame the plaintiff. Moreover, one who repeats or republishes defamatory material is liable just the same as the original publisher. This rule is called the "repetition" rule and holds that each repetition is a separate publication for which the victim can recover damages.

Another essential element to a defamation legal action is that the false statement of fact harms the reputation of the aggrieved plaintiff bringing the lawsuit. As such, the nature of the statement must expose the plaintiff to hatred, contempt, scorn, ridicule, or shame, or must harm the plaintiff's reputation, injure his or her business or occupation, or contain an assertion that the plaintiff committed a crime, as stated by the Florida supreme court in the case of *Jews for Jesus, Inc. v. Rapp* (2008). For example, in the federal district court case of *Addison v. City of Baker City* (2017), applying Oregon law, the court ruled that the statements that the employee, a news reporter, got into a fight with a former employer and that the employee had "mood swings" harmed the employee's reputation because this type of information would tend to diminish the esteem, respect, goodwill, and/or confidence in which the employee) was held as well as to motivate adverse, derogatory, or unpleasant feelings or opinions against the employee. To compare, in the federal district court case of *Wilson v. New York* (2017), applying New York law, the statements by a school administrator that a faculty member should no longer be a professor because he is no longer interested and that he should be an entrepreneur were not deemed to be defamatory because nothing about these statements could have exposed the professor to public hatred or contempt or harm his business reputation. However, the statement that the professor was engaging in criminal activity was deemed to be defamatory because it was the type of statement that would tend to harm a person's professional reputation (*Wilson v. New York*, 2017).

Moreover, in certain cases, harm to reputation is presumed. That is, the harmful false statements of fact will cause others to not have a good opinion of or associate with, the employee. However, according to one federal district court, applying New Jersey law, mere name-calling, even the use of reprehensible and morally repugnant racial epithets, will not in-and-of-itself constitute defamation due to superseding concerns about protecting freedom of speech and expression, including even unpopular, ugly, and/or hateful, political, religious, and/or social opinions (*Harley v. City of N.J. City*, 2017, applying New Jersey law).

The "injury to the reputation" requirement of defamation presents a problem, since now one must carefully distinguish between two types of defamation – libel and slander – because the plaintiff's burden of proof as to damage to the plaintiff's reputation may differ on the nature of the defamation. *Libel* is a defamatory statement recorded in writing or some other permanent form, such as a picture, statue, movie, television, or radio. There are two important kinds of libel. The first is called "*libel per se*." Libel *per se* occurs when a statement is defamatory and libelous on its face, without the need for any extrinsic facts or explanation. The rule of law is that in such a case damage to the plaintiff's reputation is presumed by the law, and accordingly the plaintiff can recover damages without the necessity of proving harm. The second kind of libel is called "*libel per quod*." This form of libel is not defamatory on its face, and as a result requires reference to additional facts to establish its defamatory nature. In such a case, most courts will not presume damage to the plaintiff's reputation, and thus the plaintiff will be required as a general rule to plead and prove special damages, for example, that the defamation caused the loss of employment or a business opportunity.

Slander is spoken defamation; it is oral and heard; it is in less permanent and less broad areas of dissemination. As a general rule, damage to the plaintiff's reputation is not presumed, and thus the plaintiff has to plead and prove special damages. However, there are four categories of slander that are considered so harmful they are called "*slander per se*." The legal consequence of uttering a slander *per se* is that damage to the plaintiff's reputation is presumed. The four slander *per se* categories involve defamatory statements that: 1) a person is guilty of a serious crime of moral turpitude (and not a minor offense); 2) adversely affect a person's profession, business, or trade; 3) impute a loathsome disease to a person; and 4) historically impute that an unmarried woman is unchaste. The law regards these types of slander, called slanders *per se* (or in-and-of-themselves), to be so harmful to a person's reputation that actual damages are conclusively presumed; that is, no extrinsic or additional evidence as to the aggrieved party's damages are required. An example would be a false allegation that the employee committed a crime; as such, no tangible adverse consequences to the employee's reputation or career need be demonstrated; the harm to the employee is presumed. A slander *per se* can consist of imputing to a person a criminal offense which is a felony or an offense involving moral turpitude, according to the Florida appeals case of *Spears v. Albertsons, Inc.* (2003). Imputing to a person conduct, characteristics, or conditions that would be harmful to the person's lawful business, trade, occupation, office, or profession because the statements impugn the person's professional competence or character, impute incapacity or unfitness for the position, or impute dishonesty or fraud. Subjecting a person to hatred, distrust, contempt, ridicule, or disgrace, such as imputing fraud or dishonesty to another person. An example would be the California appeals court case of

Redfearn v. Trader Joe's, Inc. (2018), where a representative of the defendant company falsely accused a food broker of spreading rumors that the company's representatives were soliciting bribes and that the only way to do business with the company was to pay the bribes demanded. The court in *Redfearn* deemed these comments to be an accusation of "unethical behavior" which would have a natural tendency to harm the broker in his trade or profession; consequently, the comments were deemed legally actionable as slander *per se*. To compare, saying that a girls' basketball coach did not meet the school's "core beliefs and mission," and thus a change was necessary to more closely align the program with the school's values was not deemed to be defamatory because the statements said "nothing about (the coach's) credentials or other qualifications as a coach" (*Carrington v. Carolina Day Sch., Inc.*, 2020, applying North Carolina law).

Consequently, the employer making false statements that the employee has been convicted of a crime or is accused of committing a crime will be regarded as slanders *per se*, for example, accusations of theft of company property, according to the Kentucky supreme court in the case of *Virginia Stringer v. Wal-Mart Stores* (2004), or that the employee was stealing from her employer (for example, in the New York appeals case of *LaBozzo v. Brooks Brothers*, 2002). Also, the fact that the employee supervisor made anti-Semitic remarks to Jewish volunteers at her employer's museum, according to the New York appeals court in the case of *Herlihy v. Metro Museum of Art* (1995), would be deemed to be a slander *per se* because the logical conclusion of defendant's statements was that plaintiff was anti-Semitic and biased based on her treatment of Jewish volunteers. Such anti-Semitism would be incompatible with the proper conduct of the plaintiff's duties as she was in a position where she had regular and substantial interaction with the public as well as the museum's volunteers. Also, comments that an employee lacked the necessary knowledge and skills for his or her job or profession or lacked good character and integrity would be construed as slanders *per se*. Another example is the federal district court case of *Manswell v. Heavenly Miracle Acad. Servs.* (2017), applying New York law, where a supervisor's statements to a parent and to an employee of another day care facility that the plaintiff employee, a preschool teacher, was fired for hitting a student were regarded as defamation *per se*. The court explained that such a serious statement regarding a daycare teacher constitutes defamation *per se* because it would clearly injure plaintiff in her profession, because hitting a child is incompatible with the proper conduct of a childcare provider. Moreover, in the aforementioned case, the court in addition to damages for economic harm upheld an award of $25,000 just for the harm to the plaintiff employee's reputation since the amount was a reasonable amount of damages (*Manswell v. Heavenly Miracle Acad. Servs.*, 2017). Similarly, in the New York appeals case of *Conklin v. Laxen* (2020), a statement by a veterinarian to the board of directors of an animal shelter that the director had euthanized several cats who had ringworm without the approval of a veterinarian was construed as defamation *per se* because such a statement would purportedly injure the plaintiff director in her "professional standing." To compare, in the New York state appeals case of *Wideberg v. Tiffany & Co.* (1992), the court pointed out that the mere expression of dissatisfaction with a person's job performance does not constitute slander *per se*.

When a defamatory statement is in written form the general rule is that the defamation is actionable *per se* or in-and-of-itself without the need to prove any special harm or damages; that is, harm to reputation is established from the very fact of the written defamatory statement and the jury can award damages at is discretion (*Virginia Stringer v. Wal-Mart Stores*, 2004, applying Kentucky law). An example would be when an employee is discharged for poor or inferior performance with an explanation that would harm a person in his or her office, trade, profession, business, or otherwise means of making a living (*Frank Samuels v. James D. Tschechtelin*, 2000, applying Maryland law). However, if a defamatory statement is not libelous on its face and proof of additional facts is necessary to supply the defamatory meaning to the statement then the libel is deemed to be *per quod* and the general rule is proof of harm to reputation and special damages is required. For example, in a New York state case the court ruled that the employer sending an email to a client apologizing for the unauthorized and unprofessional communication by an employee and the employee's "lack of professionalism" was not a defamatory communication *per se* (*Menelly v. Willex Indus. Corp.*, 2011). It is a function of a judge to decide the question of law as to whether an alleged defamatory statement is *per se* or *per quod* (*Frank Samuels v. James D. Tschechtelin*, 2000).

There are four chief defenses to defamation: 1) consent, 2) truth, 3) absolute privilege, and 4) *qualified or conditional privilege*. Consent by the plaintiff to the publication of the defamatory statement will be a defense. Consent also will be discussed in a forthcoming section of this chapter in conjunction with other intentional torts. Truth is a total defense to a lawsuit for defamation; no matter how defamatory the statement is, if it is true, the truth will be a complete defense to a cause of action for defamation, though not necessarily for other intentional torts. An absolute privilege to defame arises in court trials, including the discovery process, and other government hearings proceedings, and protects litigants, witnesses, attorneys, judges, and other government personnel. An example of the absolute privilege is the New York state appeals case of *Ifantides v. Wisniewski* (2020), where in the context of an employment dispute, the defendant's statements that the plaintiff was a "concubine" and a "mistress," even if construed as defamatory, were nevertheless deemed to be protected by the absolute privilege because the statements were made in a deposition, though never completed, as well as repeated in a letter but the letter was to the federal court.

A qualified or conditional privilege will operate as a complete defense; but it may be forfeited by the presence of malice, in the sense of spite or ill-will, or abuse; that is, the publishing of the defamatory statement occurred with an improper motive or for an improper purpose. An example is the North Carolina appeals case of *Brodkin v. Novant Health, Inc.* (2019), where the statements in an email by an oncology doctor to a hospital administrator, the hospital's head of oncology, which statements expressed the concerns of another oncology doctor's treatment of cancer patients, were deemed to be protected by the qualified privilege, even assuming the statements were false and defamatory, because proper medical treatment of patients is "unquestionably" an important and legitimate interest for all the parties concerned and society as a whole. Moreover, there was no evidence of malice or bad faith, but rather just good faith and honest disagreements as to the appropriate course of treatment for cancer patients. The qualified privilege can be used to protect not only the public interest, but also the private interest, for example, to protect a statement by a former employer to a prospective employer regarding a job applicant. In the absence of malice or abuse, the qualified privilege will even protect defamatory and false statements by the former employer concerning the former employee. However, regardless of the existence of such a common law privilege to defame, which some states have formalized in statutory form, most employers are very fearful of being sued for defamation by former employees, and thus are very reticent to be expressive, let alone expansive, in communications regarding former employees.

As emphasized, it is a fundamental principle of defamation law that truth is an absolute defense to a lawsuit for defamation. For example, in the New York state case of *Priore v. N.Y. Yankees*, 2003), the purportedly false statement that an employee was terminated for petty larceny was found to be true when the employee admitted guilt to petty theft, thereby, obviously, vitiating his defamation case. Even if the truth "causes needless embarrassment" to a person, for example, where a director of libraries told library personnel at other libraries that a librarian was "subject to disciplinary proceedings," truth is still an absolute defense (*Smith v. Library Board of Homestead*, 2018, applying Alabama law). Moreover, truth is a defense in some jurisdictions even if the statement is substantially true. In other jurisdictions, however, the statement even if true must be made with "good motives" (*Lipsig v. Ramlawi*, 2000, applying Florida law). It is also important to point out that the law presumes defamation to be false; thus, the defendant has the burden of proof and persuasion to show that the defamatory statements were true. Consent is another absolute defense to defamation. Consent can arise, for example, when the employee has waived his or her right to sue for defamation based on any comments or information provided by the employer in a reference. Another example of consent would be when the employee hires a relative, friend, or private investigator to solicit a reference from a current or former employer.

Judges are completely immune from liability for defamation for their "judicial acts," that is, actions regarding a case pending before the judge that are within a judge's normal judicial functions whether the event occurred in the courtroom or the judge's chambers, for example, according to the Florida case of *Kalmanson v. Lockett* (2003). Statements made during the course of judicial proceedings are also absolutely protected (*EEOC v. Day & Zimmerman NPS, Inc.*, 2017, applying Florida law; *Florida Evergreen Foliage v. E.I. DuPont de Nemours & Co.*, 2001, applying Florida law). These protected statements include statements made by judges, lawyers, parties to judicial proceedings, and witnesses; and these statements are not restricted to formal proceedings but rather can include communications preliminary to proposed judicial proceedings (*EEOC v. Day & Zimmerman NPS, Inc.*, 2017 *Florida Evergreen Foliage v. E.I. DuPont de Nemours & Co.*, 2001). Moreover, statements made by witnesses in legislative proceedings are protected if the statements are relevant to the legislative proceedings and the witness appeared pursuant to a legal subpoena. Statements made in labor grievance procedures are protected so long as the statements are relevant to the proceedings, are made during the proceedings, and are not transmitted beyond parties who have some relation to the proceedings. Finally, statements made in administrative proceedings, to unemployment-related agencies, and to state human rights commissions are absolutely protected too (*EEOC v. Day & Zimmerman NPS, Inc.*, 2017; *Porietis v. Tradesmen Int'l*, 2017, applying Maine law). The objective of affording absolute immunity to those who provide information in connection with judicial and quasi-judicial proceedings is that in certain situations the public interest in having people speak freely supersedes the risk that individuals will occasionally abuse the privilege (*EEOC v. Day & Zimmerman NPS, Inc.*, 2017).

A qualified privilege will afford complete immunity for defamatory statements if certain conditions are met. Accordingly, the statement must be made in good faith, on a proper occasion, published in a proper manner, by one who has an interest in the subject matter (either public, private, or personal interest) or a duty to speak (either legal, moral, social, judicial, or political duty), and to a person who has a corresponding interest or duty, then the statement is protected even if false. This privilege is also called the "common interest" privilege (*Brian A. Mastro v. Potomac Electric Power Company*, 2006, applying District of Columbia law) or the "conditional privilege" (*Theriault v. Genesis Healthcare LLC*, 2017, applying Maine law). For example, a statement in a report after an investigation that the plaintiff employee had "performance issues," even if defamatory, would be protected by the conditional privilege since the report was just distributed to "interested parties" of the employer (*Sullivan v. City of Frederick*, 2018, applying Maine law). Another example of communication protected by the conditional privilege would be a report mandated to be made to the government, for example, reports required to be made to the Department of Health and Human Services that a nursing assistant at a nursing home was abusive to a patient. The rationale is that such reports were legally mandated reports to a government agency regarding an issue of public concern, even if information in the reports was not technically accurate (*Theriault v. Genesis Healthcare LLC*, 2017).

The burden of defeating the privilege lies with the plaintiff employee suing for defamation (*Brian A. Mastro v. Potomac Electric Power Company* (2006). It typically is the function of a jury to decide if a false defamatory statement of fact is nonetheless protected by the privilege, which role for the jury would encompass any finding of malice or abuse (*Doe v. John Hopkins Health Sys. Corp.*, 2017, applying Maryland law). An interesting case is the aforementioned federal district court case of *Walter v. Jet Aviation Flight Servs*. (2017), applying Florida law, where there was evidence that the defamatory statement that a pilot engaged in unsafe flying conditions was made for personal and malicious purposes by the co-pilot/co-worker against the pilot employee and also by the employer who republished the statement in an attempt to get the pilot fired. As such, there was evidence that the co-pilot and the employer were motivated by a combination of malice and a genuine yet misguided belief that the pilot was engaging in unsafe flying conditions; and, accordingly, the court ruled that a jury must determine what was the primary motive in making the statements and thus whether the qualified privilege protected the statements (*Walter v. Jet Aviation Flight Servs*., 2017, applying Florida law). Another example of the qualified or conditional privilege being lost is the federal district court case of *Porietis v. Tradesmen Int'l* (2017), applying Maine law, where the court ruled that there was evidence of "malicious intent" in the statement by a supervisor that the plaintiff employee was fired for making a false report when the employee's supervisor regarded the employee as a "troublemaker" and also that the supervisor wanted to retaliate against the plaintiff employee for making a complaint about the negative conduct of a co-worker.

When defamation occurs on the Internet, unique problems emerge, especially with the "repetition" rule and the liability of re-publishers of defamatory statements. In particular, the legal issue arose as to whether an Internet service provider (ISP) could be construed as a "re-publisher" and thus potentially liable for defamatory statements made by users of their online services. This perplexing question was resolved by a federal statute in the United States, The Communications Decency Act of 1996, which holds that the provider as well as the user of an "interactive" computer service shall not be liable as a publisher or speaker for information provided by another content supplier. Moreover, the courts have ruled that even when an Internet service provider becomes aware of the defamatory statements on its online system, and fails to promptly remove them, the ISP is still not legally liable, though one would assume that ethically the ISP would feel duty-bound to remove the offensive material as soon as possible.

Defamation can also occur against one's property, and at times this tort is called "disparagement of property," which can include a variety of legal wrongs, such as slander of quality, trade libel, or slander of title. The essence of this type of defamation is that the defendant makes an intentional, false, accusation impugning the quality or ownership of another's goods or property. Ordinarily, the standard defamation rules apply to this variant of the tort, but with one major exception. In the "property" form of defamation, in order to recover damages, the aggrieved party will not have any damages presumed; rather, the plaintiff will have to prove that the disparagement to his or her property or ownership rights caused an actual property loss.

Management Implications and Recommendations:

Managers must be keenly aware that defamation law clearly applies to the workplace – and to both private sector and public sector workplaces. Typically, defamation cases arise when the employment relationship ends, usually when the employee is fired, and the discharged employee is seeking some sort of legal redress to sue for "wrongful discharge." In such a situation, employees who are discharged or demoted following a negative performance review will very likely include a defamation claim in their complaints if they are contemplating legal action for wrongful discharge. Another frequent occurrence of defamation in the workplace is when the employee asks for a job reference or recommendation for a prospective employer, and then the former employee claims that the information therein, usually negative reasons about why the employee was discharged and/or the employee's performance, were false and harmed the employee's job or career prospects. As such, the harm claimed by the employee usually is premised on the fact that another company did not hire the employee because of the allegedly defamatory statement (Guerin, 2020). However, from the employee's perspective defamation lawsuits can be difficult to win because the allegedly false statements usually take place in a context that the employee was not privy to, and even if stated to the employee it is usually just to the employee, thereby obviating the publication requirement. In addition, the employee will need to demonstrate that the allegedly defamatory statement was the cause of his or her being discharged or turned down for another job. Finally, in those states that afford the employer a qualified privilege to make false and defamatory statements, for example, in references, the employee would then have to prove that the employer in so doing acted with malice in the form of hatred or spite (Guerin, 2020).

Defamation claims in the private as well as public employment sectors frequently do arise, and are at times successful, especially when a prospective employer attempts to seek information about or verify the background of a job-seeker by asking for a reference or letter of recommendation from the employee's current or former employer. As such, the employer must decide if it merely will send a statement indicating basic information as to the tenure of the employee and his or her position and duties, or if the employer will send a true reference with information regarding the capabilities, competence, and character of the employee, or a true recommendation endorsing the employment to the prospective employer. The employer must be well aware that if a manager or employee of the employer provides a false reference or recommendation that falsely maligns the employee, harms his or her reputation, and thus hinders or prevents the employee from securing employment, there very well could be a lawsuit against the employer for defamation unless the employer can take advantage of a statutory 'common law privilege'. Similarly, false and derogatory information in an employee's performance review should also be protected by a privilege unless the employer was motivated by malice, bad faith, or an intent to harm the employee.

Managers, moreover, must be aware that defamation lawsuits by an employee can arise in an employment at-will situation, particularly in the private sector. Pursuant to the employment at-will doctrine, which is based on the old English common law and is still a governing principle in the vast majority of states in the United States, if an employee is an employee at-will he or she does not have any contractual protection regarding employment tenure and discharge. Consequently, the employee at-will can be discharged for no reason, no good reason, even a morally bad reason, such as nepotism, and, moreover, the employee is not entitled to any warning, notice, or explanation. Of course, the doctrine is defended as being a balanced one since the employee can quit at any time without any notice. Accordingly, if an at-will employee is terminated, and he or she wants to challenge the discharge as being a "wrongful discharge," the employee must come up with some legal doctrine and the facts to support it to challenge the termination. These legal doctrines can encompass violations of statutory law, such as civil rights and labor relations acts or whistleblowing statutes, as well as common law doctrines, such as negligence, fraud, invasion of privacy, infliction of emotional distress and, for the purposes herein, defamation. Without a legal avenue to proceed the at-will employee risks being fired legally as well as perhaps immorally; thus, an employer not acting ethically in terminating an employee is insufficient for a "wrongful discharge" claim as the latter is "purely" a legal doctrine.

Furthermore, managers must be cognizant of the fact that since defamation law is highly dependent on state law – case law and statutory – the employer must consult with an attorney in that particular jurisdiction. However, to avoid attorneys and legal problems the employer must clearly and firmly tell managerial and other employees to be truthful and accurate in transmitting information about employees as well as to have witnesses, evidence, and/or documentation to substantiate negative information about the employee. Have a complete, accurate, and substantial record of the facts. Tell the managers, human resource, and other pertinent personnel not to discuss the reasons for an employee's termination beyond those with a "need-to-know" and not to discuss the reasons beyond the organization. All employers should have policies regarding the criteria and procedures for termination, the relevant personnel to be involved, and the communication of the fact of as well as information about the termination of employees. In letters of recommendation, references, and performance reviews, the employer must make certain that there are no unfounded allegations of wrongdoing or misconduct that would harm the reputation of the employee and hinder his or her job prospects, particularly if the allegations involve criminality, theft or other dishonesty, workplace violence, incompetence, or sexual or other misconduct. Remember that disseminating false and derogatory information about an employee may be construed as a publication for a defamation claim, though the disclosure may be protected by a privilege. Regarding references for current and former employees and associates, even though certain states laws provide some legal cover, generally, many firms "err on the side of caution" and thus only state the dates of employment, title, and salary of a former employee to prospective employers.

Fraud

A very significant legal doctrine impacting business, particularly contractual relations, is *fraud*. Yet "fraud" is a very general legal formulation which covers a wide variety of legal wrongs based on misstating or misrepresenting facts. The first important point is to recognize that if fraud is committed in the contract inducement, execution, or performance, that legal wrong can be used in four main ways: 1) the victim of the fraud can interpose the fraud as an affirmative defense in a breach of contract lawsuit for non-performance; 2) the victim of fraud, instead of waiting to be sued for breach of contract, can proceed to a court and ask the court to rescind the contract on grounds of fraud; 3) if the contract is executed, the victim can sue at law to recover money or goods turned over to the wrongdoer as well as to sue for contract damages; and 4) the fraud may rise to the level of the legally actionable tort of fraud and the victim thereof can sue the perpetrator of the fraud for the intentional tort of fraud.

The second important point is to recognize that there are three types of misrepresentation wrongs: 1) fraud in the old common law sense of "deceit"; 2) negligent misrepresentation; and 3) innocent misrepresentation. Fraud in the sense of *deceit*, to be accurate, is called *intentional fraudulent misrepresentation*, and, as will be seen, requires evidence of an intent to deceive. The remedies for deceit encompass the full range of contract remedies and defenses, equitable rescission, and tort relief and tort damages, including punitive damages. Fraud in the sense of *negligent misrepresentation* is premised on a misrepresentation made not intentionally but by carelessness. The party making the misrepresentation does so not purposefully, but because of a failure to exercise reasonable care before making the misrepresentation, for example, by not uncovering crucial underlying facts. An example of negligent misrepresentation in the employment context would be when an employer provides pertinent job information to an applicant, but then subsequently there is a change of circumstances, such as a lack of funding for the position transpires or the employer decides to move to a different location. In such situations, if the change of circumstances is not communicated to the applicant before he or she has accepted the position, the employer could be liable for the tort of negligent misrepresentation (Morrison, 2016). Negligent misrepresentation provides contract remedies and rescission and also tort damages, but not punitive damages. The last generic "fraud" category is called "*innocent misrepresentation*," and it is a most interesting legal notion indeed. In this situation, a party does make a misrepresentation, but the party honestly believes that the statement is true and there is no negligence in making the misstatement. In such a case, the aggrieved party can rescind the contract and receive restitution, but there is no damage recovery.

The fraud legal wrong of greatest consequence is fraud in the sense of an intentional misrepresentation, that is, deceit. This type of fraud is, in essence, lying; but legally recognized lying, as not every lie is illegal in the "eyes" of the law, just fraudulent lying! Fraud thus can be defined as knowingly and purposefully inducing a person to enter into a contract as a result of an intentionally or recklessly made false statement of material fact. Fraud makes the resulting contract voidable; and affords the victim restitution and damages as remedies; and also fraud serves as the basis for a weighty intentional tort lawsuit. However, there are many elements to the legal wrong of fraud-deceit-lying that must be satisfied before the aggrieved party can interpose or sue on the doctrine.

Fraud is premised on a false statement of material fact; that is, any words or conduct that likely would cause an innocent party to reach an erroneous conclusion. Actively concealing material facts, and thereby preventing the other party from discovering the truth is treated as fraud, even though there are no express misrepresentations. It is, however, critical to note that the misrepresentation must concern "fact," that is, actual, historical events, circumstances, or occurrences, and not mere opinions or predictions, which are not legally actionable, unless perhaps made by an "expert." The person making the false statement must know that it was false at the time made, or that he or she made the statement in reckless disregard of its truth or falsity. Deceit is an intentional legal wrong and accordingly there must be evidence that the wrongdoer possessed an "evil mind," called the *scienter* requirement. That is, there must be evidence of a purposeful intent or design to deceive and to induce the innocent party to act. Finally, the allegations of fraud – the false statements, by and to whom made, and how it is made - must be pleaded specifically and with particularity in order to sustain the cause of action (*Stepanovich v. Houchin,* 2019).

Even if the preceding requirements are met, there still must be a showing that the aggrieved party justifiably or reasonably relied on the misrepresentation. For example, one cannot rely on the alleged misrepresentations in a company's privacy policy when one did not actually read the policy (*Terpin v. AT&T Mobility, Inc.*, 2020, applying California law). Similarly, one cannot reasonably rely on a person's erroneous representation of the taxable status of providing security services since the party is just giving a mere legal opinion, and the other party is in an equal position to ascertain the applicable law (*ISS Action, Inc. v. Tutor Perini Corp.*, 2019, applying New York law). Moreover, if the party making the misrepresentation can show that the other party knew or should have known of the true facts before taking the action, for example, entering into a contract, then there is no reasonable reliance present and thus no deceit. Employment examples could be when the applicant and potential employee is very experienced and knowledgeable about the position and/or company, or he or she is capable of making his or her own investigation as to the claims or information provided by the employer; because in such situations, a jury or court may find that the potential employee did not reasonably rely on the inaccurate information, even if the misstatements were carelessly or even purposefully made (Morrison, 2016). However, in one federal appeals case, the Fourth Circuit Court of Appeals, in *Fessler v. IMB* (2020), applying Virginia law, held that an employee, a sales information specialist with eight years of tenure, justifiably and reasonably relied on the company's representations in a Power Point presentation that repeatedly informed him that his commissions would not be capped. Important to the finding of reasonable reliance was the fact that the employee had no knowledge of the company ever capping commissions until the employee encountered it (*Fessler v. IBM*, 2020).

Moreover, if a buyer is given an opportunity to view and inspect goods, the buyer is presumed to know about any obvious or patent defects; consequently, the buyer cannot accept "blindly" whatever the seller misrepresents. Finally, if the person bringing the fraud lawsuit seeks to recover monetary damages based on the fraud, he or she must show some type of financial harm or physical injury as a result of the misrepresentation. Such a showing might be difficult for a job applicant who was previously unemployed or under-employed, since even though the actual position with the employer did not conform to the "glowing" statements made about the job, the employee may now be better off financially despite the misrepresentations (Morrison, 2016). As such, employers must be very careful to not make misrepresentations, either through carelessness or purposefulness, that induce the employee to leave a previous position or to move in order to work for the new employer (Morrison, 2016). For example, in the case of *Gupta V. Eli Global, LLC*, (2019), applying North Carolina law, the plaintiff, a mechanical engineer and a successful global entrepreneur, argued that he was fraudulently induced to enter the employer's medical and financial research business based on the following misrepresentations: that he would initially receive modest compensation but if the business was expanded he would receive substantial rewards, including stock appreciation rights; that the employer would never restructure the company that would deprive him of any monies earned, and that the employer would not interfere with his management of India operations.

Management Implications and Recommendations:

First and foremost, employers and managers must take reasonable measures to fully and accurately inform job applicants, potential employees, and current employees regarding information that might affect their decision to take the job or position; and if there is a change of circumstances, employers and managers must promptly notify applicants and candidates of the changes that might also affect their decision-making (Morrison, 2016). Also importantly, employers and managers must be aware of the common instances where fraud or misrepresentation claims can arise in the workplace based on representations made to employees or applicants that are false and either intentionally or negligently made. These fraudulent misrepresentations can be made to induce an employee to work for an employer or they can be made during the course of employment to induce the employee to change his or her position in a detrimental manner (LeWitter, 2020). Some typical examples of workplace fraud include the following misrepresentations regarding: the salary or amount of pay for the job; the existence of work, the kind of work and the duties therein, the length of work, or long-term job security or commitment to the employee, especially if relocation is involved; statements that at-will employment status would not apply to the employee; promises of higher salary, promotions, commissions, or guaranteed bonuses, particularly if they induce a person to quit a current job or close his or her business; promises of specific authority, especially in the form of managerial or supervisory authority; promises of a severance package or other retirement benefits that induce an employee to retire early; the existence or non-existence of any strike, lockout or labor dispute; the safety or sanitary conditions at work; statements regarding relocating or closing a plant, facility, department, and/or division of the company; and statements regarding the status of the company and/or its products or services, and statements regarding the financial strength, future viability, and successful performance of the company (Legal Aid at Work, 2020; LeWitter, 2020; Resnick Law Firm, 2020). However, if the fraudulent misrepresentations were made during the course of terminating the employee, and if the employee was an at-will employee, then generally there is no liability for fraud since the employer has the legal right to terminate the employee at-will, unless perhaps, the employer's misrepresentation which causes harm to the discharged employee is separate from the termination, for example, inducing the employee to give up a severance package which he or she is entitled to upon termination (LeWitter, 2020).

Of course, as emphasized, for an employee to successfully sustain a lawsuit for intentional misrepresentation, that is, fraud in the form of deceit, the plaintiff employee must demonstrate that the misrepresentations were either intentionally or recklessly as well as knowingly made by the defendant employer or its managers. This evidentiary task can be a very difficult burden because such a showing requires some evidence of the defendant's "evil" and purposeful state-of-mind or evidence that the defendant acted in bad faith and/or in reckless disregard of the truth or falsity of the statement. However, fraudulent intent may be inferred by a jury based on indirect or circumstantial evidence, for example, the quick insolvency of the employer, the rapid repudiation of a promise to the employee, the failure to attempt any type of performance, or the continued assertions of performance when the evidence is clear that a party would not perform (DeWitter, 2020).

Managers must be cognizant of a major principle in the law of fraud. That is, generally, silence is not fraud. The rationale for this old common law rule goes back even further to Roman times and the Roman saying Caveat Emptor, that is, "Let the buyer beware." Consequently, refraining from disclosing pertinent facts unknown to the other party is not fraud. Under the common law, again, as a general rule, there is no duty to volunteer information. Another reason given for this rule is that the essence of fraud is the affirmative misleading of one person by another. For example, there is no duty for a seller of a pre-owned car to tell a prospective buyer that the car was previously in an accident. There are, however, many exceptions to this rule. One common law exception arises if one is deemed to be a fiduciary, that is, one is in a relationship of trust and confidence with another party, such as: the attorney-client relationship; between partners; shareholders in a small, closely-held corporation, even if they are also in the employer – employee relationship (Stepanovich v. Houchin, 2019); the stockbroker- customer relationship, the real estate broker-customer relationship; the corporate director-corporation relationship; and/or the principal-agent relationship. In such a case, there is a duty to speak and silence will equate to fraud. In the employment context, managers must be aware that an aggrieved employee likely will argue that he or she was in a fiduciary relationship with his or her employer and thus entitled to disclosure about the facts and circumstances of the job, position, and company. However, the fact that the parties are about to enter into an employer-employee relationship or are in one is as a general rule not sufficient to establish a fiduciary relationship (LeWitter, 2020); but there may be exceptions among the several states and thus reference must be made to the pertinent state's law.

In addition to the fiduciary exception, several states by statutes have modified the old common law, and now hold, for example, that the seller of real property has an affirmative duty to disclose latent and hidden defects which a basic inspection would not disclose, such as subsoil conditions or termite infestation, as well as in the case of goods whether a vehicle was a Hurricane Katrina (or otherwise) flooded vehicle. There are also federal statutes, for example pertaining to securities fraud, in which the old common law "silence" rule has been changed by legislative pronouncement and thus where silence can be fraud.

Another aspect of fraud that managers should be aware of is the general rule that misrepresenting the law is as a general rule not grounds for fraud. That is, generally, one can lie about the law, for example, whether an area is zoned for a business to sell alcohol. The (perhaps a bit "twisted") rationale for this rule is the old maxim that "ignorance of the law is no excuse"; consequently, everyone is presumed to know the law, and thus reliance on a lie about the law is not reasonable. An exception deals with attorneys and other non-lawyer experts in certain legal fields whose misrepresentations of the law will be deemed to be fraud, such as real estate agents regarding real property law.

Breach of the Duty of Loyalty

The focus of this section is on the duty of the employee to act in a loyal manner while being employed by the employer. This *duty of loyalty* was created by and principally today is based on the common law, that is, judge-made decisions that interpret and apply the duty of loyalty to employment cases and controversies. The violation of this duty is construed as a breach of a fiduciary duty, and thus a tort, as well as a breach of contract.

The fundamental common law rule is that an employee has a legal duty not to engage in any disloyal acts against his or her employer during the employment relationship. This duty of loyalty does not depend on the existence of a written employment contract. The employee can be an employee at-will and he or she is still bound by the duty of loyalty. The duty is implied by virtue of the common law. As such, the employee must act in an honest, faithful, and loyal manner and must discharge all of his or her employment duties for the sole benefit of the employer. If the employee acts in a self-serving manner which is contrary to the employer's interests, the duty of loyalty is violated. Similarly, if an employee fails to disclose matters that are inimical to the interests of employer, the duty is violated. If the employee takes an undisclosed payment or receives an undisclosed benefit from a third party the duty is violated.

However, merely being a poorly performing employee does not automatically equate to a breach of the duty of loyalty to one's employer. To illustrate, in one federal case, *Laba v. Chicago Transit Authority* (2017), the federal district court in Illinois dismissed the employer's breach of loyalty claim against multiple employees who were allegedly sleeping, using their personal cell phones, reading personal mail and newspapers, and viewing pornography in an electrical breaker room for extended periods of time, which went well beyond any break periods. According to that court, such activities by these employees did not amount to a valid disloyalty action, even if their misconduct occurred on-the-job. That court relied upon prior precedent which established that an employee who fails to perform his or her work, whether he or she spends time and "work" sleeping on the job, day-dreaming, or "surfing" the internet is not disloyal; nonetheless, the employee still receives a full paycheck; yet this conduct, according to the court in *Laba*, simply is not comparable to an employee who steals or embezzles from his or her employer when analyzing breach of loyalty claims against regular employees

Of course, once the employee leaves the job (that is, the employer's employ) he or she no longer owes the duty of loyalty and thus is free to compete against his or her former employer, absent any contract provisions to the contrary, for example, a covenant-not-to-compete or a non-solicitation (non-piracy) agreement. Note that even if the duty of loyalty is not one premised on a fiduciary duty, the more "generic" and general duty of loyalty still exists to be applied to a case, and which will give rise to tort liability. This common law general duty of loyalty presupposes faithful, honest, ethical, diligent, and attentive conduct on the part of the employee.

There are several factors to be taken into consideration when determining if an employee has breached the duty of loyalty. First and foremost, directly competing against one's employer while working for the employer clearly violates the duty of loyalty. The employee's commencing and carrying on a competing business while working for an employer will be deemed to be a disloyal and illegal act. Mere preparation, however, to open a competing business, even active preparation while in the employer's employ, may be permissible. Merely making "preparations" or "arrangements" to compete, including planning on buying or even buying a rival business may be permissible, so long as no customers are solicited for the rival business, no confidential information is misappropriated, no conduct directly damaging the employer or directly competing with the employer is done while in the employer's employ. Similarly, organizing the competing business, opening a bank account, as well as securing office space, will likely not be deemed to be disloyal acts. Moreover, incorporating a business to compete with the employer as well as developing competing products or designs may also be permissible so long as the employer's time and resources are not utilized and no confidential information is wrongfully used, such as the employer's new product pipeline and plan and pricing proposals and data.

However, soliciting customers, clients, and co-workers, diverting business to the new firm, as well as using the employer's resources for the purpose of starting a competing company, will rise to the level of improper competition and thus disloyal acts.

The following cases will illustrate the "competition" vs. "preparation" factors: For example, in the federal district court case of *Viken Detection Corp. v. Videray Techs, Inc.* (2020), applying Massachusetts law, the defendant former employee, the director of engineering for the employer, argued that while working for the employer he was merely engaged in "mere preparation" and in "logistical arrangements" in forming a company to prepare to compete with the employer. However, the evidence indicated the following actions taken by the defendant employee: 1) meeting with potential investors to solicit funds; 2) soliciting a co-worker to join his new company; 3) collecting the employer's customer accounts; 4) accessing confidential employee salary and equity information to entice employees to join his firm; 5) failing to share customer feedback relating to product improvements and intending to use this information for his competing product; and 6) asking co-workers to help him collect confidential customer information. Accordingly, the court in *Viken Detection Corp.* ruled that these actions were not mere preparation but rather active competition, and thus a breach of the duty of loyalty. Similarly, in a South Carolina supreme court case, *Futch v. McAlister Towing, Inc.* (1999), the court ruled that the duty of loyalty was breached when the employee initiated a competing business, undercut his employer on pricing, targeted current customers of the employer asking them to commit to the new company, and lured co-workers to work for the new company. However, even if the competition against the employer is indirect a court may still find that the duty of loyalty was breached. As such, the employee cannot act to harm the employer to benefit a competitor of the employer or to otherwise benefit the competitor, which may be a potential employer for the employee. In another state supreme court case, from New Jersey, *Cameo, Inc. v. Gedicke* (1999), the court ruled that assistance provided to a competitor of the employer, for example, by co-mingling shipments of goods of the employer and two competitors and by having the competitors' goods delivered first, although indirect behavior nonetheless harmed the employer and thus violated the employee's duty of loyalty. The New Jersey supreme court also pointed out that if the assistance to a competitor of the employer is direct but even slight a breach of the duty of loyalty nonetheless could occur; whereas if the assistance is indirect the employer would have to show that the competitor received substantial assistance. Accordingly, this line separating "mere" preparation from "active" competition is difficult to ascertain. Consequently, this critical issue is often considered to be a "question of fact" to be decided by the trier of fact, typically a jury, which will have to look at all the facts and circumstances of the case.

Whether the employee's allegedly disloyal activities were done in secret or known by the employer is another factor in determining liability. Secrecy may imply active wrongdoing and may make the case stronger that the duty of loyalty has been breached. However, an employee may be able to secretly prepare for and incorporate a competing business prior to departing, so long as the employee did not use his or her employer's time, facilities, or confidential information or solicit the employer's customers. For example, in *Techno Lite, Inc. v. Emcod, LLC* (2020) a California court of appeals case, the court held that two employees surreptitiously incorporating a competing business selling the same products as their employer, soliciting and diverting customer accounts to their business, including sending emails to customers to replace their employer with them, as well as asking customers to change the purchase orders they had in their computers with the employees' firm, violated the duty of loyalty.

Another factor is the knowledge of the employer. To illustrate, in one federal appeals court case for the Third Circuit, *Colgate Palmolive Company v. Tandem Industries* (2012), applying Pennsylvania law, the court upheld a finding of disloyalty by the employee when the employee sold certain second-hands products to retailers of the employer even though the employee thought the products were his own because the employer was not informed of the sales. To compare, in a federal district court case applying New Jersey law, *Hahn v. OnBoard, LLC* (2011), the court dismissed the employer's disloyalty claim based on the employee promoting at focus group meetings his own blog and distributing his own blog cards, which did not mention the employer, while attending a trade conference on his employer's behalf, because the employer had pre-existing knowledge of these activities and did not object to these actions.

There also is a relationship between the position and responsibility of an employee and the duty of loyalty. Accordingly, the duty of loyalty is more likely to be applied to higher level employees who are in a position of trust and confidence and thus who have access to confidential information than to lower-level employees who perform basic tasks. To illustrate, in one federal district court case, *Numeric Analytics, LLC v. McCabe* (2016), applying Pennsylvania law, the court was dealing with multiple claims by an employer against five non-resident ex-employees who allegedly breached their duty of loyalty by violating non-solicitation agreements by leaving the plaintiff company's employ, starting a competing business, and poaching plaintiff's clients. The five non-resident defendants worked remotely outside of the state of Pennsylvania where their employer's principal place of business was located and where the employer filed suit. The court held that the e-commerce activities by the ex-workers were too tenuous to support personal jurisdiction over them, *except* one who was the president of the company. Another example where the position of the employees was a factor was the New Jersey court of appeals case of *Comet Mgmt. Co. v. Wooten* (2020), where the office manager and financial manager of a property management firm while working for the employer formed a competing company and solicited and accepted business from the employer's clients. The defendants argued that some of the clients were dissatisfied with the employer's services. The court nonetheless found a violation of the duty of loyalty, stressing the high-level management positions of the defendants as well as the fact that they were in relationship of trust and confidence and thus owed a "higher duty" to the employer as opposed to employees performing "low-level" tasks. To compare, in the California court of appeals case of *Arriaga v. Lara* (2020), the low-level position of the employees was the critical factor in the disposition of the case in favor of the employees. In the *Arriaga* case, the court first generally noted that an employee does not breach the duty of loyalty by preparing to compete with his or her employer. The case involved two security employees of the employer who while working for the employer submitted a bid for security services to a major customer of the employer. The employees also did not tell their employer that the customer was looking for alternative security service providers and was accepting bids. Normally, one would think that the duty of loyalty would be breached based on the preceding facts. However, the fact that the employees were low-level, part-time, at-will, security guards and not managers, supervisors, or high-level employees was the critical factor in the court's determination that the duty of loyalty was not breached (*Arriaga v. Lara*, 2020). Nevertheless, it is important to note that an employee does not necessarily have to be a management employee or a high-level employee to have the duty of loyalty imposed by the courts on the employee. Even non-management employee can perform certain duties and obligations that involve the duty of loyalty. Therefore, the employee violating the loyalty duty can be a lower-level one.

The employee's soliciting co-workers prior to the end of his or her employment to join a new competing company likely will be construed by the courts as a violation of the duty of loyalty. However, whether the solicitation of co-workers is a breach of the duty of loyalty is a fact-intensive examination requiring consideration of several factors, to wit: 1) the nature of the co-worker's employment relationship with the employer, that is, whether at-will or pursuant to a contract; 2) the impact of the solicitation on the employer's operations; 3) the extent of any promises or inducements made to co-workers; 4) whether the co-workers were key officers or employees; 5) whether the co-workers left simultaneously; and 6) whether the employer was given an opportunity to hire and train replacements. To illustrate, pertaining to solicitation situations, in one federal court of appeals case in the Eighth Circuit, *Stuart C. Irby Company v. Brandon Tipton* (2015), applying Arkansas law, the court ruled that there was sufficient evidence for a trial on the issue of the duty of loyalty being breached when the employee, while still being employed by his employer, solicited fellow employees to work for a competitor of the employer, whom the employee resigned to work for, by means of several telephone calls, emails, and text messages to the co-workers as well as arranging a meeting at the competitor's facility which included "beer and a tour." In another federal district court case, *Riggs Investment Management Corp. v. Columbia Partners*, LLC (1997), applying the law of the District of Columbia, the employee provided to a competitor of the employer confidential and detailed information about co-workers before resigning to work for the competitor's company. The competitor then used the information to recruit employees away from the former employer. The district court ruled that the employee violated his duty of loyalty because he did not act for the benefit of his employer and that he acquired in interest adverse to his employer. However, when the employee leaves the employer's employ the former employee is allowed to state to his or her former co-workers that he or she is commencing a new business, give them a business card or the equivalent, and asks them to join the former employee's new firm. Of course, such solicitation will not be permitted if the former employee is bound by a non-solicitation or non-piracy clause in the contract with the former employer.

A violation of the duty of loyalty clearly occurs if the employee while working for the employer uses customer lists and customer contact information to contact the employer's customers to lure them to the employee's competing business. As a general rule, the employee may not use written lists of clients or customers which he compiled during the course of his employment and took with him or her on departure, because such lists will be construed as the confidential and proprietary property of the former employer. However, if the former employee has developed the list himself or herself and there are no contractual restrictions on the employee's taking and using the list there is some authority that the employee can take and utilize the list. Similarly, if the employee developed the list by soliciting clients on his or her own, or before her employment with the employer, then there would be no violation of the duty of loyalty. The duty of loyalty may be breached by the employee using, disclosing, or otherwise misappropriating confidential information. For example, an employee sending confidential emails to herself with client information could be a breach of the duty of loyalty if the email information was used by the employee to compete with her employer.

The employee's soliciting of clients and/or customers of the employer prior to the end of employment will also be construed by the courts as a disloyal act. Moreover, it is irrelevant that the employee did not initiate the contact with the employer's customer. There is still a breach of the duty of loyalty if the employee agrees to do the work for the employer's customer without informing the employer. To illustrate, the court in the aforementioned *Riggs Investment Management Corp.* case also found that the duty of loyalty was breached because the former employee also provided to a competitor of the employer detailed information about his employer's clients before he resigned to join the competitor, which information the competitor used to solicit and obtain clients from the former employer. Another example is a federal district court case, *Shamrock Power Sales, LLC v. John Scherer* (2015), applying New York law, where the employee, a sales representative, while being employed, secretly set up a competing business, misappropriated and copied client contact information, price lists, and other sensitive and proprietary information, secretly contacted customers and tried to lure them away from the employer, deleted the employer's name from purchase orders, and instructed customers not to send their purchase orders to the employer. The court ruled that the evidence showed that this conduct was unfaithful, disloyal, not isolated, and thus substantially violated the duty of loyalty. In another federal district court case, *Audio Visual Group, LLC v. Christopher Green* (2014), applying Virginia law, the court ruled that the employee, a sales engineer breached the duty of loyalty by invoicing for a separate business 34 customers who were also customers to whom his employer had provided quotations; moreover, the employee was in the process of quoting 29 separate projects to existing or potential customers of his employer. Nevertheless, when the employee leaves the employer's employ the former employee is allowed to state to his or her former clients or customers that he or she is commencing a new business, give them a business card or the equivalent, and ask them to be served by the former employee's new firm or position. Of course, such solicitation will not be permitted if the former employee is bound by a non-solicitation or covenant-not-to-compete clause in the contract with the former employer.

Management Implications and Recommendations:

Managers should take heed of a pronouncement by the New Jersey court of appeals, in Comet Mgmt. v. Wooten (2020), that duty of loyalty cases can be very "fact-specific" ones that require "rules of reason and fairness." Nonetheless, managers can take certain proactive steps to bolster a duty of loyalty lawsuit. As such, managers are advised whenever possible under state law to attempt to characterize the breach of loyalty as a breach of a fiduciary duty since the latter is viewed as a tort with more expansive tort damages. Such a characterization would have greater weight when applied to higher level employees. Managers are also advised to be wary of inserting arbitration clauses in contracts since if a breach of the duty of loyalty is viewed as a contract dispute it may be governed by the arbitration clause and the arbitration process, where the damages and right to appeal are limited. However, if the breach of the duty of loyalty is viewed as the violation of a fiduciary duty then a tort remedy is available, which is one that will be independent of any arbitration clause in the contract. The contract between the employer and employee may be able to emphasize as well as to define the duty of loyalty, for example, by spelling out the confidential nature of the employee's position. Similarly, the contract may be able to state the fiduciary nature of the employment relationship and thus help to create a fiduciary relationship between the employer and employee. Managers also should use confidentiality and non-disclosure agreements to enhance contractual and trade secret protection of confidential information as well as to define the parameters of the duty of loyalty.

Customer lists and contact information and other confidential and sensitive information, such as price lists, should be clearly designated as valuable confidential and proprietary information, and then reasonable measures should be instituted to maintain the secrecy of such information in order to take advantage of trade secret law protection. Managers also should use non-solicitation and non-piracy agreements to contractually prevent the employee from contacting clients and customers of the employer and to further define the duty of loyalty. Managers, moreover, should use covenant-not-to-compete agreements to prevent the employee from unreasonably competing against the employer. The aforementioned contractual agreements should specifically and explicitly cover social media and Internet communications and competition. Managers, furthermore, should use "works-for-hire" provisions within written employment agreements to set expectations with their workforce that all intellectual property developed by employees or independent contractors belongs exclusively to the employer. The aforementioned contractual provisions are particularly important in contracts with higher-level and/or technical employees who typically would have access to confidential information.

Violation of Public Policy

The *"public policy" doctrine* is a tort-based, common law doctrine which is adhered to, though in varying degrees, by all the states in the United States. The "public policy" doctrine maintains that an employee, even an *at-will employee* (that is, one without any contractual protection regarding termination), cannot be discharged for engaging in an activity that public policy encourages, or conversely for not engaging in an activity that public policy discourages, such as illegal and immoral conduct. The definition of "public policy" is not clear, but generally it includes activities that promote the health, safety, and welfare of the citizens and residents of a state as well as activities that encourage lawful and ethical conduct. Ultimately, the high court of each state, the state supreme court, will determine what "public policy" means on a case-by-case basis, though the courts are guided by the state's constitution, statutes, and prior judicial decisions. So, for example, firing an at-will employee for serving on a jury or grand jury, for filing a Worker's Compensation claim, or for filing a safety report with state regulators are all violations of public policy since the law favors all those activities. Similarly, firing an employee for refusing to violate a statute or to participate in illegal activity will typically trigger the "public policy" doctrine. For example, the California appeals court ruled that the firing of a union employee for refusing to pay money to three union officials, which money purportedly was to be used for political campaign contributions, was in essence the crime of extortion, and thus there was a violation of public policy for the employee's discharge (*Gaelotti v. International Union of Operating Engineers Local No. 3*, 2020). Furthermore, the supreme court of South Carolina ruled that a town's firing of a building inspector, who was an at-will employee, for issuing a "stop-work" order on a construction project violated "a clear mandate of public policy" of the state because the state statute required the inspector to do so when an inspector determines there are building code violations (*Donevant v. Town of Surfside Beach*, 2018). Also, the preceding *Donevant* case is noteworthy because of the fact that there was a discretionary element to the building inspector's issuing stop-work orders; but nonetheless the state supreme court stated that it was the inspector's legal duty to take action when she believed that unpermitted construction was occurring in violation of the building code. Finally, whistleblowing, that is, disclosing wrongdoing by the employer or fellow employees, even if not protected by a state whistleblower protection statute, may afford the whistleblowing at-will employee the legal recourse to challenge a discharge.

In one interesting public policy case, an employer fired an armored truck driver who left his vehicle unguarded while he attempted to rescue a woman from a knife-wielding robber. The supreme court of the state of Washington, however, ruled that the defendant company wrongfully terminated the plaintiff employee for violating the company's work rule, which prohibited armored truck drivers from leaving their vehicles unattended. The state supreme court decided that a discharge for saving a woman from a life-threatening situation violated public policy, which encourages such "heroic" conduct. The court emphasized that society values and thus should encourage voluntary rescues in life-threatening circumstances (Cavico and Mujtaba, 2014). To compare, in a Massachusetts case, a female employee who worked in a computer store was told she had to work long work shifts as the company was going through a merger. She refused, saying that she was a single-mother and if she had to work such long-hours she would barely see her child awake. She was fired; and then sued for wrongful discharge based on a contravention of the state's public policy doctrine, contending that the public policy favors taking care of children. However, although expressing sympathy for her and parents in general, the supreme court of Massachusetts ruled that the public policy doctrine was not violated by her discharge. In another often-cited and noteworthy case, an at-will employee, an engineer in a defense and technology company, was encouraged to "speak his mind" in company employee forums, called Dialog, All-Hands, and Straight-Talk. The company even provided a "facilitator" to encourage employees to speak up. The employee did in fact speak up, criticizing his employer's upper-level managers for receiving "enormous" bonuses at a time of poor economic performance, layoffs, and budget reductions, and without regard to the fate of lower level company employees, the interests of shareholders and the public good. The employee was discharged and sued for a violation of public policy, contending that he was commenting on important public issues; but the court ruled that the expression of his opinion of his company's management was merely "a matter between him and his employer" and thus not a public policy violation (Cavico and Mujtaba, 2014).

A public policy claim, if successful, in most states, is a tort violation, which means that the wrongfully discharged employee has a tort lawsuit against his or her employer for tort damages, including damages for "pain and suffering" and punitive damages. For example, in one noteworthy case, an employee, a gastro-intestinal research scientist, was fired by his pharmaceutical company employer for protesting the company's alleged failure to disclose the adverse side-effects of an anti-ulcer drug it was developing. The employee complained to the Food and Drug Administration. A California jury found that the scientist had been discharged in violation of the fundamental public policy of the state of California and awarded him $2.5 million for economic loss and emotional distress as well as $15 million in punitive damages (Cavico and Mujtaba, 2014). In another California court of appeals case, *Colucci v. T-Mobile USA, Inc.* (2020), the court ruled that a manager willfully and consciously firing an employee who complained about discrimination was a public policy tort violation and one sufficiently oppressive and reprehensible to justify an award of punitive damages as well as compensatory damages.

Management Implications and Recommendations:

Managers must be aware that the critical term "public policy" is a very nebulous and amorphous concept, which is highly dependent on state law, primarily legislative enactments and judicial interpretations thereof. Accordingly, reference must be made to the pronouncements of the high court in the pertinent state to secure guidance on the meaning of "public policy." Some situations are relatively easy to decide, for example, discharging an employee for doing his or her civic duty of jury service, filing a Worker's Compensation claim, refusing to lie to government regulators, or "blowing the whistle" on the employer's or co-worker's illegal conduct. Other situations are more problematic. For example, in the aforementioned armored car-driver and single-mother cases, if one was going to make reasonable predictions, one would think that the armored car-driver who disobeyed company policy would lose whereas the single-mother, especially in a "liberal" state such as Massachusetts, would prevail. Yet the result was just the opposite! And that is one major reason why cases get settled. Finally, it is important to point that as noted in most states a public policy violation is a tort, and an intentional one, thereby subjecting the employer to the full range of potential tort damages. Yet if the conduct by the discharged employee is "whistle-blowing," that is, informing on illegal conduct, the employee's common law tort claim may be preempted by the state's Whistleblower Protection Act, assuming a state has one. Such preemption of the tort claim by the statute can be very beneficial to the employer since in most states the remedy for the statutory whistle-blowing violation is a compensatory one, that is, reinstatement with back pay, seniority, benefits, etc., but not damages for emotional distress or punitive damages.

Wrongful Institution of Legal Proceedings

The final intentional tort to the person is the *wrongful institution of legal proceedings*, also called "*malicious prosecution.*" This tort is based on the premise that under the common law people have a right not to be sued for unjust, unfair, or improper reasons, but rather only for legally just reasons. Accordingly, this tort arises when a private party (and not a government prosecutor) wrongfully institutes criminal or civil proceedings against another party, which terminate in that party's innocence or exoneration, and when the defendant initiating the legal proceedings lacked probable cause to proceed and also possessed an improper purpose for instituting the criminal action or civil action. Evidence of malice, typically in the form of ill will, hatred, or spite, also may be a required element in some jurisdictions (Stimmel, Stimmel, and Roeser, 2020).

Malicious prosecution must be differentiated from *abuse of process*, which is a broader tort in that it covers the wrongful use of any aspect of the legal process, for example, the deliberate and wrongful use of subpoenas, summons, liens, attachments on property, and executions on property, in order for the wrongdoer to attempt to accomplish an improper purpose for which the legal process was not intended, typically the payment or performance of some collateral obligation. The tort neither requires prior institution of a lawsuit, litigation, nor prosecution. However, depending on the jurisdiction, evidence of malice may be required. Both torts recognize that under the common law people have a right to be protected from misuse and abuse of prosecution, litigation, and the misuse of the legal system and processes. However, merely because a person has a weak case, or is mistaken, stubborn, and/or stupid does not necessarily mean that there has been malicious prosecution or abuse of process, even if that person eventually loses his or her case (Stimmel, Stimmel, and Roeser, 2020). Finally, it again must be emphasized that, as with so many aspects of the common law of torts, reference must be made to the specific *corpus* of law in a particular jurisdiction.

Intentional Torts to Property

The preceding analysis has focused on intentional torts to the person as they are most pertinent to business and employment. However, the authors would be remiss if they did not briefly examine the second category of intentional torts – intentional torts to the property of a person. The law recognizes that there are protected interests regarding not only one's person but also one's property. Accordingly, there are four main types of intentional torts to property: 1) trespass to land, 2) trespass to chattels, 3) conversion, and 4) defamation to property (which latter tort was previously covered in the defamation section).

A *trespass to land* happens when a person purposefully and physically invades another's land or real property. The interest protected by this tort is the interest of exclusive possession of real property. Some physical invasion of the land is required, though it is not necessary that the defendant actually comes on the premises. For example, a defendant can be liable for a trespass by intentionally causing objects or third parties to come upon the plaintiff's land. A trespass can exist, moreover, when a defendant remains on a plaintiff's land after the defendant's original lawful right of entry has ended. However, if no physical object or person enters the land, then there is no "invasion" and thus no trespass; however, the defendant may still be liable under nuisance law if the plaintiff's use and enjoyment of the premises is materially and unreasonably impeded, for example, by noise or odors. There is one caveat regarding the intent requirement to trespass to land. That is, although intent is required, the intent to trespass is not required; rather, only the intent to do the act that constitutes the trespass is sufficient. A mistake, therefore, as to the lawfulness of the defendant's entry on the land is not a defense. Finally, there is no requirement of actual damages in order to have a cause of action in trespass; that is, actual injury to the land or real estate is not required; damages, at least nominal damages, are presumed. In addition, if the trespass continues, it may evoke a lawsuit in equity by the landowner for an injunction.

The next type of intentional tort to property is *trespass to chattels* or, in more modern parlance, trespass to personal property (as opposed to real property). This tort requires a purposeful act by the defendant which interferes with the plaintiff's right and interest in the possession of a chattel (or thing). This type of trespass can arise by intermeddling, that is, conduct which directly damages the personal property, such as intentionally "keying" another's automobile, or by dispossession, that is, by temporarily depriving a person of his or her right to possession of a chattel, such as "borrowing" another's bicycle for a ride. As with trespass to land, a mistake is not defense; however, contrary to the "land" tort, trespass to chattels requires some actual damage to the property or a dispossession for an appreciable length of time; nominal damages are not presumed for a trespass to chattels. Note that if the interference with, or dispossession of, the chattel is so serious or so long, the tort may be "upgraded" to the intentional property tort of conversion, which may require the defendant to pay the full value of the property as damages.

The intentional tort "cousin" to trespass to chattels is the tort of *conversion.* The essence of conversion is a purposeful act by the defendant which amounts to an exercise of dominion and control over a chattel of the plaintiff's, which is so long or serious in nature that the defendant must pay the full value of the chattel as damages. Conversion may be effectuated by a variety of methods: 1) wrongfully acquiring the property (for example, by theft or embezzlement, which also makes the civil wrong of conversion a crime); 2) wrongfully transferring the property, such as by selling or mis-delivering it; 3) wrongfully detaining the property, such as refusing to return it to its rightful owner; 4) substantially changing the property; 5) destroying or severely damaging the property; or 6) misusing the property. The property, of course, converted must be tangible personal property, and not land or real property. Recall also that conversion is an intentional tort; and thus "merely" causing accidental damage to or loss of the property is not sufficient for the tort of conversion, though, it may be grounds for the tort of negligence. At times, it is difficult to draw the line between "mere" trespass to chattels and the more serious legal wrong of conversion. The more serious the damage to the property is, the longer the time that the defendant holds the property, and the more extensively the defendant uses the property, the more likely that a jury will find that the conversion tort has been committed. Assuming a conversion, the aggrieved party gets as damages the fair market value of the property at the time and place of conversion. This means of redress can in essence be a "forced sale" even if the defendant offers to return the property, as a plaintiff is not obligated to take an item back. Finally, the plaintiff, if he or she does want the item back, can seek a writ of "replevin" from the court, ordering the defendant to return the item.

Management Implications and Recommendations:

Managers should be aware that there is currently a legal controversy as to whether "spam" and "spamming" can be conceived as a trespass to property. Spam, of course, is bulk, unsolicited, and "mass" email. Because of the burden in time, effort, and money that "spamming" may inflict on an online user or an Internet service provider, some courts in the United States have stated a willingness to accept "spam as trespass" lawsuits. The courts, though, typically will require a showing of material economic harm produced by voluminous spamming, and not mere annoyance, before imposing tort damage liability under a trespass to chattels theory or issuing an injunction. Moreover, due to the uncertainty of tort law as well as the many, and at times conflicting, state statutes regulating spam, the U.S. Congress in 2003 enacted the CAN-SPAM Act, fully known as the Controlling the Assault of Non-Solicited Pornography and Marketing Act, which went into effect on

January 1 of 2004. This federal statute applies to any electronic and commercial mail messages; and it also preempts any state anti-spam laws (except state laws prohibiting false and deceptive email practices). The CAN-SPAM Act, it is essential to underscore initially, does not prohibit spam; rather, the federal law prohibits certain types of spamming practices, such as not having a return address or having a false return address on the email, "harvesting" email addresses from others' Web sites, as well as sending mass emails to randomly generated email addresses. The Act also requires an "opt-out" provision, thereby enabling a recipient to block further emails from the same source, as well as the appropriate labeling of any sexually oriented materials appearing in the email message. While the federal statute certainly will preempt conflicting state anti-spam statutes, it remains to be seen whether CAN-SPAM will also override the old common law of torts, especially the "virtual" use of the trespass to chattels intentional tort doctrine. It also should be mentioned that another anti-spamming statute was promulgated in 2006, the U.S. Safe Web Act (also known as the Undertaking Spam, Spyware, and Fraud Enforcement with Enforcers Beyond Borders Act), which is designed to prevent spam originating from servers in other countries. The U.S. Safe Web Act enables the U.S. Federal Trade Commission to share information and cooperate with foreign government agencies to investigate and eventually prosecute spamming, spyware, and other instances of fraud and deception on the Internet.

Defenses to Intentional Torts

Although the discussion of the intentional torts to persons and property in this chapter has touched on several defenses germane to specific torts, mention should be made of three general categories of intentional tort defenses: 1) consent, 2) self-defense, and 3) defense of property.

The *consent* defense holds that as a general rule, a defendant is not liable for a wrongful act if the plaintiff has consented to that act. Consent may be given expressly or impliedly. Implied consent is often referred to as "apparent consent," that is, the consent that a reasonably prudent person would give in such circumstances, for example, when engaging in a bodily contact sport, or shopping on "sale day" in a crowded shopping mall. Consent, moreover, will also be implied by the law, for example, in an emergency situation where some type of action, such as medical care, is necessary to save an unconscious person's life. Similarly, pursuant to many states' Good Samaritan statutes, a rescuer who voluntarily assists at the scene of an emergency may be absolved from intentional tort liability by statute, though typically the rescuer is still obligated to effectuate the rescue or render aid in a careful and non-negligent manner.

Self-defense is an ancient, common law, legal doctrine; and is one that still affords a viable defense to intentional tort liability. Today, self-defense common law principles are typically embodied in statutes (see, for example, New Jersey Statutes, 2020). When a person possesses reasonable grounds to believe that he or she is being attacked, or about to be attacked, that person may use such force as reasonably necessary to protect against the potential harm. This defense is available when one has a reasonable belief as to another party's hostile actions. A work example would be when an employee physically attacks his or her supervisor; then the supervisor would be entitled to use a reasonable amount of force to defend himself or herself (Legal Aid, 2020). The "apparent necessity" of defending oneself is all that is required, not actual necessity; and, therefore, a reasonable mistake as to the existence of the danger does not negate the defense, with the "classic" example being the "unloaded gun" case. Moreover, under the old common law, though with some differences among the states today, there is no duty to retreat. Thus, most courts would hold that there is no duty to try to escape; rather, a person may "stand your ground," and thereby defend oneself. Yet how much force can be used in this self-defense? As a general rule, only that force which reasonably appears necessary to prevent the harm will be authorized; consequently, one may not use force likely to cause death or serious bodily injury unless one reasonably believes that he or she is in danger of serious bodily injury. If more force than necessary is employed, the actor will lose his or her legal right to self-defense. As a result, he or she become the potentially tortious aggressor. Finally, it is important to note that if properly used, the right to self-defense extends to third party injuries. Accordingly, when in the course of reasonably defending oneself a person accidentally injures a bystander, the actor is still protected by the defense.

The common law right to self-defense encompasses a person's right to defend his or her property. Accordingly, one may use reasonable force to prevent the commission of a tort against his or her property, including trespass, as well as theft, criminal mischief, or other criminal or civil interference. There are material limitations, however. First, the property, whether real property (land and/or dwelling) must be in one's possession (or in possession of an immediate family member or member of the household). Second, a request to desist must precede the use of force, unless it appears futile or dangerous to do so. Third, this type of defense is limited to preventing the commission of a tort against the property; and as such, once the tort is completed or the plaintiff is permanently dispossessed of his or her property, he or she may not use force to recapture it or avenge the tort. Yet there is a "hot pursuit" exception, which arises when a person is in "hot pursuit" of someone who wrongfully dispossessed him or her of the property. Once again, only reasonable force can be used; but in the case of defending property, "reasonable" does not include force which will cause death or serious bodily injury, though there are exceptions permitting the use of deadly force in order to protect one's home (but this subject matter, though obviously important, is beyond the purview of this book). However, if utilized successfully, the defense of property operates as a complete defense to civil as well as criminal liability (Hussein and Webber, 2020).

Summary

This chapter to the book first covered the older common law intentional torts of battery and assault and false imprisonment. The authors treated the civil law aspects of these torts, though their commission may also be a crime. The authors mentioned an important business ramification to these torts, which deals with the defense afforded to merchants under the common law, and now mainly by statute, typically called Merchants Protection statutes, to detain and to make reasonable investigations of suspected shoplifters. Next, the authors examined the tort of intentional infliction of emotional distress, which was differentiated from the tort of negligent infliction of emotional distress. Although rare in a business context the tort of intentional infliction of emotional distress can arise, particularly in the context of "bullying" and harassment in the workplace, as the authors pointed out.

We analyzed four intentional torts with clear business consequences – invasion of privacy, interference with contract or business relations, defamation, and fraud. Note that fraud was principally treated in the old common law sense of "deceit," that is, purposeful, knowing misrepresentations. Note too that regarding defamation the important qualified privilege was fully explicated and illustrated in the context of employment. Next, the authors covered the breach of the duty of loyalty by employees, which in some states is considered the breach of a fiduciary duty and thus the equivalent of an intentional tort. The authors then covered the violation of public policy doctrine, which similarly in some states is viewed as an intentional tort violation. Brief mention was made of the tort of wrongful institution of legal proceedings, also called "malicious prosecution," as well as the related and broader tort of "abuse of process."

Although the bulk of this chapter dealt with intentional torts to the person, the authors briefly examined the three main intentional torts to property – trespass to land, trespass to chattels, and conversion, which also can be crimes. Specific defenses to certain preceding intentional torts were stated as were the general defenses applicable to all intentional torts. Finally, the authors provided suggestions and recommendations to employers and managers on how to avoid liability for these intentional torts. This chapter to the book, therefore, examined intentional torts to the person and to a person's property. These common law intentional torts protect against intentional infringements of legally protected interests. When injury to a person or harm to his or her property occurs not through intentional or purposeful conduct, but rather by means of unintentional but careless conduct, another vital area of the law - for business, employment, and otherwise - is brought forth – the tort of negligence.

CHAPTER IV - NEGLIGENCE

The legal wrong of *negligence* is an unintentional tort. The actor does not want to bring about the injurious consequences of his or her act, but the conduct creates a risk of harmful consequences. This tort derives from the very old common law, with recorded decisions dating back to the 1300s in England; but the tort is even older than that time period, as evidenced by the fact that the word "tort" is a Norman-French term, thereby dating this body of law way back to 1066 and William the Conqueror. The purpose of this body of the law is to protect a person's interest in being free from harm carelessly caused by another party's conduct. As one "price" for living in a civilized "kingdom," a person is held to a fundamental duty; that is, when one decides to affirmatively act, regardless of the activity, one owes an obligation to others to act in a reasonable, prudent, and careful manner. The failure to exercise this requisite degree of care will subject the careless actor to legal liability for the tort of negligence.

Accordingly, this chapter will examine the tort of negligence. Negligence will be defined and the elements of negligence – duty, breach of duty, causation, and damages – will be explained and illustrated. The meaning of the critical "reasonably prudent person" standard as well as the important distinction between causation-in-fact and legal or proximate causation also will be explained. Negligence will be differentiated from malpractice. The primary defenses to negligence – comparative negligence and assumption of the risk – will be explained and illustrated. The authors, in addition, will analyze two specialized negligence doctrines – *res ipsa loquitur* and negligence *per se*. Moreover, the specialized tort of negligent infliction of emotional distress will be explained and differentiated from the intentional tort of infliction of emotional distress. The authors then will examine in depth negligence law as applied to the hiring, supervision, and retention of employees. The authors, furthermore, will address negligence principles as applied to premises liability. Finally, the authors will provide suggestions and recommendations on how employers can avoid and minimize liability pursuant to negligence law.

The Common Law Tort of Negligence

"Negligence" is a legal term that is used in two ways. First, it is the name given to the civil wrong tort lawsuit for acting unreasonably; and second, it is a type of wrongful conduct which is itself a component of the tort cause of action. In the latter sense, negligence is the conduct that falls below the standard of care imposed by the law for the protection of others from the risk of harm. Intent is not an issue in a negligence case. Even though an actor does not intend a harmful outcome, even though he or she may be morally blameless, nonetheless he or she may be liable civilly for committing a legal wrong. The common law will not allow a person to defend his or her behavior on the ground that his or her subjective personal intent or frame of mind was to act in a careful and non-negligent manner. The ultimate issue, therefore, is not the reasonableness of the defendant's state of mind, but the reasonableness of his or her conduct. Negligence, however, is not absolute liability or even liability without fault. In every case, it must be demonstrated that the defendant was at fault by failing to comply with the legal duty to conduct himself or herself in a reasonably prudent manner under the circumstances. Intent is immaterial; conduct is critical. The duty of due care, and thus potential negligence liability, applies to anyone who acts, whether driving a car, operating as a surgeon (in which negligence is treated as malpractice doctrine with certain specialized rules), manufacturing or selling goods, providing services, or hiring, retaining, supervising, disciplining, and discharging employees.

In order to prevail in a negligence lawsuit, a plaintiff must establish the four key elements to the cause of action: 1) duty of care, 2) breach of duty, 3) causation, and 4) damages. The first component of negligence is the "*duty of care*." The plaintiff must show the existence of a duty, recognized by the law, requiring the defendant to conform his or her conduct to a legally established standard in order to protect the plaintiff from an unreasonable risk of harm. When a person engages in an activity, he or she is held to a duty of due care to act as a reasonably prudent person. As such, the "actor" must take precautions against creating unreasonable risks of injury to other people or their property. However, there is no legal duty imposed upon a person to take precautions against events which cannot be reasonably foreseen. This standard of care from the old common law days had been characterized as the "reasonably prudent man" (and now in modern times called the "*reasonably prudent person*" standard). This "mythical" legal person is an average person in the community acting under circumstances surrounding the defendant. It is important to note that the defendant's individual characteristics are not considered, for example, whether the defendant is stupid or excitable; rather, the defendant's conduct is measured against this "reasonable prudent person." In the case of a manufacturer of goods, generally, a manufacturer will be held to a standard of care of reasonableness to see that a consumer is not harmed by the goods. Consequently, there may be liability imposed against the manufacturer for failing to inspect and/or test the goods and to maintain suitable quality control, for failing to disclose and to warn of known defects in the goods, and the failure to use due care in the design, manufacture, and sale of the goods. This duty of due care extends to all people who might foreseeably be injured by the goods, and not just the buyer of the goods.

Also, it is important to point out that there are certain standards of conduct for some people that are different from the normal reasonable person standard. For example, members of a profession, such as doctors and lawyers, are deemed to hold and to exercise the knowledge and skills of a typical member of that profession. Such a specialized standard of care brings the negligence doctrine into the realm of *malpractice* law, which essentially is based on common law negligence principles, but which usually requires expert witnesses to educate the jury as to the particular standard of care in the profession. For example, in a nursing malpractice case against a nurse who is accused of conduct falling below the professional standard of care for "blindly" following and not questioning a doctor's orders, an expert witness will have to testify before the jury to state and explain to the jury what the nurse's duty of care is in such a situation, which obligation is beyond the common knowledge of a lay jury.

The second element to a lawsuit for negligence is the breach of the duty of due care. *Breach of duty* occurs when the defendant's conduct fails to conform to the required standard of care. That is, when the defendant's conduct falls below the level required by the applicable standard of care owed to the plaintiff, the defendant has breached his or her duty. This breach can be triggered by an act or by a failure to act when the law imposes an affirmative obligation to act. This key negligence question is regarded as a "question of fact," and thus for the jury to decide, although guided by expert witnesses, most notably present in malpractice cases. That is, in a malpractice case the jury will decide if a nurse acted not as a reasonably prudent person but as a reasonably prudent professional nurse based on the standards and scope of practice of the nursing profession.

The third requirement to a negligence cause of action is *causation.* The law requires a sufficient causal connection between the defendant's careless conduct and the resulting harm. The causation element is satisfied by a showing of two elements: 1) the existence of *actual causation*, called *"causation-in-fact,"* and 2) the presence of *legal causation*, called *"proximate cause."* It is very important to note that the common law not only requires causation, but also that the common law makes a critical distinction between the two types of causation. Causation-in-fact is really a matter of physics. That is, there occurs a series or chain of events, with one event leading to another and ultimately producing a final result. Before legal liability can be imposed on a defendant, there must be sufficient evidence that the defendant's careless action was a cause in fact of the plaintiff's injuries. The standard legal test for establishing causation in fact is called the *"but for" test*. This legal test holds that an act is the cause in fact of an eventual consequence if the latter would not have occurred "but for" the first act. However, when there are several forces that combine and bring about the plaintiff's injuries, and any one of them would have been sufficient to cause the plaintiff's injuries, a special causation test is used, called the *"substantial factor" test*. This test holds that causation in fact is established in a multiple causation situation when the defendant's conduct was a substantial factor in causing the plaintiff's injuries. The causation-in-fact requirement to a negligence lawsuit has been at issue in several recent cases against Johnson & Johnson, wherein women plaintiffs who had contracted ovarian cancer have contended that their cancer was caused by asbestos in talcum powder manufactured by the company. Johnson & Johnson is defending the lawsuits by asserting that there is not asbestos in the talcum powder; and that the talcum powder does not cause cancer. The problem is that scientific studies and the scientific community are split on these issues. Although there have been some jury verdicts against Johnson & Johnson, some have been reversed on appeal, principally on the causation-in-fact requirement. However, in one notable recent case, a court of appeals in Missouri upheld a jury verdict against Johnson & Johnson based on cancer claims linked to its talcum-based powder products which were tainted with asbestos. The jury verdict in favor of the 20 female plaintiffs included compensatory damages of $500 million as well as $4 billion in punitive damages, which latter amount was reduced to $1.6 billion by the court. Important to the case, and relevant to the causation discussion herein, was the finding of the court of appeals that "reasonable methodology" was provided to the members of the jury to support their determination that causation-in-fact existed. Johnson & Johnson is appealing the case to the state supreme court (Feeley, 2020).

In addition to demonstrating causation-in-fact, the plaintiff also must show as part of his or her negligence lawsuit that the defendant's careless conduct was also a proximate cause of the plaintiff's injury. Whereas causation-in-fact is a matter of physics, the doctrine of proximate cause is more a question of policy. *Proximate cause* is a most interesting common law formulation, because it is a doctrine that protects careless people! Even if one acts carelessly, the doctrine of proximate cause maintains that not all of a plaintiff's injuries and harms in fact caused by a carelessly acting defendant will be proximately caused. Rather, the doctrine holds that a careless defendant is not legally responsible for the unforeseeable, remote, or unusual consequences of his or her careless act. Accordingly, proximate cause serves as a limitation on the defendant's liability. It is the function of the jury in a common law system to determine whether proximate cause and also causation-in-fact are present.

The fourth and final element to a cause of action for negligence is the requirement of damages; that is, the plaintiff must prove some type of actual loss or damage. Damages are not assumed in a negligence case; nominal damages are not awarded; rather, some type of actual harm or injury to a legally protected interest is necessary. The objective of damages is compensatory; that is, to restore the plaintiff insofar as possible to his or her condition before the injury or harm occurred. Damages include special damages, such as economic losses, lost wages, medical expenses, business profits, and future expenses, Moreover, additional damages for "pain and suffering" or emotional distress are recoverable, as are damages for disability and disfigurement. Finally, if the defendant's careless conduct is grossly negligent or reckless in nature, then the plaintiff can recover an extra award of damages, called punitive damages, at the discretion of the jury to punish the defendant and to deter others from engaging in such grossly negligent behavior. It is necessary to point out that several states in the United States have by statute curtailed the jury's power to award unlimited punitive damages, for example, by requiring that punitive damages not exceed five times the amount of the compensatory award. It is also necessary to point out that the United States Supreme Court has ruled that punitive damages cannot be extreme or excessive, that is, they must bear some reasonable relationship to the harm done, or otherwise they will be unconstitutional as violating the Due Process clause of 14th Amendment to the Constitution.

Generally, damage liability for the tort of negligence is deemed by the common law to be "*joint and several.*" That is, when there is more than one defendant who have caused the plaintiff's damages, they are all equally responsible for paying the judgment, regardless of the percentage of fault attributed to them. As such, for example, a defendant who is accorded only 20% of the fault may nonetheless have to pay 100% of the damages if the other and more culpable defendant cannot pay. The first defendant is the proverbial "deep pocket" defendant who ends up paying. The policy behind this old common law rule is that it is preferable for a party who is at least partially at fault to pay all, as opposed to the innocent and injured plaintiff only receiving partial compensation; and the "deep pocket" defendant can always proceed, at least theoretically, against his or her co-defendants. However, it must be noted that several states in the United States have now by statute changed this common law rule; and as a result hold that a defendant only has to pay his/her apportioned share of the damages regardless of the ability of his or her co-defendants to pay the plaintiff fully.

Specialized Negligence Doctrines

1. Res Ipsa Loquitur

There are a variety of special negligence doctrines, each with its own peculiar rules, but with far-reaching consequences, that must be addressed. One that is potentially very beneficial to an aggrieved plaintiff, who is having difficulty obtaining evidence of carelessness, is called the doctrine of *res ipsa loquitur*, from the Latin meaning "the thing speaks for itself." This doctrine may emerge as a very critical one for a plaintiff seeking to establish the breach of duty element to negligence. In essence, *res ipsa loquitur* maintains that the fact that a particular injury occurred may in and of itself establish a breach of the duty owed to the plaintiff. This doctrine is a legal device that a plaintiff may be able to use to permit a jury to consider the issue as to whether the defendant was negligent where the facts of the case indicate that the plaintiff's injuries resulted from the defendant's negligence, the jury may be able to infer the defendant's liability. There are two critical components that a plaintiff must be able to demonstrate in order to take advantage of the *res ipsa loquitur* doctrine: First, the accident causing the plaintiff's injury is not the type that ordinarily would occur unless someone was negligent, for example, when an auto abruptly swerves off the road in "good" driving conditions, or a bottle or can of soda sitting on a supermarket shelf suddenly explodes. Second, evidence exists showing that the instrumentality that caused the injury was in the sole control of the defendant, such as the defendant driving the erratic car, or the defendant had the power and opportunity to exercise control. Another example of control is when at a Lowe's store a large piece of metal shelving out of a typical customer's reach became dislodged when a customer, who was the only one in the vicinity, tried to remove it, causing it to fall and hit the customer on the head (*Turley v. Lowe's Home Ctrs*, 2020, applying Kansas law). Yet, to compare, a "heel-fall" injury in a hotel bathroom which supposedly had a slip-resistant floor, although the type of accident that would not ordinarily occur unless someone was negligent, was nevertheless not grounds for a *res ipsa loquitur* finding because the plaintiff could not prove that the instrumentality, that is, the bathroom floor was in the exclusive control of the defendant hotel (*Williams v. Paris Las Vegas Operating Co.*, 2020).

If the two *res ipsa* requirements are present, the legal effect of the doctrine is that the plaintiff has thereby established an initial case for negligence, and accordingly the judge will send the case to the jury. The causation and damages elements still must be found, of course. However, the *res ipsa loquitur* inference of negligence is rebuttable; that is, if the defendant can submit evidence of due care, the jury has the power to reject the plaintiff's *res ipsa loquitur* inference of negligence, and as such ultimately find in favor of the defendant. Moreover, the inference of negligence can be rebutted if the defendant can provide evidence of other possible explanations for the harm. For example, in the Alabama supreme court case of *Nettles v. Pettway* (2020), the plaintiff was struck by the wheel of a tire that had become detached, due to a shearing of the studs, from a car that was driven by its owner. The plaintiff asserted the doctrine of *res ipsa loquitur* against the defendant auto-body shop that installed the wheel, claiming that the only plausible explanation for the accident was the negligent installation of the wheel due to the careless inspection of the integrity of the studs. However, the defendant countered the assertion of *res ipsa loquitur* by saying that the wheel detachment could have been caused by latent internal defects in wheel-assembly parts, by the manner in which the owner of the car operated it during the 10-12 hours before the accident, as well as the fact that the car had been released to the owner and thus at the time of the accident was not in the exclusive control of the defendant. Consequently, the Alabama supreme court dismissed the *res ipsa loquitur* claim, explaining that "any number of significant factors could have proximately caused the accident" (*Nettles v. Pettway*, 2020).

The rationale behind the doctrine of *res ipsa loquitur*, which also is a older common law precept, is that it may be quite difficult in certain circumstances for a plaintiff to acquire adequate direct evidence to show a breach of the duty of due care. Examples are as follows: when a patient awakes from surgery with a sponge or surgical instrument in him or her, when a car goes inexplicably off the road and injures a pedestrian on the sidewalk, when the plaintiff is injured by a poorly made product but the plaintiff cannot show the careless situation that existed at the defendant's manufacturing facility, such as when a soda can explodes on a supermarket shelf injuring a shopper, when a load of bricks falls on a passerby at a construction site, or, in the original *res ipsa loquitur* English case in 1863, when a barrel of flour fell out of a bakery window injuring a passerby (Lorenz and Lorenz, 2020). In the preceding examples, though there may be no direct evidence of negligence, it can be reasonably and logically inferred that some person in charge of the instrumentality was careless since there is no other reasonable explanation as to why the type of harm occurred.

2. Negligence Per Se

Another specialized negligence doctrine is called *negligence per se*. At times, the standard of care in a negligence case is determined by proving that a safety type of statute which provides for a criminal and/or regulatory penalty applies to a particular case. The legal result is that the duty enumerated in the statute will replace the more general common law duty of due care. In such a case, the plaintiff must prove that the plaintiff is in a class intended to be protected by the statute and that the purpose of the statute was to prevent the type of harm that the plaintiff suffered. That is, generally speaking, the statute must pertain to the plaintiff's injury, for example, when a consumer is injured by an inadequate warning label on a drug when a statute or regulation sets forth the warning, or when an auto driver is injured by another driver who has violated traffic control laws. Other examples are the selling of liquor or firearms to a minor in violation of state and/or federal statute, the violation of a building code by a construction company, improper maintenance and unsafe operation of an elevator by a building owner in violation of a statute (Baik and Caldwell, Jr., 2020; Legal Match, 2020). The notable effect of establishing the violation of a statute is the occurrence of "negligence *per se*." That is, the plaintiff will have established a conclusive presumption of the duty and breach of duty elements to a negligence lawsuit. Of course, the plaintiff still must plead and prove the remaining elements of the cause of action - causation and damages. Defenses to negligence *per se* lawsuits are difficult to assert since the gravamen of the lawsuit is the violation of the statute and not the general reasonable person standard. However, potential defenses might be the standard negligence defenses of comparative negligence and assumption of the risk (Legal Match, 2020), as well as the fact that compliance with the statute was impossible under the circumstances, or that a party did not know or should have not known of the duty to comply with the statute or regulation (Baik and Caldwell, Jr., 2020)..

3. Negligent Infliction of Emotional Distress

The next special negligence area is the doctrine of *negligent infliction of emotional distress*. When can a victimized plaintiff recover mental anguish damages? That is always a key negligence issue. There are several legal interpretations of the negligent infliction of emotional distress doctrine, thus making this legal doctrine highly dependent on state law. First, if there is a physical injury, then damages for the attendant emotional distress are recoverable as part of the physical injury. This rule is the traditional "pain and suffering" rule. Second, if there is a physical impact to the plaintiff, even if minor or slight, which by itself causes no actual physical injury or harm, but which is accompanied or followed by emotional distress, then damages are permitted for such emotional distress. An example would be when a defendant negligently drives his or her car into the plaintiff, who is not harmed in any way or physically injured in any way, but is impacted, even if slightly, but who does suffer fright and shock. This rule typically is designated as the *"impact rule"* and is a means to tort recovery. These "impact" states thus require the "impact," even if just a mere "touching," before any recovery can be obtained (assuming, of course, that the defendant's conduct was negligent) (Goguen, 2020). Third, the more modern rule is that even if there is no physical impact, but the plaintiff nonetheless suffers physical disorders due to emotional distress, such as shock to the nervous system, then damages are permissible for the emotional and mental suffering. Note that some states also require that the symptoms be severe, such as shock to the nervous system, especially if there is no accompanying personal, physical injury (*Dokes v. Safeway, Inc*., 2018, applying California law). Yet other states maintain that the symptoms need not be severe, such as anxiety, sleeplessness, and loss of appetite, so long as the symptoms are objectively observable (Goguen, 2020). Moreover, certain states also require that the symptoms manifest themselves immediately after the defendant's negligent act (Goguen, 2020). Other states use a "zone of danger" rule, which requires that the plaintiff seeking emotional distress damages was in close proximity to the negligent act and thus was at an immediate risk of physical harm (Goguen, 2020). Yet other states just use the traditional "foreseeability" test of negligence law, and thus simply ascertain whether the emotional distress was a foreseeable consequence from the negligent act, thereby precluding the requirement in the "zone of danger" test that there be an immediate risk of physical harm (Goguen, 2020). Some states still adhere to the older interpretation, to wit: if there is no impact, and the plaintiff does not suffer any physical disorders, but the plaintiff does suffer emotional distress, then nevertheless there is no recovery permitted. An example of the last rule would arise when the defendant negligently "sideswipes" the plaintiff's auto but does not hit it, and the plaintiff is very frightened and upset, but does not suffer any physical disorder or illness, which means the plaintiff has no cause of action. Finally, mention should be made of the so-called "bystander" cases, which typically involve close family members experiencing emotional distress not directly by the negligent act but indirectly by witnessing a severe injury to a close family member. Such bystanders may be able to recover even in some states if the bystander is not technically within any "zone of danger" (Goguen, 2020). As emphasized, this area of the law is not only very variegated, but also highly dependent on discrete state law. Moreover, since the cause of action of negligent infliction of emotional distress is a variant of the negligence doctrine, when it is asserted in an employment context the lawsuit like any other negligence claim may be preempted and thus obviated by state Worker's Compensation law (*Kamdem-Ouaffo v. Balchem Corp.*, 2018, applying New York law). Finally, as previously underscored, any "impact" requirement for negligent infliction of emotional distress is not applicable to the tort of intentional infliction of emotional distress, where no "impact" at all is necessary, though the wrongful conduct must be severe and cause actual and severe emotional distress.

4. Negligent Hiring, Supervision, and Retention

The negligence doctrine most certainly can, and is, applied to the employer's hiring of employees. Consequently, the employer can be deemed negligent if it does not use due care in the hiring of its employees, for example, choosing the wrong person for a specific job. The rationale is that the employer has a duty to customers, clients, and the general public to act with due care and as a reasonably prudent employer when it comes to hiring the employees to staff its business. For example, if the employer is contemplating hiring a person for a position that requires driving a vehicle, the prudent employer would ask about driving accidents, tickets, driver license status, and any license suspensions, as well as drug or alcohol use; and the employer also should check with the Department of Motor Vehicles for the pertinent jurisdiction. If the employer breaches this duty, and harm is caused to a customer, client, or other third party, he or she can sue the employer for negligence. This lawsuit, it should be noted, is one directly against the employer for its own negligence; it is not a vicarious or imputed liability lawsuit, as will be seen (though there may be such a lawsuit if the carelessly selected employee carelessly injures a third party in the course of employment).

Negligent hiring typically is based on the employer failing to investigate or failing to do a careful investigation on the background – work, professional, personality – of the employee, and a proper investigation would have discovered some troublesome or problematic fact about the employee. Recall, however, that the employer, as does any person or business that acts, does not have to act perfectly. Negligence law does not require that a party be, in effect, an insurer against harm. The fundamental legal duty is "merely" to act carefully. So, regarding hiring, if the employer does conduct an investigation, and it is a reasonable one, the employer would not be directly liable even if a more thorough or different type of investigation would have discovered a problem regarding the employee.

An employer has a legal duty to make an appropriate investigation of the employee and failure to do so can lead to liability. Then the employer is liable in tort for the negligent hiring of an employee who is incompetent, unfit, and/or dangerous when the employer knew, or through the exercise of reasonable care, should have known that the hiring of the employee created a risk or danger to third parties. The aggrieved plaintiff also must show that his or her harm was factually and proximately caused by the employer's carelessness in hiring the employee. Thus, the employer owes a duty to exercise reasonable care in hiring an employee. Yet, how much care is "reasonable"? The amount of care deemed to be "reasonable" depends on the risk of harm inherent in the employment situation; that is, the greater the risk of harm, the higher the degree of care necessary to constitute ordinary and thus "reasonable" care. Accordingly, an employer is required to conduct an appropriate investigation of the employee; and if the employer fails to do so he, she, or it may be liable directly for the tort of negligence. Important factors in determining the reasonableness of the investigation are the nature of the person hired, the type of work the employee is to be doing, and who the employee will have to interact with. The "classic" negligent hiring example being the lack of a reasonable pre-employment investigation resulting in the hiring of an ex-offender with a record of violent crimes and then carelessly placing such a dangerous person in a position having contact with customers, clients, and other third parties as well as co-workers.

A review of cases reveals a wide variety of factual patterns underlying negligent hiring tort claims. However, essentially, in a negligent hiring claim, the question is asked: Did the employer have notice of the potential employee's dangerous nature or propensity to cause harm or damage to fellow employees, customers, clients, the public, or elsewise? In one Indiana court of appeals case, *Interim Healthcare of Fort Wayne, Inc.* (2001), the plaintiffs alleged that a healthcare agency negligently hired a home health aide, who later injured a child patient. The defendant employer's motion to dismiss the case was denied because there was no evidence that the employer contacted any of the aide's previous employers, and thus there was an issue of fact for the jury to decide relative to the negligent hiring claim. Another example of the negligent hiring tort is a case stemming from injuries sustained by invitees to a house party which increased in size to over 200 teenagers and young adults. In *Gregor vs. Kleiser* (1982), an Illinois court of appeals case, the host, a teenager, hired a "bouncer" who was known to be predisposed to physical aggressiveness and who apparently lived up to his reputation when attempting to control the crowd. The "bouncer" without cause or provocation attacked a party-goer and caused him serious injuries. In holding that the injured guest's negligent hiring complaint was sufficiently pleaded to avoid the case being dismissed, the court explained that the party host knew well of the bouncer's reputation and vicious propensity for physical violence on others as well as his body-building and weight-lifting achievements and extraordinary strength.

When determining negligent hiring claims, the subject employee's prior conduct, along with the job function he or she was contemplated to perform, are factors that weigh heavily on a court's determination. To illustrate, in *Oakley vs. Flor-Shin, Inc.* (1998), a Kentucky court of appeals case, an 18-year-old worker was locked inside a K-Mart store after hours with a cleaning crew member from another company who raped her in the store overnight. The Kansas appeals court recognized that there was a genuine issue of material fact; consequently, the plaintiff's negligent hiring claim against the cleaning company should have proceeded to trial. In doing so, the court pointed to several factors, to wit: the worker had an extensive criminal record prior to being hired by the company, including convictions for burglary, theft, and bail-jumping; he was arrested for criminal attempt to commit rape and for carrying a concealed deadly weapon; and the employer had knowledge of his criminal background due to his relationship with his brother-in-law by marriage, who was a regional manager and who hired the worker, and who knew or should have known of his criminal propensities; and also that the employer knew that he would literally be locked into a store to be cleaned with a single employee.

An employer, however, may not blindly rely on an applicant's bare affirmations of a "clean" criminal record or rely solely on listed job references when hiring employees who are performing certain sensitive services to customers or patients (*Spenser vs. Health Force Inc,* 2005). In the *Spenser* case, the supreme court of New Mexico held that the dismissal of a case on summary judgment for a home health-care employer was inappropriate; and that a jury should have decided if the employer negligently hired a domestic home health care worker who allegedly killed his thirty-six-year-old quadriplegic patient by way of an illegal morphine injection. The court in *Spenser* held that the pre-employment inquiry should have included a background check, which would have revealed the worker's prior convictions for burglary, aggravated assault, armed robbery, credit card fraud, embezzlement, and shoplifting, all of which were not disclosed on the job applicant's application; and such information would have disqualified the worker from the home-care aide profession under the law.

Likewise, employers who hire employees who handle financial affairs must reasonably seek out and recognize "red flags" in that job applicant's past-history in order to avoid a negligent hiring claim. To illustrate, in *Owens vs. Stifel Nicolaus & Company Inc.* (2016), the federal Court of Appeals for the Eleventh Circuit, applying Georgia law, recognized that an employer stock-broker company owed a duty to investors who relied upon the investment guidance given to them by an employee stockbroker. Here the securities broker employee recommended to his employer that it should promote a certain investment in a questionable company to its investor client base. The employer refused to list the investment on its list of investment opportunities; and the employer also refused the employee's request to officially recommend that particular investment to the firm's clients. Nevertheless, the employee broker induced third parties to invest about $350,000.00 in the questionable scheme by way of his position with the securities firm. The investment was later deemed a fraudulent scheme, apparently created by the employee broker, but the employer disclaimed knowledge that its employee broker was acting as its agent when recommending the failed investment product. Specifically, the employer defended itself by arguing that the employee broker acted beyond the scope of his authority and, furthermore, no professional duty was owed to the damaged investors as they were not an official client of theirs. The Eleventh Circuit Court of Appeals concluded that even if no typical professional heightened duties existed from the employer to the investors, the negligent hiring tort claim (along with negligent retention and supervision claims) could exist under the circumstances. Reflecting upon the fact that the broker used his current position to approach the victim investors and induce them into the investment with apparent authority, the court held that a jury could find it foreseeable that a financial advisor with "red flags" in his employment and investment management history would use his position to identify, build relationships with, and exploit "marks," regardless of whether the "marks" ever formalized a client relationship with the brokerage. Therefore, the court ruled that the negligent hiring, retention, and supervision claims should have survived dismissal by means of summary judgment.

Yet, when there is no evidence in a potential employee's background to place the employer on notice of a dangerous propensity to the public, its employees, or its customers, then an employer will generally not be held liable for negligent hiring. The burden lies with the plaintiff to prove that the defendant employer knew or should have known the standard. For example, in the California court of appeals case of *Jane Doe v. Walmart Stores, Inc.* (2018), the court ruled that the company was not liable for the sexual assault of a co-worker by another employee because the assault occurred 45 minutes after the employees left work and were off-duty, they were out of the workplace (though in the company's parking lot), and, most importantly, the company did not know of the co-worker's criminal history. Similarly, in the California court of appeals case of *Juarez v. Boy Scotts of America, Inc.* (2000), the plaintiff, a former boy scout, failed to carry that burden in his claim for negligent hiring and retention against the Boy Scouts of America as he was unable to prove that organization knew, or should have known, that one of its troop leader's had a propensity to molest children prior to the time he was hired and before the molestation occurred. Thus, dismissal of the case by means of summary judgement was properly ordered in favor of the Boy Scouts of America and against the plaintiff's negligent hiring and retention claims. Similarly, in *Bell, IV v. Geraldine et. al.* (2003), a federal Court of Appeals case in the Ninth Circuit, applying Nevada law, there were no "red flags" warning the employer of any possible risk of hiring a teacher. Consequently, the school district was entitled to dismissal of the case by means of summary judgment as to the plaintiff's negligent hiring claim. The court's rationale was that the school conformed to the mandatory finger-print pre-screening process under the state statutory guidelines and reasonably relied upon the "clean" results it received that erroneously detected no prior criminal record of the job applicant. In the *Bell* case, the school district forwarded the teacher's fingerprints to the Nevada Highway Patrol's central repository for a criminal history check which apparently failed to forward the fingerprints to the Federal Bureau of Investigation (FBI) because a prior out-of-state conviction of the teacher for lewd conduct was not discovered. Moreover, since the Nevada statutes imposed on the Nevada Highway Patrol, a central repository, the duty to submit fingerprints to the FBI, the school district was entitled to rely on the Highway Patrol's presumptive fulfillment of its statutory responsibilities. As a result, the school employer could not be held to have negligently hired the teacher since it fulfilled its pre-request background checks duty properly.

Furthermore, in a negligent hiring claim where an employee's criminal past is overlooked by an employer, there must be proof that such criminal past was logically and foreseeably related to the harm caused by the worker to the injured third party under this tort (*CSX Transportation Inc. vs. Pyramid Stone Industries, Inc.,* 2008). For example, in the federal Seventh Circuit Court of Appeals case of *Anicich v. Home Depot USA Inc.* (2017), applying Illinois law, the court ruled that the defendant company was liable for hiring a supervisor who had a history of harassing female subordinates, which the company knew of, and then allowing him to supervise a pregnant employee whom he murdered. The court found the company liable even though the murder occurred off-site and did not involve company property because some type of harm could have been reasonably foreseen by the company's actions. To compare, in the previously cited *CSX Transportation*, a federal court of appeals case in the Eleventh Circit, the court held that the negligent hiring claim could not survive because of the lack of "foreseeability" on the part of the employer that a quarry worker would damage railroad tracks off-duty with company-owned heavy equipment. The court explained that it would be illogical to jump to the conclusion that it would be negligent for any employer whose business includes dangerous machinery to hire an employee who has a criminal record. Here, the employee had prior experience working with heavy and dangerous equipment, which was similar to the machines he used at the quarry; and, furthermore, none of the employee's past criminal conduct occurred during his prior work with such equipment. Thus, the court explained that it could not see how a reasonable jury could find that the employee's criminal history rendered him unsuitable for quarry work, especially considering that his prior experience indicated that he was specifically suited for the job.

This necessity to prove the "foreseeability" and the "causation" element was not overlooked by the Arkansas Supreme Court in addressing a negligent hiring claim against Comcast Cable, when one of its cable installers entered a women's home to check the television reception and attempted to rape and kill her (*Saine vs. Comcast Cablevision of Arkansas Inc*., 2003). In affirming the summary judgment in favor of Comcast and thereby dismissing the negligent hiring claim, the court in *Saine* explained that there must be a direct causal connection between an inadequate background check and the criminal act for which the plaintiff is attempting to hold the employer liable. This requirement, however, was absent in this particular case. The court explained that Comcast provided documentation that the employee had passed a pre-employment drug screen and had been honorably discharged from the military. Furthermore, Comcast's background check of the employee showed experience in wiring and pole-climbing; and checks with two previous employers gave no indication that the employee might be a risk to customers. Consequently, the court ruled that the plaintiff failed to meet her burden of proof on this issue because she had not demonstrated anything in the employee's background that could have alerted Comcast to the possibility that the employee was predisposed to commit a sexual assault. Accordingly, it is at times difficult to prove the "causation" element of a negligent hiring claim and failure to do so would be fatal to a plaintiff's claim against an employer under this theory. For example, the Texas supreme court held that an employer's failure to screen a driver's illegal immigration status and thus that employer's failure to discover the driver's inability to work in the United States was not relevant evidence in a negligent hiring case against that employer because the driver's immigration status did not cause the vehicle collision (*TXI Transportation Co. v. Hughes,* 2010).

To compare *negligent supervision* and *negligent retention* with negligent hiring, the principal distinction between negligent supervision/retention and negligent hiring as grounds for the liability of the employer is premised on the time at which the employer is charged with knowledge (actual or "should have known" knowledge) of the employee's incompetence, dangerous propensities, or unfitness (*Peschel v. City of Missoula*, 2009, applying Montana law; *Garcia v. Duffy*, 1986, applying Florida law). That is, the employer has carelessly placed the employee in a position, and/or inadequately supervised the employee, so that the employer knows, or should have known, that the employee would be predisposed to commit a wrong or harm to a third person, and that wrong has occurred. The Illinois court of appeals case of *Denton v. Universal AM-CAN, LTD* (2019) well illustrates both negligent hiring and negligent supervision and retention aspects. In the *Denton* case, a truck driver caused a very serious accident resulting in personal injuries and a subsequent lawsuit and jury verdict of more than $54 million. The driver who had a "disturbing" and "negative" record, and was deemed to be a "marginal driver," and one who had a felony conviction within 10 years, which precluded hiring as *per* company policy; yet he was nonetheless hired due to a shortage of drivers. The evidence brought forth at trial indicated the following: the driver had a truck driver license from another state even though he never completed a truck driving course; within three years of applying he had been involved in four accidents, but his application listed only two accidents as well as a license suspension; within ten years he had been employed by 10 different companies; he was terminated from four of those seven companies; for seven years prior to applying he was convicted of nine traffic related offenses as well as four counts of felony aggravated assault; he waited a month to attend the required safety orientation course though he was supposed to attend one week after hiring; he received five warning violations and was put on probation for six months; he failed to attend a mandatory safety meeting after receiving a speeding ticket, a moving violation, and a logbook violation; he had his license suspended for nine months, yet the defendant company continued to dispatch him; and he accumulated 36 points on his record but was not terminated though the company's policy was that 30 points would cause a dismissal. Accordingly, the Illinois court of appeals not only upheld the jury verdict for compensatory damages but also upheld the jury award of $35 million in punitive damages since the company's conduct was deemed to be "willful and wanton" (*Denton v. Universal AM-CAN, LTD*, 2019).

The employer's liability for a negligence lawsuit premised on negligent supervision or retention is thus based on evidence that the employer knew, or through the exercise or reasonable care by means of a reasonable investigation, should have known that the acts or omissions of its employee would subject third parties to an unreasonable risk of harm. The aggrieved plaintiff also must show that he or she was harmed and that this harm was factually and proximately caused by the employer's careless supervision or retention of an unfit, incompetent, and/or dangerous employee (*Gresham v. Safeway,* Inc., 2010, applying Oregon law; *Saine v. Comcast Cablevision of Ark., Inc.*, 2003, applying Arkansas law; *Shanks v. Calvin Walker & Doctor's Assocs.*, 2000, applying Connecticut law). An important factor in determining negligent retention is the gravity of the misconduct. As such, a single isolated incident of prior misconduct (of which the employer knew or should have known) may support a negligent retention claim, provided the prior misconduct has a sufficient connection to the ultimate harm.

Critical to the cause of action is that the harm caused be a foreseeable result of the employee's retention; in this vein, some courts dictate that to be liable an employer must have actual knowledge of an employee's habit of misconduct, while others provide that an employer may be also liable if it should have known or had reason to know of the misconduct. For example, the Tenth Circuit Court of Appeals case of *Hansen v. Bd. of Trs. of Hamilton Southeastern Sch. Corp.* (2008), where the court explained that some Indiana courts require actual knowledge of an employee's conduct to prevail on negligent retention claim, while others do not. Much of the case law thus turns on this key issue of foreseeable harm. Negligent retention and supervision cases frequently fail because the plaintiff lacks sufficient evidence of foreseeable harm. For example, in *Regions Bank & Trust v. Stone Co. Skilled Nursing Facility, Inc.*, (2001), applying Arkansas law, the supreme court of Arkansas held that an employer was not liable for negligent supervision of a newly-certified nursing assistant that had sexually abused one of the patients because the abuse was not foreseeable: The court explained that to find a cause of action under negligent supervision of an employee, one must find that the probable consequence of negligent supervision in allowing a newly hired and untried nurse's aide to care for an immobile, semi-comatose female patient was sexual abuse by that nurse's aide. Absent some form of notice that the employee posed a danger, such an act is not foreseeable. In the case there was no indication of a prior criminal record or patient abuse. There was nothing to put the nursing facility on notice that the employee might do such a thing as sexually assault a patient. The fact that the employee was an inexperienced nursing assistant did not give rise to a reasonable probability that he would commit criminal sexual assault. Accordingly, it was not foreseeable that the employee would commit criminal sexual assault (*Regions Bank & Trust v. Stone Co. Skilled Nursing Facility, Inc.*, 2001). Similarly, in a 2010 federal court of appeals decision, a black employee sued his employer for negligent retention of a white employee who had allegedly engaged in racial harassment against the plaintiff. Specifically, the alleged harasser hung a noose from a piece of work equipment near where the plaintiff normally parked; inside the noose was a piece of black drainage pipe protruding from the hood of a black sweatshirt. The plaintiff described the display as an effigy depicting a black man with a hangman's noose around his neck. According to the plaintiff, this was not the first time he had been harassed by this employee (*Alford v. Martin & Gass, Inc.*, 2010). In its analysis, the Fourth Circuit Court of Appeals in *Alford* explained that under Virginia law, an employer may be subject to liability for harm resulting from the employer's negligence in retaining a dangerous employee who the employer knew or should have known was dangerous and likely to harm others; in other words, the harm suffered by the plaintiff must be a foreseeable result of the negligent retention. In this case, although the plaintiff may have been previously harassed by the alleged harasser, he failed to report the earlier incidents for fear of losing his job. As such, the court could not find evidence of foreseeable risk based on the earlier harassment (*Alford v. Martin & Gass*, Inc., 2010). Likewise, in a 2009 federal court of appeals pregnancy discrimination case, the plaintiff lost her claim for negligent retention because she presented no evidence that the employer knew or should have known of her supervisor's tendency to discriminate against pregnant women. Her first complaint about her supervisor to her employer did not occur until after she returned from leave, at which point she met with Human Resources to discuss the problem and was reassigned to work under another supervisor in a different department. Complaints by another employee about earlier animosity towards the plaintiff were similarly dealt with when the plaintiff returned from leave. Additionally, because the employer was not on notice about a hostile work environment before the plaintiff went on leave, the court found that it could not be held liable for negligent retention. Moreover, the plaintiff's supervisor was terminated shortly after the employee complained, even if for unrelated reasons (*Hyde v. K. B. Home, Inc.*, 2009, applying Georgia law).

These cases indicate that it may be at times difficult for plaintiffs to produce evidence of foreseeable harm. Also important is the fact that these cases show that employees who wait too long to report incidents of harassment may risk losing legal battles later because they failed to put their employers on notice of the foreseeable risk. Unfortunately, this inaction puts many workers in a paradoxical situation, that is, fearful that reporting the incident will result in termination, yet worrying that not reporting the incident will limit legal recourse. Indeed, in the aforementioned *Alford* case, the plaintiff made a claim for retaliation, arguing that his very fears had come true - he was retaliated against when he finally reported the harassment. The plaintiff lost this claim, along with all the others he asserted, on summary judgment (*Alford v. Martin & Gass, Inc.*, 2010).

As with all negligence cases, negligent retention and negligent supervision claims will fail if the plaintiff cannot show actual harm. For example, in *Jones Express, Inc. v. Jackson* (2001), the parents of a motorist brought a wrongful-death action against the trucking company and truck driver involved in the accident in which the motorist was killed. The plaintiffs alleged that the trucking company had negligently retained and supervised the truck driver and that the truck driver had negligently collided with the motorist's car. The jury found in favor of the plaintiffs on their negligent hiring, retention, and supervision claims. However, the jury found in favor of the truck driver on the negligence claim. On appeal, the Alabama supreme court held that the jury's finding that the truck driver was not negligent was inconsistent with a finding that the trucking company was negligent in hiring and supervising the driver; consequently, the case was remanded for a new trial (*Jones Express, Inc. v. Jackson*, 2010). Similarly, in *Bruchas v.*

Preventive Care (1996), a Minnesota court of appeals case, the court held that the employee's claims for negligent retention and negligent supervision failed as a matter of law, because she failed to show that she suffered personal injury or a threat of physical injury as a result of the alleged sexual harassment (*Bruchas v. Preventive Care*, 1996). In the aforementioned *Saine* case, the employer's worker, a cable installer, raped and attempted to kill a woman whose home he had entered to work on cable. The victim filed suit, alleging the employer's liability for her injuries based on multiple claims including negligent retention and negligent supervision. In court, the plaintiff presented evidence of another customer who had tried to report the perpetrator's suggestive behavior; that customer claimed that she had spoken with three people at the employer's office and given her contact information, but that no one had returned her call. Based on this evidence, the court reversed the lower court's partial summary judgement for the defendant, finding that there were issues of fact as to whether the employer was on notice that the perpetrator might harm a female customer and, therefore, there were issues of fact regarding the reasonable foreseeability of the perpetrator inflicting such injuries. Further, the court asserted that it is not necessary that the employer foresee the particular injury that occurred, but only that the employer reasonably foresees an appreciable risk of harm to others (*Saine v. Comcast Cablevision of Ark.*, 2003). In *American Auto. Auction, Inc. v. Titsworth* (1987), the Arkansas supreme court affirmed a jury verdict of liability for negligent supervision, where two bouncers (who were ex-convicts) hired by an auction company had severely beaten customers while forcibly removing them from an auction. The president of the defendant auction company had told one of the plaintiffs to leave the premises, but then watched him walk into the auction area. The court reasoned that the president knew or should have known that his employees might forcibly eject the plaintiffs, since that was the job they had been hired to perform. Further, the court emphasized that the president did not exercise any supervisory care to ensure the safety of the plaintiffs. The court explained that an employer who hired two ex-convicts, one of whom was normally drinking, and entrusted to them the job of forcibly ejecting patrons, had a duty to exercise reasonable care to avoid harm to those patrons by exercising supervisory care when the employer knew or by the exercising of reasonable diligence should have known, that such employees were about to forcibly eject a patron (*American Auto. Auction, Inc. v. Titsworth*, 1987, applying Arkansas law). In *Doe v. Centennial Indep. Sch. Dist. No. 12* (2004), a Minnesota court of appeals case, the plaintiff alleged that when she was a high-school student a teacher touched her inappropriately and later initiated a sexual relationship. The defendants argued that they could not be held liable for negligent retention because they did not have actual notice of an improper relationship between the teacher and the student. The court disagreed, explaining that actual knowledge is not required for liability under a negligent retention theory. Case law established that being reasonably on notice of a problem with an employee so that the employer should have been aware of an employee's propensities is adequate to sustain a cause of action (*Doe v. Centennial Indep. Sch. Dist. No. 12*, 2004, applying Minnesota law).

Accordingly, it is at times necessary to distinguish between the negligent supervision and negligent retention claims. Negligent supervision, as noted, is the failure of an employer to exercise ordinary care in supervising the employment relationship in order to prevent foreseeable misconduct of an employee from causing harm to others. Negligent retention, however, arises when an employer becomes aware or should have become aware that an employee poses a threat and fails to take remedial measures to ensure the safety of others. The focus in a negligent-retention claim is what the employer knew or should have known about the employee's propensity to engage in improper conduct, and if there was such knowledge, whether the employer acted reasonably to prevent such conduct toward the harmed plaintiff (*Doe v. Centennial Indep. Sch. Dist. No. 12*, 2004, applying Minnesota law).

Negligent hiring and negligent supervision and retention lawsuits as examined in the direct negligence context require more than just an employer-employee relationship; rather, as emphasized, the employer itself must be directly negligent in that the employer knew, or should have known, that the employee was incompetent, unfit, and/or dangerous and consequently posed an unreasonable and foreseeable risk of harm to third parties. For example, in the federal district court case of *La Rocco v. Harley-Davidson Motor Corp.* (2020), applying Pennsylvania law, the court ruled that it was for the jury to determine if the employer knew or should have known of the continuing sexual harassment and sexual assaults of an employee by a co-worker and thus whether the employer was directly liable under negligence law for the resulting harms to the employee, including assault and battery, false imprisonment, and intentional infliction of emotional distress. There is also confusion in the specific area of the employer's direct negligence for the negligent hiring and supervision/retention of employees caused by the fact that the courts frequently use the vicarious or imputed liability term "course and scope of employment" as a factor in determining direct liability. As emphasized, the employer's negligence for the careless hiring, supervision, or retention of employees is direct. However, the fact that the unfit or dangerous employee harmed a third party while acting in the "course and scope of employment" makes the aggrieved plaintiff's case much stronger as evidence of the "course and scope" helps to establish both of the aforementioned foreseeability tests. Accordingly, the "course and scope" requirement is a necessary one for vicarious liability, but merely one factor in determining direct negligence. Vicarious or imputed liability will be covered extensively in a forthcoming chapter to this book.

The negligence doctrine clearly can, and has been, applied to the employment sector regarding the hiring, supervision/retention, and discharge of employees. Consequently, an employer can be deemed negligent and liable civilly in damages if it does not act reasonably and use due care in the hiring and supervision/retention of its employees, for example choosing the wrong person for a specific job. The critical element for recovery is the employer's prior knowledge, actual or inferential, of the employee's propensities to create the specific risk of harm resulting in damages to the third party. The rationale for tort liability pursuant to the law of negligence is that the employer owes a duty to its customers, clients, and other third parties to act in a reasonably prudent manner when it comes to the employment aspect of its business. Of course, the aggrieved party bringing the lawsuit must prove in addition to the direct negligence of the employer the underlying tort committed by the employee and the relationship of the underlying tort to employment (*Joseph V. Dilliard's, Inc.*, 2009, applying Arizona law). Accordingly, in determining whether the employer should be held *directly* liable in negligence in hiring, supervising, or retaining an employee one Louisiana appeals court provided the following four-factor test: When determining whether the employer is liable for the negligent acts of an employee, the factors to be considered are whether the tortious act was: (1) primarily employment based; (2) reasonably incidental to the performance of the employee's duties; (3) occurred on the employer's premises; and (4) occurred during hours of employment. However, it is not necessary that all factors be met in order to find liability; rather, each case must be decided on the merits. Moreover, the fact that the primary motive of the employee is to benefit himself or herself does not prevent the tortious act from being within the scope of employment. If the purpose of serving the employer's business motivates the employee to any appreciable extent, the employer is liable (*Bourgeois v. Allstate Ins. Co.*, 2002). Other courts, however, simply use a "totality of the circumstances" test. For example, one Minnesota appeals court stated that liability for negligent hiring is determined by the totality of the circumstances surrounding the hiring and whether the employer exercised reasonable care (*L.M. v. Karlson*, 2002). Such a general pronouncement from a court would perforce give a great deal of discretion to a jury to ascertain liability.

Regarding the hiring of employees, if during the hiring process of an employee a reasonable investigation would have disclosed the unfitness or unsuitability of the employee for a particular duty or task to be performed or for employment generally, and the evidence also shows that it was unreasonable for the employer to hire such an employee based on the information that the employer knew, or should have known, then the employer is liable directly for the tort of negligence for any harm foreseeably caused to third parties by the employee. For example, if the employer is considering hiring a person for a position that requires the use of a motor vehicle, the reasonably prudent employer would investigate such matters as driver license status, driving accidents, tickets, license suspensions, as well as drug and alcohol use. Moreover, the employer would check with the Department of Motor Vehicles in the pertinent jurisdiction. Regarding the hiring of supervisors, since there is the potential for greater legal liability, it is recommended that more than a routine background check be conducted.

Note, however, and this point again must be underscored, that negligence law does not require the employer to act perfectly; the employer is not an insurer against harm; rather, the employer "merely" must act carefully. Accordingly, regarding hiring of employees, if the employer does conduct an investigation, and it is a reasonable and careful one, the employer would not be directly liable even if a more thorough or different type of investigation would have discovered a problem with the employee. When supervising an employee the failure on the part of the employer to take prompt remedial action, such as an investigation, reassignment, suspension, discharge, or otherwise control of the employee, after the employer becomes aware, or should have been aware, of the problems with the employee indicating unfitness, unsuitability, or dangerous propensities, such inaction is grounds for direct negligence liability on the part of the employer. The central factor is whether the employer had, or should have had, knowledge of the need to exercise supervision and control of the employee. Accordingly, ultimate liability depends on whether the risk of harm from the incompetent, unfit, and/or dangerous employee was reasonably foreseeable as a result of the retention of the employee and the lack of reasonable supervision.

Management Implications and Recommendations:

Management initially must discuss the company's hiring, supervision, and retention policies and practices with legal counsel. Managers very basically need to comply with the general tort requirement of acting in a "reasonable" manner under the circumstances in all aspects of the employment relationship. Managers must make sure all candidates and employees are screened and supervised in a consistent manner, for example, by asking finalists for employment the same questions. It is always a good practice to secure adequate insurance policies that specifically define negligent hiring as a covered "occurrence"; that is, as an accidently caused event that will trigger the insurer to defend the business entity should such a claim arise. The employer, in addition, must conduct a reasonable and careful investigation of potential employees. Managers should have each applicant fill out a detailed job application; and avoid just asking applicants for resumes as they are susceptible to exaggeration and fabrication. In so doing, it is important to confirm work history and verify educational degrees, licenses, and/or certificates conferred. Managers must conduct an interview of the prospective employee and ensure that questions pertain to the specific job qualifications, knowledge, skills, performance, attitude, attendance, and the ability to work as part of a team as well as independently. In the application and during the interview process ask the candidate why he or she left the former employer. Moreover, managers must be wary of the following explanations for leaving the prior employer as they are "red flags": "personality conflicts," especially with managers and supervisors, as well as "disagreements," especially with managers and supervisors.

Managers must make a reasonable effort to contact references and former employers; and keep written documentation of any reference check. As such, ask the applicant if he or she has ever been fired or asked to resign from a job. Also ask the applicant how he or she thinks the former or current employer will respond to a request for a reference. Typically, the former employer will not respond favorably to such a request; and if so, ask the former employer if the applicant would be eligible to be rehired by the former employer. It is also very important to conduct a criminal background check and investigation of applicants, but it is critical to do so in conformity with the Equal Employment Opportunity (EEOC) guidelines for criminal background checks. Accordingly, Clark (2019) recommends that the relevance of the crime to the job is the critical factor in deciding whether to hire a candidate with a criminal record. Consideration of such relevance, including any remoteness of the criminality, should satisfy EEOC guidelines, negligent hiring laws, fairness and ethics, as well as the "recommended best practices" of the Society for Human Resource Management (Clark, 2019). Furthermore, inquire as to any civil lawsuits and obtain the details thereof as well as obtain the driving record of the applicant if relevant to the job (but first obtain written permission from the applicant to release the record). Conduct, moreover, an Internet investigation of the job applicant, but be careful not to violate federal and state anti-discrimination laws or to commit the tort of invasion of privacy. Also conduct a credit check on the applicant but make sure to comply with the requirements of the Fair Credit Reporting Act as well as EEOC guidelines for conducing credit checks.

Managers, moreover, must make a reasonable effort to determine if the employee is competent to perform the work he or she is being hired to do. As such, ask the applicant what his or her strengths and weaknesses are. Ask the applicant how well he or she got, or gets, along with managers, supervisors, co-workers, customers, and/or clients. Also ask the applicant if he or she works well under pressure. Ask if the applicant if he or she is presently using illegal drugs and ask if the applicant would be willing to take a drug test. Make sure the employee is competent to use any dangerous instrumentalities or products which could cause harm to third persons. Finally, include in the application a statement that the information supplied by the job candidate is true and correct; and make the candidate understand that the failure to provide full and truthful information is grounds for sanctions, including immediate termination.

Regarding supervision of employees, managers must adequately supervise an employee so as to become aware of any subsequent conduct on the part of the employee that would place the employer on notice of the incompetent or dangerous character of the employee. Accordingly, managers should take adequate steps to remedy the situation when the employer becomes aware that the employee is engaging in tort-like conduct and/or has dangerous propensities. If the employer becomes aware of the employee's incompetence or unfitness, management must take immediate corrective action by means of coaching, mentoring, reassignment, or termination. Finally, managers must document the investigation as to the employee's continuing fitness to continue employment.

5. Negligence and Premises Liability

The principles of negligence have long been applied to the owners of land in order to ascertain the duties of landowners to those people who come upon their land. This area of law is also called "*premises liability*." The fundamental principle is that an owner of land owes a duty to exercise reasonable care to safeguard people who come upon the land. This duty extends to landowners who are also landlords and thus have a legal duty to exercise reasonable care to safeguard their tenants and their tenants' guests in the common areas of the leasehold, such as entrance ways, parking areas, laundry rooms, pools, and clubhouses.

Under the common law, the basic duty of the landowner was more precisely defined by the status of the person who came upon his or her land. The first category is called "*business invitees*." These are the people who are invited to come upon the land for the benefit of the landowner. Initially it must be pointed out that a landowner, for example, a store owner, is not a general insurer of its customers' safety on the premises (*Flores v. Wal-Mart Store Tex., LLC*, 2020, applying Texas law). However, the landowner has a duty to protect invitees from dangers that the landowner knew of or should have known by means of a reasonable inspection. That is, for a business invitee there is an affirmative duty to discover and remedy or at least warn of any hidden dangers that might harm the business invitee and thus to keep the property in a reasonably safe condition. Accordingly, this aspect of premises liability could be construed as another exception to the aforementioned nonfeasance doctrine since the owner of the land would be held liable for the failure to take measures to make the property safe (*Inthalangsy v. Wal-Mart Stores Texas*, 2020, applying Texas law). Examples would be for the property owner to take reasonable measures to safeguard against such foreseeable types of crime such as muggings and car break-ins at commercial shopping centers and parking lots and pickpocketing at crowded events and theme parks (Rinaldo Law Group, 2020). Similarly, a supermarket must continually inspect its premises for wet spots on the floor or banana peels or broken glass or any other hazardous conditions that could cause injury. The supermarket would be required put up warning signs, cones, or tape until the dangerous condition is corrected. For example, not discovering and remedying on a rainy day a wet, slippery, and bunched up floor mat where customers wiped their feet, and where a customer tripped and was injured, would be a violation of a legal duty if the defendant store knew about the condition or the condition existed long enough to give the owner of the premises a reasonable opportunity to discover it (*Flores v. Wal-Mart Stores Tex., LLC*, 2020, applying Texas law). However, if a landowner had neither actual nor constructive knowledge of a risk of harm then there is no legal duty of care to a person coming on the premises. For example, in the Illinois court of appeals case of *Pearson v. Pilot Travel Ctrs.* (2020), the plaintiff using a public bathroom at a Pilot truck stop was injured when she was struck on the head by an industrial-sized roll of toilet paper. Apparently, a third party somehow obtained the roll of toilet paper and balanced it on top of the restroom stall door so as to "boobytrap" the entrance way into the stall as some sort of prank or maybe an intentional attack on the plaintiff. There were no witnesses and no complaints from other customers; but the testimony at trial indicated that the foregoing cause was the only possible explanation for this type of injury, which no witness had ever heard or seen before. Accordingly, the appeals court ruled that there was no premises liability since the defendant Pilot had neither actual nor constructive knowledge of the hazard. Moreover, the appeals court also ruled generally that there was no duty of care, and thus no negligence liability, since the incident causing the injury was not reasonably foreseeable, but rather occurred in circumstances deemed "freakish, bizarre, or fantastic" (*Pearson v. Pilot Travel Ctrs.*, 2020). In one other example, a supermarket employee improperly bagging a heavy item, which fell on a customer's foot and caused injury, would not be construed as a premises liability case, but rather as a potential negligence case based on the careless performance of an affirmative act (*Inthalangsy v. Wal-Mart Stores Texas*, 2020, applying Texas law).

The second category of people that can come upon the land is called "*guests*." These are people who come upon the land with the owner's permission for the primary benefit of themselves and not the landowner. Examples would include social guests of the landowner as well as salespeople, who solicit the landowner on their own motivation. The landowner owes a duty to warn guests of hazards or dangers that the landowner is aware of or should be aware of, but there is no affirmative duty to inspect for unknown dangers or hazards or to maintain or repair the premises. Note that some states instead of a "guest" category use a "licensee" category; and then furthermore make a distinction between "invited licensees," who are treated as business invitees, and "uninvited licensees," which are people who are permitted to be on the premises, but who are not explicitly invited for the benefit of the property owner, for example, a door-to-door salesperson as well as in most cases social guests at a party on the property (Boeschen, 2020; Find Law, 2020; Rinaldo Law Group, 2020).

Finally, the third category is "*trespassers*." These are people who come on the land without the landowner's knowledge and/or consent. In most states, based on the old common law, the landowner does not owe the trespasser any duty except not to intentionally harm the trespasser, for example, by means of hidden devices or traps, such as "spring-guns." However, in some states, even the trespasser has the right to be warned of hidden or latent dangers which the landowner was aware of and which could not be readily seen on the surface or readily discovered. However, if a risk or hazard is so obvious, such as a pond, big pit, heavy machinery, or a construction site on the property, then the landowner need not as a general rule warn of the dangerous condition. However, note that the landowner may have liability to children, even trespassing children, who are injured by a condition on the land attractive to children, who thus can recover based on the "attractive nuisance" doctrine, for example, the typical, very appealing to children, swimming pool situation (Boeschen, 2020; Find Law, 2020; Rinaldo Law Group, 2020).

Defenses to Negligence

There are three main defenses to a lawsuit for negligence: 1) contributory negligence, 2) comparative negligence, and 3) assumption of the risk. *Contributory negligence* is careless conduct on the plaintiff's part that is a contributing cause to his or her own injury. Contributory negligence is a very harsh common law doctrine because it acts as a complete bar to recovery regardless of how slight the plaintiff's own negligence. At times called "pure contributory negligence," the doctrine in its most "pure" and harshest form means that even if a plaintiff is only1% negligent in causing his or her harm the plaintiff cannot recover (Justia, Comparative & Contributory Negligence, 2020; Find Law, Comparative Negligence, 2019). However, in the vast majority of the states in the United States today, by statute, the defense of contributory negligence has been abolished and replaced by the doctrine of *comparative negligence*, which doctrine is also referred to as "apportionment of fault" or "allocation of fault"

(Justia, Comparative & Contributory Negligence, 2020; Find Law, Comparative Negligence, 2019). Comparative negligence is not a complete defense; rather, the plaintiff's damages are determined, the jury makes a finding on each party's fault, and the plaintiff's damages are accordingly reduced by the proportion the plaintiff's own fault bears to the total amount of the plaintiff's harm. There are two types of comparative negligence; pure comparative negligence, in which a plaintiff can be even 99% at fault and still sue to recover for his or her injuries; and modified comparative negligence, which holds that a plaintiff must be less than 50% at fault (or in some states 51%) before the plaintiff can recover any damages (Justia, Comparative & Contributory Negligence, 2020; Find Law, Comparative Negligence, 2019). *Assumption of the risk* arises when the plaintiff encounters a known risk voluntarily, for example, by going on stairs that are visibly being repaired. When the plaintiff thereby in essence consents to assuming the risk of injury from a particular hazard, this "assumption" of the risk is a complete defense for the defendant. For example, a roller-skater assumes the risk of damage and injury resulting from contact with other people roller skating (*Huston v. Brookpark Skateland Social Club, Inc.*, 2020, applying Ohio law). Another example arises when one plays a sport, such as softball, where a player is deemed to assume the risk of being hit by a ball as well as playing on an uneven field (*Steven v. Piper*, 2020, applying Minnesota law). The traditional example of assumption of the risk doctrine occurs when one goes to a baseball game as a fan. That is, the baseball fan is knowingly and voluntarily taking a known risk, that is, being hit by a baseball. Yet what about being hit by a hot dog thrown by a vendor? There actually is a precedent in that the Missouri supreme court has ruled that a fan hit and injured by a flying hot dog does not assume a risk that is tied to an essential character of watching a baseball game (Cavico and Mujtaba, 2014). Accordingly, the injured fan could sue the ballpark for negligence, but of course would have to sustain that cause of action. Regardless, there now is precedent that a ballpark will have to train its vendors on how to properly transmit hot dogs to the fans in the stands.

Summary

This chapter examined the tort of negligence. Negligence was defined and the elements of negligence – duty, breach of duty, causation, and damages – were explained and illustrated. The meaning of the critical "reasonably prudent person" standard as well as the important distinction between causation-in-fact and legal or proximate causation were explained. Negligence was differentiated from malpractice. The primary defenses to negligence – comparative negligence and assumption of the risk – were explained and illustrated. The authors also analyzed two specialized negligence doctrines – *res ipsa loquitur* and negligence *per se*. The specialized tort of negligent infliction of emotional distress was explained and differentiated from the intentional tort of infliction of emotional distress. The authors, moreover, examined in depth negligence law as applied to the hiring, supervision, and retention of employees. The authors furthermore addressed negligence principles as applied to premises liability. Finally, the authors made suggestions and recommendations on how employers can avoid and minimize liability pursuant to negligence law. This chapter and the previous chapters to this book dealt with torts – negligence and intentional torts - that are premised on degrees of culpability and fault. In the next chapter, the authors will examine another common law tort – strict liability – which is not premised on fault but rather on Utilitarian safety, risk-avoidance, cost-distribution, and insurance rationales.

CHAPTER V - STRICT LIABILITY TORTS

Strict liability, or liability without fault, is a special type of liability imposed by the common law. Although an actor not only did not intend any harm, and even though he or she acted in a careful and prudent manner, the actor is nevertheless legally responsible for any injuries caused by his or her conduct. Strict liability is imposed in three types of situations. One instance involves activities that the law regards as "ultra-hazardous," such as construction blasting, crop-dusting, fumigation, and reservoir and dam construction and maintenance. These activities and conditions are potentially so highly dangerous and threaten substantial injury to the public, so that regardless of how much care is exercised, the duty of safety is an absolute one. Insurance is the only "answer" in such a case. Another category of strict liability case deals with the liability of the owners and possessors of dangerous animals, which as a topic is most interesting but beyond the purposes of this handbook. The final category of strict liability is the highly significant and consequential business law and consumer protection doctrine of strict tort liability for the manufacturers and sellers of defective products.

Strict Liability for Products

Strict liability in tort is a relatively new, at least compared to negligence and fraud tort law, cause of action for the aggrieved consumer. Strict liability is a very important and far-reaching legal doctrine, one created to advance consumer safety and to protect the consumer; and thus strict liability is a doctrine that is very frequently asserted by consumers harmed by products. The doctrine is a common law formulation; it was first promulgated by the supreme court of California in 1963, in the seminal case of *Greenman v. Yuba Power Products, Inc.*; and for an additional time frame point of reference, the doctrine was adopted in

Florida by that state's supreme court in 1976. All states in the U.S. now have adopted strict liability, though in varying formulations.

The doctrine was first enunciated in the *Restatement (Second) of Torts*, a compendium of existing law as well as recommendations of what the law should be, drafted by legal experts, and published by the American Law Institute. Restatements of the Law are not law *per se*, but they are very persuasive legal authority. The *Restatement* formulation for strict liability now has been adopted in varying forms by virtually all the states in the United States. Strict liability in tort holds that one who sells any product in a defective condition unreasonably dangerous to the user, the consumer, or his or her property is liable to the ultimate user or consumer if: 1) the seller is engaged in the business of selling such a product, that is, the seller is an entity of the marketing chain; and 2) the product is expected to, and in fact does, reach the user or consumer without substantial change in the condition in which it was sold. Moreover, the doctrine of strict liability in tort applies although: 1) the seller has exercised all possible care in the preparation, distribution, and sale of the product, thereby clearly distinguishing strict liability from the tort of negligence; and 2) the user or consumer has not purchased the product from, or entered into any contractual relationship with, the seller of the product, thereby obviating the old contract "privity" requirement. Strict liability regarding products has been applied to manufacturers, wholesalers and distributors, retailers, as well as commercial lessors of products. Traditional tort damages, including damage to property, are recoverable elements of damages in a strict liability lawsuit, but not, however, purely economic losses, that is, lost income, at least in the majority of states.

The essence of strict liability in tort for products is the finding of a "*defect*" in the product. In most jurisdictions, if a product is defective, it is presumed also to be "unreasonably dangerous" to the user or consumer. Products can be deemed "defective" in three ways: 1) the product contains a "flaw," 2) the product lacks a warning, or 3) the product is defectively designed. First, regarding *flawed products*, the main consideration is to measure the product in its manufactured state with the manufacturer's own specifications and standards for that type of product; and then if the product does not even meet the manufacturer's own "specs," the product is legally flawed, defective, unreasonably dangerous, and the manufacturer (as well as distributors and retailers of the flawed product) is strictly liable in tort for the flawed product when it causes harm. It is important to note that evidence of how the product became flawed is not an issue in a strict liability "defect" lawsuit. Strict liability is not a negligence lawsuit. Consequently, the fact that the manufacturer demonstrated that it had an elaborate inspection, testing, and quality control scheme (which obviously failed!) is irrelevant in a strict liability lawsuit (though such evidence would be critical to the disposition of a negligence lawsuit). In the U.S., the term "flaw" is used as one of the criterion for "defectiveness"; but in Germany, the term "run-a-away" product is commonly employed, and that latter term more accurately "captures" the usual situation; that is, the manufacturer, though truly striving for that "zero defect" objective (and award!) somehow allowed the product to "run-a-away" from all the manufacturer's quality control and safety checks. Finally, it is interesting to note that one ordinarily does not see "flaw" cases reported in the law reports since typically the cases are settled before an official and recorded legal disposition. What real defense does the manufacturer have if the evidence indicates that its product which caused harm does not even conform to the manufacturer's own product standards?

Second, a product can be deemed defective because the product lacks a warning or the warning is inadequate. To be legally sufficient, the warning must address the nature and severity of any risks and dangers to using the product, explain how the consumer should handle the risks, as well as indicate any reasonable alternatives. The warnings, as well as labels and instructions, must clearly, simply, and prominently warn the consumer of the dangers involved in using the product; they must be conspicuous and understandable to the reasonable consumer. The warnings should be on the product as well as in the owner's instructional manual (Peeler, 2020). If the warning is clear and visible the fact that the consumer did not see it does not mean the defendant manufacturer will be held liable (Peeler, 2020). Moreover, a manufacturer cannot avoid liability by claiming mere ignorance of the risk; that is, the manufacturer is held to a duty to exercise reasonable care to discover risks through research, testing, and investigation, for example, that a car seat might collapse backwards in an accident if the driver was overweight (Boeschen, 2020a). An interesting, illustrative, and recent case dealing with the adequacy of warnings is the Utah court of appeals case of *Feasel v. Tracker Marine LLC* (2020). In the *Feasal* case, the plaintiff, a passenger on a small boat, was fishing on a lake with a friend who was driving the boat, when the boat struck an unknown object, and both parties were ejected. The engine on the boat was manufactured by the defendant company. The boat was equipped with a "kill-switch" lanyard, which the boat operator was not wearing at the time of impact. Consequently, the boat continued to operate under power after the two men were ejected. Unfortunately, instead of moving forward away from the men, the boat turned in a tight circle, and although the boat operator managed to swim away out of the boat's path, the plaintiff was repeatedly struck and sliced by the boat's propellers as the boat continued to circle. The operator managed to rescue the plaintiff, who was flown to a hospital, very seriously injured. The phenomenon of a driverless boat circling is known as the "circle of death" (*Feasel v. Tracker Marine LLC*, 2020). The defendant manufacturer had provided warnings in the boat user's manual regarding the use and purpose of the "kill-switch" lanyard, the danger presented by a spinning propeller blade, as well as the possibility that the steering wheel may spin if released. Moreover, the defendant affixed warnings on labels near the boat's steering wheel warning users to wear the "kill-switch" lanyard, to keep a firm and continuous grip on the wheel, to make sure no one is in the water when the engine was started, and that the rotating propeller could cause injury. However, none of the warnings stated that wearing the "kill-switch" lanyard would prevent the boat from turning in circles if the driver was ejected from the boat (*Feasel v. Tracker Marine LLC*, 2020). The lower court dismissed the plaintiff's lack of a warning case, ruling as a matter of law that the warnings provided were adequate. On appeal, the plaintiff argued that the warnings were inadequate since they did not specifically and explicitly mention the "circle of death" phenomenon. The appeals court agreed with the plaintiff, and thus reversed the lower court ruling. The appeals court explained that the issue of the adequacy of a warning is typically a question for a jury, and consequently that key question could not be resolved as a matter of law by the lower court judge.

Accordingly, the appeals court ruled that the fact that the warnings provided did not specifically and explicitly warn that the failure to wear a lanyard could result in a "circle of death" situation raised a factual question for a jury as to whether more specific and explicit warnings were required (*Feasel v. Tracker Marine LLC*, 2020). Therefore, the *Feasal* case provides another evident illustration as to why manufacturers should, and do, "err on the side of caution" when providing warnings.

Nevertheless, the general rule is that the manufacturer is not required to warn of obvious or predictable risks that the reasonable and rational person should be aware, for example, a warning that lighting a match from a match book could start a fire (Boeschen, 2020a). Yet nevertheless, after such "classic" lawsuits as the McDonald's hot coffee case, in which the product was construed as defective due to the lack of a warning that the coffee was hot (actually, very, very hot!), manufacturers now "err on the side of caution" and warn of risks that one might think a reasonable person should be cognizant of. For example, warnings not to use a snow-blower on the roof, not to use a CD rack as a ladder, not to allow children to play in a dishwasher, and not to fold a baby carriage with the baby in it, seem very obvious, and one would think would be within the purview of common sense and rationality, but nonetheless the nature of a warning "defect" under strict liability motivates manufacturers to issue such warnings (Cavico and Mujtaba, 2014). An example of an obvious risk that a manufacturer would not have to warn could be in the case of a cigarette lighter which typically would ignite and cause a fire when applied to flammable material or gasoline which could be combustible and highly flammable (Peeler, 2020). Another would be a knife or an axe which is sharp and thus might strike and cut one's hand when cutting or chopping. Similarly, there is one recent legal precedent that clearly states that the risk of harm from a product can be so evident that the product does not require a warning. The case was a New Jersey one in which a college student who fell off a loft bed sued and recovered a $170,000 award from a local jury. The student claimed that his fall and injuries, mainly a dislocated shoulder, were caused by the lack of a warning label on the loft bed, which was about six feet off the floor. However, in 2006, a three-judge panel of the state court of appeals unanimously overturned the ruling, stating that the obviousness of the danger was an absolute defense. The appeals court explained that warnings would lose their efficacy and meaning if they were placed on every product that is known to be dangerous, such as a knife or scissors, glass, a bat or ball, or bicycle, that would pose a generally known risk of injury if abused, misused, dropped, or fallen from (Schwaneberg, 2006).

Causation of course will be required in a failure to warn case, that is, there must be evidence that the lack of a warning or insufficient instructions were a substantial factor in causing the plaintiff's harm (California Civil Jury Instructions, 2017). Moreover, in a strict liability case the misuse of a product is a defense. However, if a person's misuse of a product was something that a reasonable manufacturer could predict, then there could be liability for failure to warn of the predictable consequences that could cause harm (Boeschen, 2020a). A general warning will not protect a manufacturer from liability for a defectively designed or manufactured product. For example, an automobile manufacturer will not be able to obviate its liability under strict liability law for defectively designed or flawed brakes merely by stating that the brakes may fail under certain conditions. Note, though, that the obverse is not true; that is, an injured consumer can proceed with a failure to warn strict liability lawsuit even if there was neither a design nor manufacturing defect.

Third, a product can be defective because it is *defectively designed*. Yet, is that not a tautology? That is, that a product is defective because it is defective! Such a legal standard brings U.S. products liability law closer to the "old" socialist, European, insurance scheme; that is, product-causation-harm equals manufacturer-pay. However, as first enunciated by the California supreme court, there is a test, though an imprecise one, for determining whether a product is defectively designed. There are three parts to the test, all of which must be applied to the product to ascertain if it is defectively designed: First, does the product meet the "state-of-the-art"? That is, going back in time to when the product was made (and not at present time perhaps many years later during a lawsuit), and given the level of science, engineering, and technology at that time, could anything more have been done to make the product safer? As such, a manufacturer's compliance with minimum product standards in the industry is not a shield to liability in a design defect case (*Alicea v. Gorilla Ladder Company*, 2020, applying New York law). However, the burden of proof and persuasion is on the plaintiff to demonstrate the existence of an alternative design that was safer (*Great Plains Otter Tail, LLC v. Pro-Environmental, Inc.*, 2020, applying Minnesota law).

If the product could have been made safer, the next part to the test is to factor in two constraints – practicality of use and economic feasibility. That is, could the product have been made safer and still have the product function as a product of that type? For example, a knife can be designed to be perfectly safe, but then it would not cut. Similarly, a car could be designed to be totally safe to its occupants, but it would look like a tank. As to the economic variable, a similar question is posed: Could the product be designed to be safer, and still be affordable? Once again, how much does a tank cost, what is its fuel mileage? Yet, because the technology does exist to put "crash" air-bags, rear-view cameras, and all types of safety features throughout a vehicle, then how much would those safety features materially add to the cost of a car, especially an "economy" one? If the product is rendered unaffordable by the additional safety feature, the manufacturer is not legally obligated to adopt it. However, the test for a "design defect," one must underscore, is a very vague one; and, moreover, the application and ultimate decision regarding this legal theory is typically in the U.S. in the hands of a lay jury – a jury guided by experts, of course; but who knows what a jury will do in a given situation, especially when faced with an injured, and perhaps very sympathetic, plaintiff. It is also important to note that the Restatement of Torts was again amended, and in 1997 the *Restatement (Third) of Torts* was approved. Regarding design defects, the new Restatement continues the emphasis on an alternative design that was available, reasonable, and practical, but was not incorporated into the product, as the essence of "defectiveness." The "classic" design defect case was the series of Ford Pinto cases commencing in the late 1970s, where the costs of incorporating the available design improvement (structural alteration of the car) were minimal ($11.00 per vehicle) compared to the risks (ruptured fuel tanks and car fires at collisions over twenty-five miles per hour); and consequently Ford was found to be legally liable on strict liability as well as negligence grounds (and was subject to considerable punitive damage liability too). The amount that Ford had to pay in damages and settlements exceeded $50 million, which was more than double what the alternative design implementation would have cost the company. A recent design defect case arose in 2019 involving a Tesla electric vehicle which after a crash the battery caught fire, but rescuers were stopped from pulling the driver from the burning vehicle due to the automatic door handles which failed to automatically extend from their retracted positions, making it impossible for anyone on the outside to open the doors. Rescuers and bystanders watched helplessly as smoke filled the interior causing the eventual death of the driver. Tesla stated that the door handles, which require a fob to open, are designed for efficiency and to make the vehicle more aerodynamic and that the company's vehicles are designed to make them the safest vehicles in the world. One of the issues in the lawsuit will be whether the vehicle is defectively designed due to the type of door handles utilized as well as whether the battery will cause a fire after a crash (Boryga, 2018). Typically, whether a product is defectively designed is a question of fact for the jury, unless reasonable minds could not differ on the issue when the question then becomes one of "law" for a judge to resolve (*Great Plains Otter Tail, LLC v. Pro-Environmental, Inc.*, 2020, applying Minnesota law).

Today, an interesting products liability dilemma – legally and scientifically – is emerging – the "hacking" of cars, particularly whether a "hacked" car is a defective product pursuant to strict liability law, as well as the concomitant need for cyber-security for cars and other vehicles. The fear, of course, is that hackers might be able to hack into a car's engine and brakes remotely from a laptop and perhaps even to commandeer the vehicle. The concern is that hackers might be able to take over a vehicle while one is driving it, especially at highway speeds. Lawmakers, government regulators, car manufacturers, and consumers naturally are concerned. The Jeep demonstration and other tests have demonstrated the vulnerabilities of cars to hacking. Consequently, the apparent inability of a car to withstand a cyber-attack raises the legal issue of whether there is a safety defect in the car. If the National Highway Traffic and Safety Administration (NHTSA) deems a car to have a defect the agency can demand a recall of that vehicle line, which obviously is costly to a manufacturer's reputation and "pocketbook." However, auto manufacturers contend that a cyber-attack on a car is not a legal "defect"; rather, they say that hacking into a car is an intentional wrongful act by a bad person, comparable to someone slashing a car's tires. The proliferation of driverless features in cars, such as automatic braking and increased wireless communication, has heightened security concerns. A major problem is that the main federal law dealing with safety, defects, and recalls of autos was promulgated in 1966, long before sophisticated (and perhaps hack-prone) technology existed. Accordingly, government regulators have focused on more traditional aspects of vehicles, such as seatbelts, brakes, air bags, as well as how well vehicles can withstand crashes.

In addition to the aforementioned regulatory law administered by the NHTSA there are two bodies of common law that could apply to the hacked car controversy, and which could result in lawsuits by private parties against auto manufacturers and sellers. The first is negligence law. Pursuant to negligence law, a car manufacturer has a legal duty to act as a "reasonably prudent" car manufacturer and to exercise due care in the design and production of its vehicles. The failure to do so subjects the manufacturer to civil damages for the tort, or civil wrong, of negligence, including "pain and suffering" damages as well as additional punitive damages if the negligence is gross, for harms caused by its negligent actions. The duty of due care requires that the manufacturer guard against and warn of risks that the manufacturer knew of or should have known of and which are reasonably foreseeable. The second area of law is products liability law, specifically the doctrine of strict liability in tort. Strict liability imposes civil tort liability and tort damages on anyone on the marketing chain (manufacturer-wholesaler/distributor-retailer) who produces and/or sells a "defective" product. One recalls that there is no need for an injured party to prove negligence; the liability is "strict," that is, without fault. However, it is indispensable that the product be adjudged to be a "defective" one. One important objective of strict liability law, particularly the design defect doctrine, is to advance product safety. Yet how these common law theories will be applied to the hacked car controversy will only be determined when there are actual lawsuits instituted and judges and juries render decisions. Moreover, another most interesting and challenging ramification of the strict liability in tort doctrine will be its application to the rapidly developing field of self-driving or autonomous vehicles.

The manufacturer or seller of a product is allowed to assume the product will be used in a normal fashion. Accordingly, the manufacturer or seller generally will not be held liable for harm or injuries resulting from the abnormal use of the product. There is an exception, however, that may arise when the abnormal or unusual use of the product is deemed to be foreseeable. For example, using a lawnmower with the grass bag removed could be deemed to be a foreseeable misuse of the product, thereby resulting in the manufacturer's or seller's liability when a bystander is injured by a projectile that is shot through the unguarded lawnmower.

There are decided advantages to the consumer with the strict liability doctrine. Strict liability in tort for products is not negligence law; thus evidence of a lack of due care is not required. Strict liability is not warranty law; and thus disclaimers as well as notice and privity requirements are not operational. The injured consumer or user only must establish that the product was defective when it left the seller's hands and that the defect caused the injury. Moreover, several entities on the marketing chain can be potentially liable under strict liability law, to wit: the manufacturer of the product, the wholesaler and distributor of the product, the retailer who sells the product, as well as the manufacturer of component parts of the product and the party responsible for the assembly and/or installation of the product (Peeler, 2020). There are, however, some defenses that a defendant manufacturer (or wholesaler or retailer) can interpose, to wit: 1) assumption of the risk, that is, the user of the product assumed the risk of its use by being aware of the defect or danger and nonetheless used the goods anyway; 2) misuse or abuse of the product; or 3) disregarding the manufacturer's instructions as to proper and safe use. Finally, it must be noted that parties not on the marketing chain, that is, "casual" sellers, such as buying a product at a person's home garage sale, are not subject to strict liability law (Peeler, 2020).

The justification for the doctrine of strict liability in tort is asserted, originally by the California supreme court, as a consumer safety one. Accordingly, the doctrine is supported on Utilitarian "greater good" grounds that it will not only maintain consumer safety but also advance consumer safety since a manufacturer now will be legally obligated to "keep up" with the "state-of-the-art." There is also a "risk distribution" rationale behind strict liability law. That is, the costs of injuries for defective products should be borne by the manufacturer or seller who placed the product on the market rather than the injured consumer; and then the manufacturer in essence can "spread" the risk by factoring it into the price of the product. Moreover, the manufacturer as well as other entities on the marketing chain can obtain insurance to protect themselves, and then once again, the additional cost of the coverage can be factored into the price of the product.

Two other legal doctrines that impact strict liability law are *market share liability* and *statutes of repose*. The former benefits plaintiffs and the latter benefits defendants. Normally, an injured plaintiff must demonstrate that the defective product that caused the plaintiff harm was produced by a particular defendant manufacturer. However, in some instances, it may be very difficult if not impossible for a defendant to pinpoint which manufacturer out of the many that produced the product, or perhaps which one of the many distributors of the product, made or supplied it to the plaintiff. Accordingly, in some states a court may interpose the doctrine of *market share liability*. This legal principle holds that manufacturers who sold a defective product, or distributors who supplied it, such as lead-based paint, will be compelled to share the burden of damages based on the percentage each holds of the pertinent product or distribution market. A *statute of repose* is similar to a statute of limitations. A statute of repose is a state statute (and most states have such a statute) that holds that the manufacturer or seller of a product cannot be sued for producing or selling a product that caused harm unless the lawsuit is brought within 10 or 12 years, depending on the state statute, from the date the product was made or sold.

Management Implications and Recommendations:

Products liability litigation in the United States also has dealt with tobacco, guns, and "fast food," and particularly the relationship of these products to the design defect component to the strict tort liability doctrine. The tobacco cases are most interesting because they reveal the uncertainties and risks of the U.S. jury system to the litigants. Examine and reflect on the two Florida cases, for example. In one, in 1999, a jury in Miami-Dade County found in a class action suit against several tobacco companies that the cigarettes they manufactured and sold to Florida smokers were defective and unreasonably dangerous and caused a variety of fatal illnesses. Yet earlier, in 1997, another Florida jury, this time in Jacksonville, found that R.J. Reynolds, the maker of Salem cigarettes that the plaintiff smoked, was neither negligent in the plaintiff smoker's death nor did the tobacco company, ruled the jury, make an unreasonably dangerous and defective product (Cavico and Mujtaba, 2014). Why the disparity in outcomes? The Florida tobacco cases reveal the distinction between the roles of the judge and the jury in the United States. The judge determines questions of law and instructs the jury as to the law and the meaning of the law, for example, the design defect test part of the strict liability doctrine, but then the jury, as the "trier of fact" applies the law to the facts of the cases and renders a verdict. The design defect test, as are many legal precepts in a common law system such as the U.S., is not a precise formulation, which consequently accords the jury a great deal of discretion. Cigarettes certainly are not technically flawed, but are the warnings adequate? Moreover, most importantly, can a plaintiff sustain his or her burden of proof in convincing a jury that a tobacco company can make a safer cigarette, and do so in a practical, feasible, and economic manner? Those are difficult burdens to overcome. Moreover, these same legal and practical issues and challenges surely will arise with the increasing use of e-cigarettes and vaping.

The strict liability doctrine also has spawned a series of gun suits, in which injured plaintiffs argue that guns are defective products. The lawsuits typically are not based on the contention that guns are flawed products (and actually they seem to work very well, and therein lies the problem!), or even the assertion that warnings are inadequate (since ordinarily there are many warnings as to the proper transportation, use, cleaning, and storing of guns). Rather, the products liability lawsuits involving guns are based on the premise that guns are defectively designed products; and specifically the charge is made that the design of guns should incorporate modern "smart gun" *technology designed to prevent unauthorized users from firing the guns. One example of "smart gun" technology would be a feature, such as a fingerprint code or some type of sensor on the handle or trigger, which would recognize the unique characteristics of someone's grip. The gun industry, in defending product liability suits, argues that such "smart gun" technology is still in the developmental stage, and had not reached the scientific, as well as legally binding, level of state-of-the-art technology. Other issues involve the practicality of adopting such technology, and still having a gun that can be used efficaciously for legitimate purposes such as target shooting, hunting, and especially self-defense. There is also the economic feasibility issue of incorporating such safety features into a gun and still having the gun remain as an affordable product of that type. One very noteworthy, tragic, and very revealing gun products liability case, called the Grunow case, occurred in Florida in 2002. In that case, the widow of a teacher, who was slain in 2000 by one of his students, an irate thirteen year old forbidden by the teacher from seeing his girlfriend in class, and who used his grandfather's pistol to kill the teacher, sued the distributor of the weapon (since the manufacturer was bankrupt), claiming that the weapon was defective in design because it did not have better safety features, such as an internal locking system. The jury in West Palm Beach awarded the widow $1.2 million but also stated on the verdict form that the gun was not defective. The judge, of course, was obligated to throw out the jury's verdict, since the jury, apparently very sympathetic to the widow, nonetheless found for the defendant distributor on the critical design defect question. It is also interesting to note that in 2002 the New Jersey legislature passed into law the first "smart gun" law that mandates that all new handguns that are sold in that state be equipped with safety features that would allow only the owner of the weapon to fire it. New Jersey was the first state to enact such legislation. However, the law does not specify what "smart gun" technology must be; rather only that it must recognize the owner as well as be commercially available and feasible (Cavico and Mujtaba, 2014).*

The emerging area of products liability lawsuits in the U.S. deals with food, specifically "fast food" and soda, particularly the allegation that such food and drink cause obesity and related health problems. Several lawsuits alleging that "fast food" violates the strict liability doctrine have been filed; but none as of this writing have been successful. Yet perhaps as a result, many companies now are placing calorie and nutritional information prominently on the food labels or cartons as well as displaying such information in the restaurants at the food-counters. Such meritorious behavior is certainly "socially responsible" conduct, but also activity that will go a long way to complying with the "warning" element to strict liability. The much more interesting, as well as perplexing question, is whether "fast food" is defectively designed. Could a cheeseburger, large fries, and Coke be made safer, and still taste the appetizing same? Are there alternatives to certain ingredients of the food or the substances or manner in which it is cooked that emerge as reasonable alternatives? Are these alternatives presently available, and are they practical and feasible? These are issues that will have to be addressed and answered in this expanding area of products liability litigation.

Regarding warnings, one recalls the aforementioned New Jersey loft case, where although the seller prevailed on appeal it still had to undergo the time, expense, and effort of a civil trial and an appellate one. Consequently, manufacturers and sellers feel that it is better to "err on the side of caution" and thus to provide a warning even though a reasonable person would be aware of the risk. One example will clearly illustrate this prophylactic legal approach. In one case a woman was driving her new Winnebago vehicle back from a football game and drove it off the freeway injuring herself and harming the vehicle. Apparently, she set the cruise control at 70 mph, and then left the driver's seat to go back and make herself a sandwich, thereby causing the vehicle to crash and overturn. She sued Winnebago contending that the vehicle was defective due to the lack of a warning, specifically for the company not putting in the driver's manual that the driver should not leave the driver's seat with the cruise control set. An Oklahoma jury agreed with her and awarded her a new vehicle and $1,750,000 in damages. As a result of the jury verdict the company has changed its manuals to provide such a warning. As such, it is cheaper to warn than to defend a products liability lawsuit; and as a result one sees warnings that one would think that a reasonable and rational person would not need, such as: "Never iron clothes while they are *being worn"; "Never use hair dryer while sleeping"; "Remove child (from baby stroller) before folding"; "Do not use snow blower on roof"; and "Do not allow children to play in dishwasher" (Cavico and Mujtaba, 2014).*

Strict Liability for Ultra-Hazardous Activities

Strict liability, or liability without fault, as emphasized, is a special type of liability imposed by the common law. Although an actor not only did not intend any harm, and even though he or she acted in a careful and prudent manner, took precautions, made no mistakes, the actor is nevertheless legally responsible for any injuries caused by his or her conduct that caused harm. Strict liability is imposed in three types of situations, one of which, for products deemed "defective," has been extensively covered. Another instance involves activities that the law regards as "ultra-hazardous" or "abnormally dangerous." The courts typically use a six factor test, established by the *Restatement (Second) of Torts* (1977), to determine if an activity is ultra-hazardous or abnormally dangerous, to wit: 1) the existence of a high degree of risk of harm to the person or property of others; 2) the likelihood that the harm that results from the activity will be great; 3) an inability to eliminate that risk by the exercise of reasonable care; 4) the extent to which the activity is not a common usage; 5) the inappropriateness of the activity to the place where it is conducted; and 6) the extent to which the value to the community of the activity outweighs its dangerous attributes (Cornell Law School, Legal Information Institute, 2020). Typical examples are as follows: making, using, and transporting explosives; construction blasting and demolition; using, storing, and transporting dangerous chemicals, fuels, or radioactive materials; disposing of nuclear and chemical wastes; controlled burnings of buildings and fields; crop-dusting; fumigation; reservoir and dam construction and maintenance; and sky-diving and cliff-diving (Law Shelf, 2020; Legal Match, 2020a). These activities and conditions are potentially so highly dangerous and threaten substantial injury to the public, regardless of how much care is exercised, that the duty of safety is an absolute one. The aforementioned six-factor test would have to be applied to the preceding activities on a case-by-case basis, of course. For example, the transportation of hazardous materials on an interstate highway likely would not be considered ultra-hazardous, but its transportation near a school might be so construed (Legal Match, 2020a). Also, storage of a gas at a local service station, as opposed to a refinery, might not be considered abnormally dangerous since storing gas in underground tanks at local gas stations is a practice of common usage, the storage is appropriate, especially considering the frequency and extent of customer use, and the value of the activity to the community is very high (Law Shelf, 2020). Of course, in both the previous examples the traditional rules of negligence would apply to the transportation and storage. Moreover, causation – actual/factual and legal/proximate – must be present; and the standard tort defenses of comparative negligence as well as assumption of risk may be applicable (Legal Match, 2020; Law Shelf, 2020). Waivers of liability can also be used to prevent liability, for example, in sky-diving cases (Legal Match, 2020). Otherwise, insurance is the only "answer" in an ultra-hazardous situation. A final category of strict liability case deals with the liability of the owners and possessors of dangerous animals, which, as noted, is an interesting subject matter but beyond the purposes of this handbook.

Summary

This chapter dealt with the relatively modern tort of strict liability. The doctrine of strict liability or liability without fault or negligence was explicated and illustrated primarily in the area of defective products. The authors explained how products can be deemed defective by means of a flaw in the product, a lack of a warning or an inadequate warning, or when a product is defectively designed. The authors further explained the factors to be used to determine if a product is defectively designed. Particularly important to managers, employers, and business-persons is the fact that if a product is defective any entity on the marketing chain – from the manufacturer, wholesaler, distributor, to retailer, is legally responsible to the injured party, even though the party did not design the product or cause the defect. The authors emphasized that strict liability in tort for products is a very pro-consumer doctrine as well as one designed to advance product safety and to motivate insurance coverage. The authors discussed areas of potential future product litigation pursuant to strict liability. Moreover, in the chapter the authors briefly mentioned the applicability of strict liability to two other areas of the law: ultra-hazardous activities and dangerous animals. Suggestions were provided to managers and businesses to reduce their exposure to products liability lawsuits.

In the next chapter the authors will discuss the intersection of the field of tort law with agency law and show the potential liability of an employer for the tortious acts of its employees and in some circumstances for the employer's independent contractors as well as the liability of a principal for the torts of his or her agent.

CHAPTER VI - TORTS AND AGENCY LAW

This chapter will examine the field of agency law, how agency law relates to tort law, and the relationship of these important areas of the law to business, employment, and management. The field of agency law is a broad one encompassing three very important legal relationships, to wit: employer-employee, employer-independent contractor, and principal-agent. The authors will first define and provide examples of these three relationships. Critical to the employer-employee relationship is the doctrine of vicarious liability, that is, liability imputed to the employer, based on the ancient Roman doctrine of *respondeat superior* (meaning "let the master answer for the wrongs of the servant"). The authors will explain and illustrate vicarious liability and distinguish it from the direct liability of the employer. Essential to imputing liability to the employer is the "course or scope of employment" rule, which the authors will also explicate and illustrate. Vicarious liability for negligent as opposed to intentional torts will be differentiated. Moreover, the authors will present the exceptional situations where an employer can be held vicariously liable for the torts of his or her independent contractor. Although principal-agency law has greater ramifications in contract law, the situations where a principal can be held vicariously liable for the torts of his or her agent will be addressed. Finally, the authors will present suggestions and recommendations to employers and managers on how to avoid and minimize liability at this intersection of tort and agency law generally and regarding specific torts.

Definition of Key Terms

The field of agency law has three critical and foundational classifications: 1) the employer-employee relationship, called "master and servant" in the old common law; 2) the principal-agent relationship; and 3) the employer-independent contractor relationship.

It must be emphasized that these legal categories are not mutually exclusive ones, and thus one person, for example, a salesperson, can be both an agent and employee.

The first classification is the *employer-employee* one. An *employee* is a person who is employed to render services of any type and who remains under the control of another in performing these services. The essential characteristic of the employer-employee relationship is the power and right to control. The employer, that is, the "master," to use the old common law term, must at all times control or have the right to control the physical conduct of the employee, that is, the "servant," in the performance of his or her duties. There is no or very little discretion in the sense of independent thought and judgment exercised by one regarded as a conventional "employee" under the traditional common law.

The second relationship is the *principal-agent relationship*. An "*agent*" is a person who works for another, called the "*principal*," but who also acts for and in the place of the principal in order to effectuate legal relations with third parties. The essence of the principal-agent relationship is that the agent transacts business for the principal, represents and negotiates for the principal, and, most significantly, enters into contracts on the principal's behalf. The agent, moreover, can bind the principal to contracts with third parties. An employee "merely" works for another; whereas the agent represents another and thus ordinarily possesses a great deal of discretion in carrying out the purposes of the agency. An agent can be a "special agent," that is, authorized to bring about a particular undertaking for the principal, or the agent can be a "general agent," that is, authorized to represent the principal in any and all authorized dealings.

Finally, an *independent contractor* is a person who renders services in the course of an independent occupation. The independent contractor contracts with the employer only as to results, not how the work is to be done. Thus, the primary feature of this relationship is that the employer has no right of control as to how the work is done. As noted, a person may fulfill both roles, for example, an architect who is also empowered to make certain contracts on behalf of a property owner. Determining if a person working for an employer is an employee or an independent contractor is a crucial legal decision since many bodies of law, such as tort liability principles, as well as federal and state employment, tax, safety, and Workers' Compensation laws, will apply to "employees" but not to independent contractors.

From the employer's perspective, it may be financially advantageous to classify a worker as an independent contractor as opposed to an employee. There are several advantages to the employer for using independent contractors as opposed to employees, to wit: the employer is generally not liable for the torts committed by the independent contractor in performing the employer's work; the employer does not have to hold and pay Social Security and Medicare taxes; the independent contractor is not entitled to unemployment compensation and, usually, depending on the state, not entitled to worker's compensation; the independent contractor is not entitled to minimum wage and overtime pay requirements of federal and state labor law; the employer need not withhold income tax from the pay of the independent contractor (but may have to file an informational return with the IRS or other tax agency); and the employer will not be providing such employment benefits as health insurance, life insurance, paid holidays and vacations, and retirement plans. From the employer's perspective, therefore, it may be financially advantageous to classify a worker as an independent contractor as opposed to an employee.

What steps can an employer take to ensure that a worker is classified as an independent contractor as opposed to an employee? First, a written contract explicitly designating the worker's status as an independent contractor and spelling out his or her services and the conditions of employment is critical. However, merely calling an employment relationship an "independent" one is certainly evidentiary, but not dispositive of the issue. Other factors, which should be spelled out in the contract, include the responsibilities of the contractor, the time frame for their performance, that payment will be in a lump or divided sum for the performance of those services, and that the contractor will supply all the necessary tools, supplies, and equipment. If any other workers are to be hired, the responsibility to do so, as well as any insurance (liability and workers' compensation), benefits, and taxes must be the responsibility of the contractor. Accordingly, employers must be cognizant of the fact that even if an employer calls and names a party doing work for the employer as an "independent contractor," merely using that label is not dispositive of the issue of the status of the party. Rather, the courts will examine the actual working relationship between the parties to determine if the party is truly an independent contractor or really is an employee. Of course, though not controlling on the issue of status, the fact that a party is called an independent contractor certainly is evidence of that status.

The Doctrine of Respondeat Superior

Pertaining to vicarious tort liability the first category of relationships to examine is the "master-servant" relationship, which is now called the employer-employee relationship. The key issue is to determine the legal liability of the master/employer for the torts of his or her or its servant/employee. The governing rule, which goes back to Roman times, is called the doctrine of *respondeat superior*, which as noted means "let the master answer" for the wrongs of his or her servant. This seminal legal doctrine thus holds that the master/employer is legally liable for all torts committed by the servant/employee acting within the scope of employment. As a result, a third party injured by an employee's tort can proceed against both the employee and the employer. The employee is of course directly liable, and the employer is "merely" vicariously liable. The nature of the employer's *vicarious liability* is "strict"; that is, the employer is responsible even though the employer has exercised due care in the hiring and the supervising of the employee. This liability is also "joint and several," which means the employer can be sued alone or together with the employee. The employer, however, has the right, at least theoretically, of indemnification from the wrongdoing employee. In order for the doctrines of *respondeat superior* and vicarious liability to apply, two essential elements must be established: First, was there a master-servant relationship, as opposed to a principal-agent or employer-independent contractor one; and second, was the servant's wrongful act committed within the course or scope of his or her employment? In order to have a master-servant relationship the employer must have the power and right to control the physical manner by which the employee performs his or her job. In neither the principal-agent nor the employer-independent contractor relationship is this physical control element present. It must be noted, however, that there is a legal doctrine, called "*employment by estoppel*," at times called "*ostensible employment*," which is created when one person intentionally or carelessly creates the appearance that another person is his or her employee, and a third party reasonably relies on that "appearance" to his or her detriment. In such an "estoppel" situation, the "employer" is now legally prevented (or "estopped") from denying the employment relationship and is thus liable to the third person as if a "master." For example, if a health club advertises that it employs skilled "trainers," who wear the logo of the health club on their exercise clothes, and relying on the advertising and name recognition, a person engages the services of such a trainer, and is thereby negligently injured, the defendant health club may be estopped from denying that the trainer is its "servant."

One of the most difficult questions in agency law is to determine the status of a person employed as either a servant/employee or an independent contractor. Answering this question is crucial not only for tort liability but also for tax and Workers' Compensation liability, though the latter two fields are beyond the scope of this handbook. Regarding tort liability, recall the seminal doctrine of *respondeat superior*, which is limited to wrongful acts committed only by a servant/employee, and not by an independent contractor. As a consequence of this doctrine, vicarious liability does not apply when the tortious acts are committed by a person's independent contractor. Therefore, as a general rule, the employer is not liable for injuries and harms caused by the employer's independent contractor, even though the independent contractor was acting for the employer's benefit. As previously mentioned, the key test in determining whether a person is an employee or an independent contractor is the "right to control." That is, does the employer have the right to control the employing party's conduct in the actual performance of the work? In the master-servant relationship, the master has the right to control; whereas in the employer-independent contractor relationship, the employer is only bargaining for results, and retains no control. The classic and clear case is when a homeowner hires an electrician or plumber to do repairs; accordingly, the homeowner is hiring an independent contractor. However, if the nature of the relationship is not clear, there are several pertinent factors that the law will apply: 1) the actual extent of control over the details of the work; 2) whether the person employed has an occupation or business of his or her own which is distinct from the employer; 3) whether the type of work done is usually done under direction or independently by a specialist; 4) whether the employer provides the place of work and supplies the instrumentalities and tools for the work; 5) the method of payment, that is, whether by time or by completed project; and 6) the level of skill, knowledge, and expertise required for the work. Making this critical determination is regarded as a question of fact for the jury in a common law system to decide. However, some typical examples of independent contractors would be legal and accounting professionals hired by an employer, as well as medical professionals the employer retains to treat its employees. Also, general building contractors that a property owner hires to do work, and the sub-contractors retained by the general contractor, usually will be regarded as independent contractors since they own their own businesses and are not controlled by the property owner. However, if an employer retains the right to control the method, manner, and operative details of the work, so that the independent contractor is not free to do the work his or her own way, as opposed to the employer merely having the right to start, stop, and restart the work, retaining the right to inspect the work, and to make suggestions which need not be followed, then the employer is vicariously liable for the negligence of the independent contractor (*Devoe v. Am Eagle Energy Corp.*, 2020, applying North Dakota law).

There are, moreover, exceptional situations, based on grounds of public policy and utility, when an employer will be liable for the torts of his or her independent contractor. One exception arises when the nature of the work is highly dangerous or ultra-hazardous. The other concerns non-delegable duties, that is, where an employer is under a duty by law or public policy which is not delegable, and thus where the employer will be liable for the wrongful conduct of its independent contractor. Examples of non-delegable duties are: an employer's duty to provide and maintain a safe place of employment for its employees; a landlord's duty to provide and maintain safe rental premises and to make proper repairs; and the duty of an owner of a business open to the public to keep the premises safe for the public. Another example arises when the work is inherently dangerous and thus requires special precautions. For example, in the Ohio court of claims case of *Waitt v.*

Ohio (2020) the state Department of Transportation (DOT) could not insulate itself from liability by hiring an independent contractor for road construction work using hot and wet tar. The court explained that, as opposed to mere grass-cutting, road construction by its nature entails inherent risks, and thus the employer has a non-delegable duty to exercise reasonable care and to manage the work to see that it is done in a reasonable manner. As such, the employer cannot insulate itself from negligence liability merely by hiring an independent contractor to do the work (*Waitt v. Ohio*, 2020).

Although hiring workers as independent contractors generally can help control or manage the risk of loss under negligence and *respondeat superior* law, managers nonetheless should be aware that the tort theories of negligent hiring have been applied at times to a principal's selection of independent contractors. Many jurisdictions today have validated the cause of action of negligent hiring of independent contractors by an employer. For example, the Wyoming supreme court in so doing explained that the doctrine of *respondeat superior* does not apply to the acts of an independent contractor because the owner/operator has no control over the work performed. Negligent hiring, however, is not premised on the theory of *respondeat superior*, but instead is premised on the owner/operator's own negligent acts in hiring the independent contractor *(Basic Energy Services, L.P. v. Petroleum Resource Management, Corp.*, 2015).

Once the nature of the person employed has been established as a servant/employee, the second critical issue to resolve before imposing vicarious liability on the employer is the *scope of employment* question. That is, did the employee commit the wrongful act within the course or scope of his or her employment? In answering this question, which again is viewed by the common law as a question of fact for the jury to decide, several rules of law must be addressed. First, in order to be within the scope of employment, express authorization by the master is not necessary; that is, it is not a requirement to show that the master explicitly authorized or permitted the particular act, so long as the act occurred within the normal course of the employee's duties. For example, if the employee is hired to make deliveries using the employer's vehicles, but instead the employee uses his or her own vehicle, and negligently causes an accident, the employer is nonetheless still liable, even though the act was not authorized, because it was still within the scope of the employee's duties. Moreover, even if certain acts are specifically forbidden by the employer, the acts nevertheless still may be within the scope of employment. For example, even though the owner/employer of an automobile service franchise tells an employee not to do certain types of precision mechanical work, but the employee nonetheless does so, and thereby causes harm, the employer may still be liable if that type of mechanical work is within the scope of employment for the employee. Similarly, when a sales person defrauds a customer, the conduct is considered to be within the scope of employment, even though the misconduct was contrary to the company's policies, because the conduct benefits the employer by increasing sales (*Drew v. Pac. Life Ins. Co.*, 2019, applying Utah law). The rationale for this rule is that otherwise merely by instructing one's employees never to do certain activities, the employer could unfairly absolve itself of vicarious liability.

Under a negligent hiring tort claim, moreover, the scope of an employer's "duty" when hiring employees will not be extended beyond its natural logical limitations, especially when the employee's conduct that gave rise to the action against an employer was outside the scope or course of employment. This was clearly expressed in the Colorado supreme court case of *Raleigh vs. Performance Plumbing & Heating, Inc.* (2006), where a new-hire of a plumbing company was driving home from his shift in his own vehicle and caused a severe accident that injured two other individuals in another vehicle, who would later sue the employer for negligent hiring. Discovery during the case revealed that the new-hire had a deplorable driving record, including the following: a 1990 careless driving conviction involving an accident; a 1991 conviction for violation of a red light signal; a 1991 defective vehicle conviction; a 1992 careless driving conviction involving an accident; and driving without insurance. As a result of accumulated points, his license was suspended. Prior to reinstatement, he drove without a valid license and reinstatement was deferred for one-year until 1993. His license was reinstated later in 1993. In 1995, he received a ticket for speeding. Also, in 1995, he was convicted of failure to signal for a turn; and he also did not have liability insurance. As a result, his license was suspended until 1996. At the time the defendant employer hired him, he was eligible for license reinstatement upon providing proof of insurance coverage and paying a reinstatement fee, but he did not proceed to obtain insurance and have his license reinstated. However, in dismissing the negligent hiring claim, the court held that the plumbing company's duty was not owed to the injured plaintiffs because the employee was driving home after work and as such the company's duty of care would extend only to those members of the public exposed to the employee's unsafe driving in the performance of his job duties. Here, the defendant employer's duty pursuant to the tort of negligent hiring did not extend to the injured plaintiffs because the job for which the employer hired the employee to do did not include driving to and from work.

The "*scope of employment*" requirement to vicarious liability also presents some interesting legal and factual questions that managers need to be aware of. One concerns the employee's use of the employer's vehicle or equipment outside the scope of employment. The general rule of law is that the mere fact the employer allowed the employee to use its vehicle or equipment is not sufficient to impose liability on the employer if the use is outside the scope of employment. The employer only will be deemed liable when the vehicle or equipment is used for advancing the employer's own business rather than furthering the employee's personal interests. So, in the classic example, the employee who uses the employer's vehicle and who also has permission to take the employer's vehicle home, uses the vehicle for the employee's own recreational use, and thereby negligently causes an injury; and as such, the employer will not be deemed vicariously liable. Another "scope" issue concerns employees who commute to and from work. In such a traveling to and from work situation, known at times as the "coming-and-going" rule, the employee will be deemed to be outside the scope of employment, unless, of course, the employee in addition to his or her standard commute will also be doing a special errand for his or her employer (*Painter v. Amerimex Drilling I, Ltd.*, 2018, applying Texas law). Traveling salespersons, furthermore, are typically deemed to be within the scope while traveling, even while not technically working. For example, in the federal district court case of *Silvas v. Harrie* (2018), applying Texas law, a traveling consultant, whose employer reimbursed his mileage and other travelling expenses, but who did not control or direct the consultant's work-related travel arrangements, was not within the course and scope of employment while he was involved in a motor vehicle accident while driving between his hotel and a work site.

The departure by an employee from authorized activity has always presented a problem to the common law. The problem arises when the employee temporarily departs from his or her instructed duties and undertakes some personal business. Under the old common law, this situation was called, most quaintly though quite accurately, "*detour and frolic*." The classic case occurs when the employee, while delivering goods for the employer, goes out of his or her way to visit a "friend," and while so doing, injures a third party. The deciding legal issue, of course, is whether the employee was acting within the scope of his or her employment when the harm occurred. There are two main rules governing "detour and frolic": first, only a substantial departure will take the employee outside the scope of his or her employment. That is, if the deviation from the direct route is only a minor one, to do an incidental personal chore or act, causing just a slight delay, and the employee's principal purpose is still to serve the employer's business, then the employee is still within the scope. Second, presuming a substantial departure, when is there sufficient re-entry into the "scope" for there to be vicarious liability for the employer? For there to be a sufficient "scope" re-entry, the common law requires that the employee resume the intent to further the employer's business, physically turn back to the departure point, and come reasonably close to the departure point. For example, in the Texas court of appeals case of *Molina v. City of Pasadena* (2018), the court ruled that a city engineering inspector who was involved in a vehicle accident while driving his city-owned vehicle from lunch at a restaurant to his next inspection site was not acting within the course and scope of employment because he was returning from the personal activity of lunch and he had neither resumed his job duties, nor was he acting in the city's interests, and not yet had reached his next zone of employment. Another example is the California court of appeals case of *Marz v. Lyft* (2020), where a Lyft driver on a day not working for the company got into an accident travelling home from working at a gaming conference in order to see his family and get some sleep. He was driving not his car that he used for Lyft but a rental vehicle; however, he was reimbursed by Lyft for certain driving expenses. The court ruled that his conduct, main purpose, and ends were "purely personal" and thus the defendant Lyft was not vicariously liable under the doctrine of *respondeat superior* for the injuries he caused by his allegedly negligent driving (*Marz v. Lyft*, 2020).

Also related to the "scope" issue is the unauthorized guest problem; that is, when the employee without authority invites third persons to join the employee in the employer's vehicle, and the third party is injured due to the employee's negligence. The majority rule under the common law is that the employer is not liable because such an invitation is construed to be outside the scope of employment, even when the employee's conduct which in fact caused the harm is within the scope; but it should be noted that there is a distinct minority view that would hold the employer vicariously liable in the latter case. Finally, it must be noted that the doctrine of *respondeat superior* generally is a rule imposing civil liability; and thus it is not applicable to the criminal law. Therefore, ordinarily, a master is not criminally liable for the acts of his or her servant. Yet, there are exceptions, for example, pursuant to regulatory laws governing the sale of alcohol and tobacco to minors, as well as the sale of adulterated drugs and impure food. Also, the corporate entity, as "master," can be deemed vicariously liable for the criminal acts of its officers, agents, and employees.

Pursuant to traditional principles of agency law an employer can be held vicariously liable for the tort of intentional infliction of emotional distress. Vicarious liability means that the legal wrong is imputed to the employer even though the employer did not act in a wrongful purposeful manner and even when the employer did not act in a negligent or careless manner. Vicarious liability arises when the distress is inflicted by a manager, supervisor, or fellow employee acting within the course or scope of his or her employment and there is evidence that shows that the manager, supervisor, or employee was seeking to further the interests of his or her employer, at least in part, and not serve any personal motive or vindictive interests. The fact that the conduct was intentional, it is important to note, does not take the action out of the course or scope of employment, but there must be evidence that the wrongdoer was attempting to fulfill some type of work duty or responsibility or performing or fulfilling job functions and not acting out of pure personal animosity. Moreover, even if a manager, supervisor, or employee was not acting within the course or scope of employment and was serving his or her own personal interests in inflicting emotional distress, nonetheless the employer still can be held liable if it authorized or ratified the wrongful conduct. One court ruled that an employee's allegations could constitute extreme and outrageous behavior when an employer became aware of its supervisor's slipping a cell phone under a bathroom partition to videotape an employee's private parts and then uploading the graphic video to the internet and adding vulgar and degrading comments (*Oliver v. Walmart Stores East, LP et al*., 2017, applying Connecticut law). The court in *Oliver* ruled that the plaintiff's intentional infliction of emotional distress claim against the employer should not be struck from the pleadings since the employer continued to employ the supervisor after knowing of these atrocious actions and continued to allow the supervisor to manage the same worker in the workplace causing emotional distress to the employee (*Oliver v. Walmart Stores East, LP et al*., 2017). To compare, in the federal district court case of *Kamdem-Ouaffo v. Balchem Corp.* (2018), applying New York law, the court ruled that the tort of intentional infliction of emotional distress could be vicariously imputed to the employer based on the conduct of a manager or supervisor, but in the case herein the conduct, such as "work-related outbursts, "a verbal altercation," "an elevated voice," and the supervisor telling the employee to take his belongings to human resources and to "never to return again," failed to reach a level of extreme and outrageous conduct to impose tort liability.

Managers also must be aware that the principle of *respondeat superior* can apply to defamatory as well as fraudulent statements. Consequently, defamatory statements made by an agent or employee can bind the principal or employer if the statements are made during the course and scope of the agent's authority or the employee's employment. For example, in the federal district court case of *Lora v. Ledo Pizza Sys.* (2017), applying Maryland law, the allegedly defamatory statements made by the defendant employer's managerial employee, such as saying that another manager was a "bad manager," that he "did not care about the store," and that he was stealing from the restaurant, were imputed to the employer pursuant to the *respondeat superior* doctrine since the statements were made in the manager's "scope of employment." Similarly, in the Montana supreme court case of *Brenden v. City of Billings* (2020), a supervisor, who had a personal animus against an employee, disclosed the employee's personal information to a prospective employer; and the supervisor also made statements that maligned the employee. Although the supervisor had a personal motive for the actions, as well as the fact that the supervisor's actions were not authorized by the employer, and in fact violated the employer's guidelines, nevertheless the court ruled that the supervisor's actions were incidental to his role as a supervisor and that he also had at least a partial intent to further the interests of his employer; and accordingly the court ruled that a jury would be required to determine if the employer was vicariously liable for the supervisor's intentional torts of defamation and invasion of privacy (*Brenden v. City of Billings*, 2020). To compare, in the federal appeals case of *Lorzada v. Hobby Lobby Stores, Inc.* (2017), applying Florida law, the statements made by an employee about a co-worker that the co-worker wanted to "shoot up the store" and kill himself were not imputed to the employer because the employee had a personal motive in making the statements, the statements occurred in the parking lot when the employees were leaving work, and the statements were more in the form of "gossiping with co-workers" about the co-worker's temper; and thus the statements were not made "within the scope of employment."

Conversely, if a defamatory statement is made by an agent outside the scope of his or her authority or by an employee outside the scope of his or her employer then the employer is not liable, but the individual agent or employee may be. For example, in the New York state appellate case of *Kaiser v. Raoul's Restaurant Corp.* (2008), the statement by a manager of the employer that an employee was stealing was held to be not within the scope of the manager's employment because the statement was made to an unaffiliated third party and not to the employer. Similarly, a statement by the plaintiff employee, a social worker, that her supervisor was committing sexual harassment was not deemed to be within the scope of her employment, even though the plaintiff used the defendant medical center's whistleblowing channels to report the harassment, because the plaintiff employee was under no duty to report or complain and was not directed or ordered to do so by the employer, as held in the New York state appellate case of *Rausman v. Baugh* (1998). Vicarious liability for defamation also very likely could arise in a corporate setting as the corporation is "merely" an artificial legal person that cannot speak and act for itself; rather, it must conduct business through human beings – directors, officers, managers, agents, and employees, who may commit defamation as well as other legal wrongs when conducting corporate business.

Finally, *respondeat superior* can also apply to the intentional torts of assault and battery and false imprisonment, including punitive damage liability (see, for example, *Carnegay v. Wal-Mart Stores*, 2020, applying Georgia law). For example, in the *Carnegay* case, a suspected shoplifter was detained, held, and beaten, suffering a broken leg, by an off-duty policeman hired by Wal-Mart to police theft. The policeman was informed by one of the store's security officials that the plaintiff stole a tomato, though the plaintiff said that he purchased it but went back into the store to weigh it since he believed he had been overcharged for it, but because the line was too long he decided not to challenge the price and ask for a refund, and so he put the tomato back in his bag and walked toward the exit where he was intercepted and detained. Regarding the claims of battery and false imprisonment, the Georgia appeals court held that Wal-Mart could be vicariously liable for the intentional torts of its employee, the security official, if either the belief that the shoplifting occurred was not reasonable or that the manner of the detention was not reasonable. Also, the court held that Wal-Mart similarly could be held vicariously liable for the excessive force of the off-duty policeman hired by the company, though Wal-Mart claimed that he was an independent contractor, if there was evidence that the police officer acted pursuant to the direction of the security employee and not solely in his capacity as a police officer, thereby rendering his status as an "agent" of the employer, Wal-Mart, and resulting in imputed liability for the company. The court ruled that these issues were questions of fact and thus a jury was necessary to resolve these key issues (*Carnegay v. Wal-Mart Stores*, 2020, applying Georgia law). However, to compare, in the federal district court case of

Doe v. Hotchkiss Sch. (2019), applying Connecticut law, the court ruled that the employer school was not vicariously liable for the sexual abuse of a student by a teacher since the employee's sexual misconduct was not intended to further his employer's business and thus was outside the scope of his employment.

Management Implications and Recommendations:

Managers must be aware that vicarious liability pursuant to the doctrine of respondeat superior is different from the employer's liability based on the employer's own personal breach of a legal duty. That is, the employer will be liable for tortious acts or a person in the employer's employ when the employer is directly and personally at fault, even if the harm itself is caused through an employee. For example, if the employer directed or authorized the wrongful act, the employer will be liable as if the employer itself had committed the legal wrong. Similarly, if the employer knows that his or her employee is acting in a reckless or careless manner, and allows the employee to continue performing, then the employer, together with the employee, will be liable for careless retention and supervision. Finally, initially, the employer could be negligent in hiring the employee, if the employer or a "reasonable, prudent person" knew that the employee was not qualified or capable of doing the work in a careful manner. In such a case, the employer also may be liable for acts normally outside the scope of employment. These aforementioned types of liability are regarded as "direct" as opposed to vicarious.

Managers must know that the doctrine of respondeat superior also can apply to intentional torts committed by the servant/employee. The rule of law holds that if the intentional tort occurs within the scope of the employee's employment and is intended to further the employer's business interests, then the employer is liable. However, if the employee in committing the intentional tort is motivated to further his or her own personal interests, then the employer is not vicariously liable. Therefore, there is a major difference legally between a "bouncer" in a bar who ejects a loud and abusive patron with excessive force, thereby committing a battery, and a delivery employee who upon delivering a package to a person, recognizes this person as a "long lost enemy" and strikes this person, thereby committing a battery, since the employer in the first case will be vicariously liable for the intentional tort, but not the employer in the second scenario. Moreover, if the employer had no reason to believe that the employee would commit an assault and/or battery, the conduct was not job-related, and the conduct was not ignored, tolerated, or sanctioned by the employer (England, 2020).

Another important intersection of agency law and vicarious liability law that managers need to be aware of deals with a principal's tort liability for his or her agent's fraud and misrepresentations. The essence of the agency relationship, one recalls, is representational; that is, the agent "stands in the shoes" of the principal, negotiates for, and enters into contracts on the principal's behalf. Obviously, therefore, the agent will be making representations to a third party on behalf of the principal; and accordingly, the principal is exposed to tort liability when the third party enters into a contract and thereby sustains a loss due to the agent's misrepresentations. Again, the essential vicarious liability requirements need to be shown: Was the agent actually or apparently authorized to make representations? If so, was the alleged misrepresentation made within the scope of the agent's authority? If these requirements are present, the principal will be liable for the agent's misrepresentations, even intentionally fraudulent ones. The rationale for holding the principal liable for such an intentional tort is that the principal by using and empowering an agent has thereby placed the agent in a position to make representations and by so doing has given an aggrieved third party the impression that the agent has such authority.

Summary

This chapter dealt with intersection of agency law with the law of torts. Three critical relationships were defined and examined, to wit: employer-employee (known as master-servant in the old common law); employer-independent contractor; and principal-agent. The tort liability of the employer for the wrongs of its employees as well as of the principal for the wrongs of his or her agent was explicated and illustrated. The authors emphasized and explained the important distinction the law makes between the direct liability of the employer compared to its vicarious, or imputed, liability pursuant to the doctrine of *respondeat superior*. Applications of these agency principles were provided to specialized torts. Particularly noteworthy for managers and employers is the existence of vicarious tort liability of a principal for the intentional fraudulent acts of his or her agent. The authors concluded the chapter by providing recommendations to managers for avoiding liability, especially vicarious liability.

In the next chapter the authors will go "above and beyond" the law by examining the concepts of philosophic ethics and the notion of social responsibility in a business context. The authors will stress that a business that acts in an ethical as well as a socially responsible and sustainable manner will much more readily achieve compliance with the law and avoidance of legal problems and lawsuits, particularly pursuant to the law of tort.

CHAPTER VII - LAW, ETHICS, AND SOCIAL RESPONSIBILITY

This book has concentrated on one aspect of the law – tort law based on the common law – in the context of business, employment, and management. However, in addition to tort and the other manifold legal ramifications of management and business decision-making, managers today are being called upon to act not only legally, but also in a moral, ethical, socially responsible, and sustainable manner. Accordingly, this chapter has two main components. Initially, it will examine ethics, which is a branch of philosophy. The authors will demonstrate how ethics can be applied to management decision-making to determine if the business is acting in a moral manner. The authors will also discuss corporate codes of ethics and whistleblowing, especially morally required whistleblowing in the employment context. This chapter, furthermore, will examine stakeholder values, corporate governance, as well as the concept of corporate social responsibility, which includes in its modern conception the notion of "sustainability," which characteristically is viewed as environmental responsibility. Accordingly, the authors will discuss what it means in a modern-day management and business context for a business, particularly a corporation, to be not "merely" a legal one, but also a moral and ethical as well as a socially responsible and sustainable entity. The authors will discuss the ethical principle of Last Resort and its relationship to social responsibility, legal nonfeasance, and whistleblowing. Finally, the authors will offer a management mindset for decision-making that incorporates the aforementioned critical values of legality, morality, social responsibility, and sustainability.

Business Ethics

Determining whether an action, rule, or law is moral or immoral, right or wrong, or just or unjust perforce brings one into the realm of *ethics*, which is a branch of *philosophy*, and then logically one proceeds to ethical theories, ethical principles, applied ethics, and ethical reasoning to moral conclusions. In the ethics part to this chapter, the authors will explain four major ethical theories – Ethical Egoism, Ethical Relativism, Utilitarianism, and Kantian ethics. These ethical theories were chosen because they represent the essence of ethics as a branch of philosophy in Western Civilization, which obviously is not the only civilization, but it is one that the authors are the most familiar with, including, of course, the ethics component to Western knowledge and thought, as opposed to, for example, Confucian ethical principles and the application thereof, which, although most interesting and intriguing to learn and to apply, practically would be beyond the scope of the authors' objectives for this chapter. These four Western theories also were selected because they are reason-based ethical theories; as such, the authors assume that the readers of this book possess intellect, reason, and logic, and thus will be quite "comfortable" in following the authors' ethical "train of thought," though, of course, perhaps not agreeing with their ultimate moral conclusions. Furthermore, religion-based ethical theories were not chosen because not all the readers of this book will be of the same religion and, for that matter, some may have no religion at all; and, moreover, bringing in a religious-based ethical component to this chapter would be to expand the book beyond the authors' modest, and primarily legal, aims. The focus is on Western ethics; and the initial ethical theory to be examined will be Ethical Egoism. However, it is first necessary for the authors to explain some key foundational ethical terms and concepts.

Values

The authors believe it is very harmful for people to use continually a wide variety of very general terms without clear meanings. The lack of any fixed meaning, the inability of people to provide proper explanations, the individualistic, expedient decision-making, as well as an emphasis on rhetoric and persuasion, engenders relativism, skepticism, and a great deal of confusion, People then will be talking at cross purposes and their discussions will make no progress. Only confusion, skepticism, chaos, and perhaps even conflict, will ensue. Therefore, it is very important for a business leader, academic, and manager to look for, ascertain, and pay special attention to definitions and terms. When one initially encounters the fields of ethics, corporate governance, social responsibility, and stakeholder analysis in a business context, one is confronted with some confusion due to a lack of an agreed-upon terminology and set of definitions. Moreover, what is "social responsibility"? How does it differ from the law, ethics, and morality? What exactly do the terms "corporate social responsibility," "stakeholder values," and "sustainability" mean? Accordingly, if one is going to understand what social responsibility is and how it works in a modern global business environment, there must be some agreement on, and some insight into, the meaning and nature of the value of social responsibility especially when juxtaposed with the values of legality, based on the law, and the value of morality, based on ethics. There is, therefore, a need for words, terms, and definitions with precise meaning.

In order to arrive at a precise as possible meaning of the terms, "ethics" and "social responsibility," it is first necessary to define some fundamental terms and concepts. A value is something that possesses worth. *Values* can be *intrinsic* (also called terminal), meaning that they possess value and worth in and of themselves, for example, happiness and aesthetics. Whereas values that are "merely" *extrinsic* (also called instrumental) possess worth and are valuable because they are the means to produce something else of value, for example, money (which can buy happiness!). The value of legality is, of course, based on the law. The value of morality stems from ethics; yet the terms ethics and morals or morality are not synonymous. *Morality* is the conclusion of what is right or wrong or good or bad; whereas ethics is the philosophical framework, consisting of ethical theories and principles that one uses to reason to moral conclusions. Whether morality is an intrinsic value or merely and instrumental one is an issue which the authors will leave to the philosophers; yet even if morality and ethics are "mere" instrumental values, they nonetheless possess value and thus merit attention. Social responsibility too is a value, related to, but distinct from law and ethics. Social responsibility, particularly in a business sense, which will be addressed more fully later in this chapter, is concerned with a business going "above and beyond" the law as well as acting beyond morality by taking an active part in community and civic affairs and charitable endeavors. In the next section the authors will briefly explicate ethics as a branch of philosophy by examining the four major ethical theories in Western Civilization.

1. Ethical Egoism

The ethical theory of *Ethical Egoism* harkens back to ancient Greece and the philosophical school of the Sophists and their teachings of relativism and promotion of self-interest. This ethical theory maintains that a person ought to promote his or her self-interest and the greatest balance of good for himself or herself. Since this theory is an ethical theory, one thus has a moral obligation to promote one's self-interest; and so "selfishly" acting is also morally acting; and concomitantly an action against one's self-interest is an immoral action; and an action that advances one's self-interest is a moral action. An ethically egoistic person, therefore, will shrewdly discern the "pros" and "cons" of an action, and then perform the action that performs the most personal good, which also is the moral course of action. However, the Ethical Egoists counsel that one should be an "enlightened" ethical egoist; that is, one should think of what will inure to one's benefit in the long-run, and accordingly be ready to sacrifice some short-term pain or expense to attain a greater long-term good – for oneself, of course. Also, the prudent ethical egoist would say that as a general rule it is better, even if one has a lot of power as well as a big ego, to treat people well, to make them part of "your team," and to "co-op" them.

Why should one treat people well? One reason is certainly not because one is beneficent, but rather because one is "selfish." That is, one is treating people well because typically it will advance one's own self-interest in the long-term to do so. One problem with ethical egoism is that one's own "good" must be defined. What exactly is one maximizing? Is it one's knowledge, power, money, pleasure, comfort, prestige, success, or happiness?

Ethical egoists agree that people ought to pursue and advance their own good; but they disagree as to the type of good people should be seeking. Yet in business the "good" typically means making money! Another problem with Ethical Egoism is that the doctrine counsels that everyone should pursue his or her own self-interest. Yet what if there is just one job position or one promotion opportunity and two people want to advance themselves by attaining the job or promotion? Now, one would hope that as rational egoists there would be clearly defined, legitimate, job-related criteria for the job or promotion. Yet that is not always the case. Consequently, there is the distinct possibility that the two egos seeking self-advancement will clash; and conflict may result; but there is no mechanism in Ethical Egoism that acts as an arbitrating principle to decide whose ego gets advanced. So, who will "win" the job or the promotion? "Might makes right," the Sophists long ago said!

2. Ethical Relativism

Ethical Relativism as an ethical theory also harkens back to ancient Greece and the philosophical school of the Sophists as well as the philosophical school of the Skeptics. Ethical relativists deny that there are any objective, universal moral rules which one can construct an absolute moral system. Ethical relativists deny that there are moral rules applicable to all peoples, in all societies, and at all times. There thus are no universal moral standards by which to judge an action's morality; rather, morality is merely relative to, and holds for, only a particular society at a particular time. "When in Rome, do as the Romans," said the Ethical Relativists. Morality, therefore, is a societal-based notion; it is nothing more than the morality of a certain group, people, or society at a certain time. What a society believes is right is in fact right for that society; the moral beliefs of a society determine what is "right" or "wrong" in that society. However, different societies may have different conceptions of what is right or wrong. What one believes is right, the other may believe as wrong. Consequently, the same act can be morally right for one society but morally wrong for another. So, one society can believe that the use of partial nudity in advertising is moral; whereas another society may condemn such a practice as immoral. Since pursuant to Ethical Relativism there are no moral standards which are universally true for all peoples, in all societies, and at all times, and since there is no way to demonstrate that one set of beliefs is true and the other false, the only way to determine an action's morality is to determine what the people in a particular society believe is right or wrong at a given time. So, "simply" discern the societal moral precepts, and then conform and adapt; and one will be acting morally, at least pursuant to this ethical theory. Of course, ascertaining exactly what a society is a daunting challenge. Even within a homogeneous society, there are diverse cultures, subcultures, social classes, kinship, and work groups; and in a heterogeneous society there will be many smaller sub-societies that co-exist. All these components of society may reflect different standards, mores, customs, and beliefs, including moral standards and beliefs. Yet pursuant to the doctrine of Ethical Relativism, one must attempt to find the pertinent "society" and then try to ascertain that society's moral beliefs; but when one does ascertain the societal beliefs, standards, and practices regarding morality, one simply has to conform and adopt, and one will be acting morally, at least according to the ethical theory of Ethical Relativism.

3. Utilitarianism

Utilitarianism is a major ethical theory in Western civilization; it was created principally by the English philosophers and social reformers Jeremy Bentham and John Stewart Mill. Their goal was to develop an ethical theory that not only was "scientific" but also would maximize human happiness and pleasure (in the sense of satisfaction). Utilitarianism is regarded as a consequentialist ethical theory, also called a teleological ethical theory; that is, one determines morality by examining the consequences of an action; the form of the action is irrelevant; rather, the consequences produced by the action are paramount in determining its morality. If an action produces more good than bad consequences, it is a moral action; and if an action produces more bad than good consequences it is an immoral action. Of course, ethical egoism is also a consequentialist ethical theory. The critical difference is that the Utilitarians demand that one consider the consequences of an action not just on oneself, but also on other people and groups who are affected directly and indirectly by the action. The scope of analysis, plainly, is much broader, and less "selfish," pursuant to a Utilitarian ethical analysis. In business ethics texts and classes, the term "stakeholders" is frequently used to indicate the various groups that would be affected by a business decision. Furthermore, the

Utilitarians specifically and explicitly stated that society as a whole must be considered in this evaluation of the good and/or bad consequences produced by an action. The idea is to get away from a "me, me, me" mindset to the "we, us, and all" paradigm by considering other stakeholders and specific groups affected by an action.

Utilitarianism is a very egalitarian ethical theory since everyone's pleasure and/or pain gets registered and counted in this "scientific" effort to determine morality. Yet, there are several problems with the doctrine. First, one has to try to predict the consequences of putting an action into effect, which can be very difficult if one is looking for longer-term effects. However, the Utilitarians would say to use one's "common storehouse of knowledge," one's intelligence, and "let history be your guide" in making these predictions. Neither guess nor speculate, but act based on the probable or reasonably foreseeable consequences of an action. Also, if one is affected by an action, one naturally gets counted too, but if that same one person is doing the Utilitarian analysis, there is always the all-too-human tendency to "cook the books" to benefit oneself. The Utilitarians would say that one should try to be impartial and objective in any analysis. Next, one now has to measure and weigh the good versus the bad consequences to ascertain what prevails and thus what the ultimate moral conclusion will be. The Utilitarians said that not only was this ethical theory "scientific," but it was also mathematical ("good old-fashioned English bookkeeping," they called it). But how does one do the math? How does one measure and weigh the good and the bad consequences? And for that matter how does one measure different types of goods? The Utilitarians, alas, provided very little guidance. Finally, a major criticism of the Utilitarian ethical theory is that it may lead to an unjust result. That is, the "ends may justify the means." Since the form of the action is irrelevant in this type of ethical analysis, if the action produces a greater overall good, then the action is moral, regardless of the fact that some bad may be produced in this effort to achieve the overall good. The good, though, outweighs the bad; accordingly, the action is moral; and the sufferers of the bad, who perhaps were exploited or whose rights were trampled, got counted at least. Such is the nature of Utilitarianism. After determining the action to be evaluated, the next step in the Utilitarian analysis is to determine the people and groups, that is, the stakeholders, affected by the action, then make a determination as to how they are affected (that is, are the reasonably foreseeable consequences good or bad ones), and next make an overall determination if putting the action into effect results in more good or bad. If the former, the action is moral; if the latter, the action is immoral pursuant to Utilitarianism. The lynchpin to the Utilitarianism is the focus on consequences. Yet some moral philosophers believe that focusing on consequences is the wrong approach to take in determining the morality of an action.

4. Kant's Categorical Imperative

The German professor and philosopher, Immanuel Kant, condemned Utilitarianism as an immoral ethical theory. How is it logically possible, said Kant, to have an ethical theory that can morally legitimize pain, suffering, exploitation, and injustice? Disregard consequences, declared Kant, and instead focus on the form of an action in determining its morality. Now, of course, since *Kantian ethics* is also one of the major ethical theories in Western civilization, a huge problem arises since these two major ethical theories are diametrically opposed. Is one a Kantian or is one a Utilitarian? (Or is it all relative as the Sophists and Machiavelli stated?).

For Kant, the key to morality is applying a formal test to the action itself. This formal test he called the *Categorical Imperative*. "Categorical" meaning that this ethical principle is the supreme and absolute and true test to morality; and "imperative" meaning that at times one must command oneself to be moral and do the right thing, even and especially when one's self-interest may be contravened by acting "rightly." The Categorical Imperative has three ways to determine morality. One method is called the Universal Law test. Kant is not referring to legal law here; rather, Kant asks one to imagine what would happen if a practice theoretically could be made into a universal law. Would one want to live in such a society where the universal moral norm is that it is permissible to steal, to lie, and to cheat? Of course, one would not want to live in such a society; but then one can logically conclude pursuant to the Universal Law test that stealing, lying, and cheating are immoral actions. Now, Kant does admit that people do steal, lie, and cheat, but he calls these people immoral "parasites" for living off an otherwise moral system where the vast majority of people do not steal, lie, or cheat. Another method of determining morality is called the *Kingdom of Ends* test. Pursuant to this Kantian precept, if an action, even if it produces a greater good, such as an exploitive but profitable overseas "sweatshop," is nonetheless disrespectful and demeaning and treats people as mere means, things, or as instruments, perhaps as badly as broken pieces of office furniture, then the action is not moral. The goal, said Kant, is for everyone to live in this "Kingdom of the Ends" where everyone is treated as a worthwhile human being with dignity and respect. Related to the Kingdom of Ends precept and also part of the Categorical Imperative is the *Agent-Receiver* test, which asks a person to consider the rightfulness of an action by considering whether the action would be acceptable to the person if he or she did not know whether the person would be the agent, that is, the giver, of the action, or the receiver. If one did not know one's role, and one would not be willing to have the action done to him or her, then the action is immoral. Do your duty, be ethically strong, have a good moral character, declared Kant, and obey the moral "law," based on his Categorical Imperative, and thus do the "right" thing regardless of consequences.

The authors have attempted to explain and illustrate the field of ethics as a branch of philosophy by discussing four major ethical theories. Yet, as the discerning reader can see, these ethical theories can conflict; and there is no "Supreme Court of Ethics" to tell one which ethical theory is the correct, true, and right one! The ethical situation gets even more complicated when these ethical theories are applied to factual situations to determine whether a person or a business is acting morally. However, the authors advice to managers would be to advance their self-interest and that of their company or organization (Ethical Egoism), be culturally aware and competent (Ethical Relativism), strive to achieve the greater good with "win-win" scenarios, as well as minimize any harm caused (Utilitarianism), but to attain these objectives with neither disrespecting nor demeaning anyone (Kantian ethics). In order to achieve these goals in a business context an important aspect will be the creation of a code of ethics.

Corporate Codes of Ethics

Ethics codes long have been adopted by the profession, such as law and medicine. In recent years, however, they also have been adopted by many corporations and businesses. A strong legal impetus for codes of ethics emerged from the Sarbanes-Oxley Act of 2002 (SOX), which was promulgated as a result of the Enron and other corporate accounting and financial scandals, and which was intended to help restore confidence in the corporate financial system. SOX has many provisions; and regarding ethics codes the statute states that companies must have such a code for senior financial executives and officers, or to state (to the Securities and Exchange Commission and to the public) why they have not done so. SOX defines an ethics code as one having written standards that are reasonably designed to deter wrongdoing and promote honest and ethical conduct, as well as full disclosure, compliance with the law, prompt reporting of violations, and methods to conform to the standards of the code.

Codes of ethics usually are developed for a company as a whole and form the foundation of the company's ethics program. Codes of ethics serve as the major vehicle for stating the ethical principles, core values, and moral rules the company believes in and follows. A code of ethics helps to make managers and employees aware that moral considerations, as well as economic and legal factors, must be considered when business decisions are made. The code also demonstrates to other stakeholders that the corporation is aware of, and fully committed to, acting morally as well as in a socially responsible manner. If the corporate code of ethics is to serve as a means by which business managers legitimately can begin to claim "profession" status, like the doctors and lawyers have, the code ideally should contain: a statement of adherence, that is, a statement that the corporation, as well as its employees, will be bound by the principles of the code; an ethical preamble, stating the fundamental ethical principles and core values motivating the code; a statement and description of the corporation's basic mission and purpose, how this mission coheres with the ethical preamble, thus demonstrating that the corporation serves an inherently moral purpose; a statement and description of the main stakeholders or constituencies to whom the corporation believes it is obligated in the pursuit of its mission; an enumeration of the specific obligations the corporation believes it owes to these groups; a listing of precise standards of conduct required, permitted, or forbidden by the code; and a statement of the types and severity of sanctions the corporation will impose upon violators of these principles, obligations, and standards.

The process by which the code of ethics is put together is very important. The initial, and ultimate, responsibility, of course, lies with the company's board of directors. However, it is critical that employees and departments at all levels and sectors of the corporation take part in drawing up the code. The legal department, human resources, public and community relations, and ad hoc committees of employees from different departments, for example, must be drawn into the process. If a wide variety of employees are not drawn into the process, the company risks the perils of a code that does not address real concerns and that engenders a feeling by the employees that the code is not "owned" by them, but rather is merely another set of rules and regulations imposed on them. A company should be prepared to expect certain objections to be raised to the creation of a code of ethics. A code might invite increased scrutiny of the corporation by members of the public, the press, and consumer and environmental groups. These "outsiders" now will be able to ask if the company is complying with its code of ethics and, if there have been any violations, what is being done to rectify them. An open examination of the company, however, should be encouraged, not feared. Such an examination affords the company an opportunity to explain its positions and demonstrate its commitment to morality. If a corporation desires to maintain or regain the confidence of the public, it must demonstrate that it is taking the interests of its stakeholders into account. A code also may appear to be an act of self-condemnation on the part of the company. Of course, if the company has been acting morally, the code can be phrased as a formal embodiment of long-standing moral policies and practices. However, if the company has engaged in immoral past conduct, the promulgation of a code may appear in some sense to be an admission of responsibility. Yet, the very creation of the code clearly demonstrates that the company's problems have been confronted, that the company does not now tolerate such misconduct and intends to redress it in a formal manner, and that the company wants to signal this new attitude to managers, employees, and other stakeholders. One important part of a corporate code of ethics should deal with "whistleblowing" and the treatment of employees who "blow the whistle."

Whistleblowing

"*Whistleblowing*" may be defined as an attempt by a member of an organization to disclose what he or she believes to be wrongdoing in or by the organization. The discussion herein focuses on whistleblowing by employees of a corporation. "Wrongdoing" entails not only conduct or conditions that the employee believes are illegal, but also behavior that the employee considers to be immoral. Whistleblowing can be internal, that is, to those higher up in the corporate hierarchy; or it can be external, that is, to the government, such as a regulatory agency, to a public interest group, or to the media. A "*whistleblower*," of course, is the person, the employee, who attempts to make known the wrongdoing. He or she usually "blows the whistle" for right, as well as rightful, reasons; yet one should not always assume that the whistleblowing employee's motives are meritorious or that he or she is even correct as to the underlying premise of wrongdoing.

While there may exist federal and state statutes that protect public sector employees who blow the whistle from retaliation by their government employers, as well as statutes in the areas of civil rights, labor law, and health and safety law, that prohibit employers from taking retaliatory actions against employees who report statutory violations, there is no general federal statute, and little state law, extending similar protection to private sector employees, the vast majority of whom are "at will" employees. The state *Whistleblower Protection Acts* that do exist usually only protect disclosures of actual legal violations by a company and by its employees. Therefore, reports of suspicious unfounded illegality are usually not protected, nor are disclosures of immoral and unethical conduct which are also not illegal. Thus, the whistleblower must be certain of the legal wrongdoing, as in most states erroneous but good faith whistleblowing is not protected. Moreover, the state statutes are uniform in that to be protected the whistleblowing must be made to a government agency or public official and not to the media or a public interest organization. Some, such as Florida's, even require that the whistleblowing employee report the legal wrongdoing to his or her supervisor, then up the corporate "chain-of-command," and also give the employer a reasonable opportunity to correct the problem. Furthermore, in most states, the successful and legally protected whistleblower "only" gets his or her job back (with lost wages, benefits, seniority, etc. but no money damages (though in New Jersey, pursuant to statute, called the Conscientious Employee Act, the wrongfully discharges whistleblower can also sue for emotional distress damages). Even if a state does not have a whistleblower protection statute, the wrongfully discharged employee can attempt to bring a suit under the *Public Policy doctrine* if the employee can convince a court that his or her discharge was in violation of the "fundamental public policy" of the state, for example, when the employee disclosed pollution or workplace hazards on the part of the employer. There is also a federal whistleblowing statute in the Sarbanes-Oxley Act (SOX) of 2002, but that law only protects whistleblowing employees of public companies regulated by the Securities and Exchange Commission. Moreover, SOX only protects employees who disclose information pertaining to securities fraud or some other type of fraud or embezzlement against the shareholders. Thus, SOX provides only some protection to whistleblowers. Whistleblowing, finally, should not be confused with disclosing wrongdoing pursuant to False Claims Acts, which are federal and state statutes that provide that a whistleblowing employee who discloses wrongdoing by his or her employer in the form of embezzlement or fraud against the government, such as Medicare or Medicaid fraud, is entitled to a percentage (ranging from 10-30%) of the award or settlement against the employer that the government receives. It also should be noted that the 2010 Dodd-Frank Wall Street Reform and Consumer Protection Act has a provision that extends whistleblower protection and rewards to those employees, as well as any others, disclosing financial fraud in private sector contracting and bribery in overseas contracting with foreign governments. Thus, whistleblowing may, or may not be, legally protected, let alone rewarded; consequently, the issue arises, therefore, as to whether ethics extends any moral protection to private sector whistleblowing employees, especially in the corporate context and particularly regarding at-will employees.

As has been pointed out, there does not yet exist a uniform corpus of whistleblower law to protect private sector, at-will employees. There is yet no general federal law, though the new federal, securities fraud, whistleblower provision in the Sarbanes-Oxley Act is a start. There are some state statutes, but only a relatively small number of truly comprehensive state statutes. Most of these contain strict reporting requirements, and, moreover, are strictly construed by the courts. Finally, as was seen, there is a rather large, but loose, state-by-state collection of at times widely divergent, common law, "public policy" formulations that may encompass whistleblowing protections. The statutory and case law, of course, eventually will determine the legalities of a whistleblowing situation. Ethics, as a branch of philosophy, will be used to determine what is morally required in a whistleblowing situation. Ascertaining whether whistleblowing is morally permissible or even whether it is morally required, or concomitantly whether it is morally justified, is a very difficult task. Such a moral whistleblowing inquiry first necessitates an examination on how the general field of ethics applies to one specific practice - whistleblowing. Do employees have the moral responsibility to "blow the whistle"? There is an ethical principle that will help to answer the preceding question.

The Ethical Principle of Last Resort

As presented in the initial chapter to this book that as a general rule (though with exceptions, as noted) the common law doctrine of nonfeasance maintains that one does not have a *legal* duty to help, aid, or rescue anyone. Consequently, one, again as a general rule, cannot be held legally liable for negligence for not rescuing someone even if one is able or for not warning someone of a peril. That is the law – nonfeasance, not acting, is not actionable legally. Yet when does one have a positive moral obligation to act? Acting morally may involve more than merely avoiding negative harm; acting morally also may require one to perform an affirmative positive action, even though legally one may not be required to take the action. The ethical principle of "*Last Resort*" indicates when one has a moral duty to act, to aid another, or to rescue. One morally must act when there is a need, proximity, capability, one is the last resort or chance to avoid the peril, and when acting would not cause harm, or threaten to cause harm, equal to or greater than the original peril. The principle is based partially on Kant's admonition that "ought implies can"; that is, one is obligated to do only what one can do. Thus, if one is unable to act and help, due to lack of opportunity, means, or resources, one is not obligated morally to act.

The "last resort" principle usually involves an obligation of immediacy and high priority posed by an emergency; it thus generates a moral obligation to act that one cannot ignore without moral condemnation. The classic example is a drowning case when the five "last resort" factors are present. To answer the whistleblowing question previously posed it is certainly conceivable that if the potential whistleblower is the "last resort" to report harm or future harm by the corporation and/or its employees then the whistleblower has the moral obligation to "blow the whistle." The problem, however, in successfully applying the "last resort" principle to business, emerges the fourth and fifth factors. Who is the last resort for people unemployed and in need, business or government? Would business "rescuing" in fact harm the corporation, or its shareholders, or other stakeholders? A "friendly takeover," a corporation helping an employee pay his or her children's college tuition, may be praiseworthy actions, but are they morally required under the "last resort" principle? Is a corporation immoral for choosing not to act in the preceding circumstances? One example is the case of the Malden Mills Company, whose very compassionate owner rebuilt the facility after a fire without terminating any employees; but due in part to the added financial strain of keeping those employees, he forced his company to file for Chapter 11 bankruptcy protection in order to reorganize its finances, thereby resulting in a considerably, and permanently, diminished workforce. Another example concerns the large, multinational pharmaceutical companies who are providing for free or at greatly reduced cost their patented anti-AIDS drugs to African nations. Yet are they so doing because it is their moral responsibility as the "rescuer" of "last resort" or due to other social pressures? Similarly, corporations may not be the "last resort" to take care of their employees' children that have a disability, yet companies such as Toyota and Raytheon do provide assistance, for example, by hosting dinners with speakers and holding "networking" events, as well as expanding insurance coverage for "special needs" children. If not moral duty, what motivates these meritorious actions? A most interesting and thought-provoking example concerns Wal-Mart's very meritorious response to the Hurricane Katrina disaster in New Orleans and the Gulf Coast. Was Wal-Mart's "trucking in" tons of relief supplies (literally!) "merely" a socially responsible action, or was Wal-Mart the "last resort" to bring rapid relief to this devastated region of the country; and if the latter, what does that say about the government—all levels of government—federal, state, and local? A critical point is that even though a company or person may not have a legal obligation to help, aid, or rescue, and, moreover, even if a company or person does not have any moral obligation to act based on the Last Resort principle, nonetheless many people and businesses do "help out" in the community by taking part in charitable and civic affairs. These philanthropic and civic-minded individuals and business today are deemed to be "socially responsible" ones. This value of social responsibility will be covered later in this chapter.

In summary, what does it mean to be moral? Being moral means being ethical, that is, reasoning from ethical theories and principles to moral conclusions as to right and wrong. This chapter has introduced managers to the field of ethics, which is a branch of philosophy, and has sought to demonstrate how ethical theories can be applied to modern day business problems to reason to moral conclusions. The four ethical theories examined in this chapter – Ethical Egoism, Ethical Relativism, Utilitarianism, and Kant's Categorical Imperative – are major ethical theories in Western Civilization intellectual thought and tradition. These theories are not, of course, the only ethical theories in Western Civilization; and obviously there are many other ethical theories stemming from other civilizations as well as religions. As noted, the authors selected these four since they are very important ones as well as the fact that the basic tenets of each should be familiar to the reader. Ethics is thus a very large intellectual endeavor. And, as emphasized, to really complicate matters, there is no "Supreme Court of Ethics" to tell the readers, and for that matter the authors, which ethical theory is the "true" and "right" one. There is, however, an element of truth and rightfulness in all four theories. Accordingly, the authors would advise the reader to do the following: first, pursuant to Ethical Egoism improve oneself, empower oneself, and achieve success for oneself and one's company or organization; second, pursuant to Ethical Relativism, when achieving this success be "culturally competent" and thus strive not to contravene a society's moral norms; third, pursuant to Utilitarianism, in addition to achieving one's own and one's company's success, similarly strive to find "win-win" scenarios where the good of all the stakeholders including society as a whole is maximized too; and finally, pursuant to Kantian ethics, in attaining this individual and societal good make sure that no person or stakeholder group is disrespected or demeaned. These principles should be manifested in any true Code of Ethics. Then, one will be successful, and rightfully so, in the sense that individual and organizational success will be secured in a truly moral manner. Of course, now that one and one's company has achieved so much success, stature, and money, there very likely will emerge an expectation from the community and society that the company and organization will be not "just" a legal and moral one, but also a "socially responsible" entity as well as a sustainable one. The next part to this chapter, therefore, deals with the very current and relevant topic of social responsibility, or when the term is applied to business – "corporate social responsibility."

Corporate Social Responsibility

Stakeholder analysis has emerged as a critical concern for the modern business leader. Typically, *stakeholder* considerations, above and beyond the interests of the shareholders of the corporation, have been interpreted and examined under the concept of "*corporate social responsibility*." Corporate social responsibility (CSR) now also has become a central issue for business leaders. Moreover, today stakeholder analysis as well as CSR is converging with the notion of "corporate governance," which traditionally has had mainly legal connotations. The philosophical movement from focusing solely on shareholder wealth maximization was recently manifested by the Business Roundtable, a corporate lobbying and educational organization composed of many of the CEOs from the country's largest organizations. The Business Roundtable enunciated a new statement on corporate responsibility that expressed a company's purpose more broadly by encompassing serving all the firm's stakeholders, including employees, customers, suppliers, local communities, and society at-large. The rationale is that the long-term sustainability of business is tied directly to the society of which it is an integral part (Cassel, 2020; Ramey, 2019).

In this part to the chapter, the authors examine stakeholders and CSR in the context of corporate governance. The authors take a broad approach to corporate governance and stakeholders, encompassing legal, moral, social responsibility, and economic values. Stakeholder analysis and CSR are addressed in a global context. The authors discuss the traditional nature of the corporation, with its emphasis on maximizing shareholder value; and then examine corporate constituency statutes which allow corporate boards to consider the values of other stakeholders. Next, the authors examine new socially responsible ways of doing business, which give primacy to stakeholder values beyond the interests of the shareholders in corporate decision-making. The critical relationship of corporate social responsibility and stakeholders to corporate governance is emphasized and explicated; finally, suggestions and recommendations for business leaders are provided to incorporate not only legal and ethical values but also corporate social responsibility and stakeholder values into corporate governance. The imperative of governing the corporation in a profitable, legal, moral, and socially responsible manner is underscored. The beneficial result is that the corporation achieves sustainable economic growth and development, and that it also produces positive value for all the stakeholders of the corporation and betterment for society as a whole.

Accordingly, what exactly is a corporation's "social responsibility"? Does a corporation have a social obligation to take care of the poor, educate the public, give to charity, and fund cultural programs? Social projects and social welfare in the United States traditionally have been viewed as the appropriate domain of government, not of business. Business, of course, is taxed and such taxes may be used for social purposes. The traditional purpose of business as viewed in the U.S., moreover, is the profitable production and distribution of goods and services, not social welfare. Yet by raising the issue of social responsibility, business is forced to concern itself with the "social" dimension of its activities. This issue is now a critical one for business today. Accordingly, what is the "social responsibility" of business today? The term at a basic philanthropic level may be defined as a business taking an active part in the social causes, charities, and civic life of one's community and society. Newman's Own is a private sector company praised for its philanthropic mission since it donates all of the profits and royalties after taxes for charitable and educational purposes. However, corporate social responsibility (CSR) certainly can be more than "mere" philanthropy. The social responsibility of business can also be thought of in a broader constituency or stakeholder sense, that is, by the corporation considering the values and needs of employees, suppliers, consumers, local communities, and society as a whole. One can also take a "strategic" as well as stakeholder approach to corporate social responsibility by integrating stakeholder, social, environmental, as well as economic concerns into the organization's values, culture, governance, strategy, and decision-making.

The World Business Council for Sustainable Development views social responsibility in a corporate context as a company's continuing commitment to act legally and morally and also to contribute to the economic development of society while improving the quality of life of their employees and their families as well as the local community and society as a whole. This definition evokes another, and even more expansive, concept of the "social responsibility" of business – "sustainability." The sustainability approach to corporate social responsibility is premised on the idea that a company must remain economically viable in the long-term, and that in order to be viable the company must take into consideration other stakeholders beyond the shareholders, including, and especially, the environment. The objective is to simultaneously produce economic value for the company, but also value for society as a whole by helping to solve societal needs, particularly by improving the lives of the people (and potential consumers) who live in the communities where the company does business. "Sustainability" is often used when discussing such concepts as corporate citizenship, social responsibility, stakeholder analysis, and social enterprise. Sustainability is at times discussed as part of a broader conception of social responsibility; but it also is discussed in a narrower discrete sense of a company being environmentally responsible, that is, not "merely" obeying all environmental laws and regulations, but also seeking to reduce waste and energy and water consumption, to conserve energy and water by means of "green buildings" and "offices," and even to produce energy by wind or solar means.

Some recent examples of socially responsible and sustainable actions by companies and organizations are as follows:

- In 2019, Coca Cola and Unilever NV and more than 200 other global businesses, representing approximately 20% of all packaging worldwide, made a commitment to reduce plastic waste. Unilever said that it would reduce by one-half its use of virgin plastic by 2025 by various means, including using more recycled plastic. Coca Cola announced a goal in 2018, stating that its bottles will contain an average of 50% recycled content by 2030 (Ibukun, 2019).
- Starbucks has embarked on a program to provide free job-skills training classes to people in certain local communities. The National Urban League as well as other community organizations are partnering with Starbucks to bring in the jobless for training, especially young people, veterans, and the homeless. Starbucks views this laudable effort as not "merely" an exercise in social responsibility designed to have a beneficial social impact in the communities it serves but also a strategic opportunity to hire people, to help achieve a more diversified workforce, and to motivate employees, all of which should help to produce eventual financial value to the shareholders.
- The Carnival Corporation cruise company has embarked on a social impact "volun-tourism" program in the Dominican Republic, where travelers can choose from socially responsible shore excursions in addition to the usual "sand-and-surf" ones. Examples of the former are working on the production-line in a locally-run chocolate factory, visiting an artisan's center and working with local people to recycle products, pouring concrete in local homes, and teaching English. The company expects that the program will be fulfilling and an inspiration for the cruise passengers, will

provide a new perspective on life for them, will help the local communities and people in the Dominican Republic, as well as achieve for Carnival some very positive and appropriate publicity for being a socially responsible cruise company.

- The city of Rome, Italy, has commenced a program whereby companies can sponsor a ruin by paying into a fund to restore the hundreds of ruins, statutes, fountains, as well as other artwork and historic sites. The luxury good companies, Fendi and Bulgari, are sponsoring the Trevi fountain and Spanish steps, respectively. However, there is a concern that the big and "big-name" monuments will readily find sponsors and those smaller and less well-known ones will lack patrons.
- Disney and Royal Caribbean are no longer using plastic straws, replacing them with paper ones, because as per Disney a "commitment to environmental stewardship."
- Dell Computers has implemented a recycling program that enables the company to reuse and dispose of electronic products and parts more safely (Cassel, 2020).
- Kroger Supermarkets is discontinuing the use of plastic bags in its stores but will provide brown paper bags for free as well as sell customers reusable bags for $1 to $2 a piece.
- Kraft Heinz is now planning on using eggs only from cage-free hens in its global operations as well as only sustainably sourced palm oil. The company intends to spend $200 million on the project.
- Mondelez, the global snack food company, has as part of its broader social responsibility plan the Cocoa Life program wherein the company works with more than 90,000 coca farmers in Ghana, the Ivory Coast, and other countries to develop a sustainable network of cocoa farms for the future. As part of the program the company sends 15 employees, called "joy ambassadors" to help the local farmers and to work on local projects to improve the quality of life in their villages. Mondelez is investing $400 million over 10 years in the Cocoa Life program. To oversee the successful implementation of all those social responsibility and sustainability activities and budgetary outlays the company has a vice-president of global

sustainability. What the company gets in return is a stronger and more reliable supply chain as well as employees who are excited and motivated and a reputation for "doing good" that can be marketed to consumers.

- The Hilton Hotel in Ft. Lauderdale, Florida has a very artistic-looking wind turbine system on its roof that produces renewable, "clean" energy, will pay for itself after several years, is collapsible during hurricanes, and impresses customers, tourists, and community, not only due to the turbines unique design but also because of the company's commitment to environmental protection, conservation, and production.
- An example of sustainability as well as an illustration of social entrepreneurship is a bank in Makassar, Indonesia, called the Mutiara Trash Bank, which will take the "deposits" of recyclable trash, such as plastic bottles and paper, from poor people in the community, at designated collection points, weight it, give it a monetary value, transfer it to the government, and then make a monetary deposit in the account of the "depositor." The objectives are to help reduce pressure on the ever-growing landfills, help clean up the environment, convert the trash to energy and other products, and to introduce poor people into the country's financial and banking system.
- Another example of sustainability and social entrepreneurship is a Kenyan company called M-Kopa Solar (note that kopa means "to borrow" in Swahili) that lends money to poor people on very favorable credit terms to enable them to buy expensive solar-power systems from the company. The objectives are to improve the lives of the people and for the company to do well too.

A corporation, of course, is a profit-making entity that exists in a competitive environment, and thus may be limited in its ability to solve a multitude of social problems particularly at the expense of the owners of the corporation – the shareholders. Where are the philanthropic guidelines for corporate contributions and improvements? How should a corporation's resources be allocated, and exactly to whom, to what extent, and in what priorities? What is the proper balance between shareholder and stakeholder interests? The corporate governance policies of the organization must seek to answer these important, yet, difficult questions. If a corporation unilaterally or too generously engages in social betterment, it may place itself at a disadvantage compared to other less socially responsible business entities. Being socially responsible costs money, and such efforts cut into profits. In a highly competitive market system, corporations that are too socially responsible may lessen their attractiveness to investors or simply may price themselves out of the market. One example is the clearly socially responsible firm – Ben & Jerry's, which has long been known and lauded for its civic, community, and environmental efforts. Yet the company may have been too socially responsible and consequently neglectful of basic business concerns. Ultimately, the original former "hippies" Ben Cohen and Jerry Greenfield of Ben & Jerry's sold their interests in their company in 2000 to global consumer products giant, Unilever, which carried on the social responsibility activities of the brand to a degree, but in a more prudent and strategic manner. Nevertheless, despite the saga of Ben & Jerry's, social responsibility, at least to some reasonable degree, may be in the long-term self-interest of business, so long as these activities align with the corporation's long-term objectives. Furthermore, there is some evidence that these socially responsible strategies have been successful.

A corporation cannot long remain a viable economic entity in a society that is uneven, unstable, and deteriorating. It makes good business sense for a corporation to devote some of its resources to social betterment projects. To operate efficiently, for example, business needs educated and skilled employees. Education and training, therefore, should be of paramount interest to business leaders. A corporation, for example, can act socially responsible by providing computers to community schools and by releasing employees on company time to furnish the training. Business also gains an improved public image by being socially responsible. An enhanced social image should attract more customers and investors and thus provide positive benefit for the firm. Other examples of companies engaging in socially responsible marketing as one way to persuade consumers to spend in a difficult economy, to wit: Sketchers USA launched a brand called BOBS, meaning Benefiting Others By Shoes, which results in the company donating two pairs of shoes for every one sold; Urban Outfitters features clothes by Threads for Thought, which gives part of its sales proceeds to humanitarian groups; Nordstrom sells hats made by Krochet Kids International, which enlists impoverished people in Uganda and Peru, for example, to make hats which are sold in the U.S. for $24; and Feed Projects, which makes T-shirts, handbags, and accessories, donates a percentage of its profits to United Nations anti-hunger programs. When implemented correctly, these socially responsible retailing efforts are "good works" and also good strategies, which may be very appealing especially to young consumers who may not have the means to make large charitable contributions, but who admire brands that are "trendy" but which also reflect a save-the-planet theme. To further illustrate, the Walt Disney Company, in an effort to portray a socially responsible message, as well as to attract customers to its theme parks, commenced a program, called "Give a Day, Get a Disney Day," whereby the company will give away a million one-day, one-park tickets to people who volunteer at select charities. The strategic objectives are to protect the environment and be charity- and civic-minded, tying these good efforts to the firm's values, mission, brand, image, products and/or services, to let consumers know of these socially responsible and sustainable endeavors, and to do so, according to one commentator, without "breaking the bank" (Cassel, 2020).

A corporation that acts more socially responsible not only secures public favor, but also avoids public disfavor. To illustrate, for many years the large multi-national pharmaceutical companies were criticized for not providing AIDS drugs for free or at greatly reduced prices to African governments. In response to public criticism, the pharmaceutical responded in a socially responsible (and also egoistic manner) by giving the drugs away or selling them at cost. Moreover, certain pharmaceutical companies, such as Roche and GlaxoSmithKline, on their social responsibility and sustainability websites, have statements indicating preferential pricing and accessibility as well as limited patent policies for AIDs drugs going to African and other less developed countries. Accordingly, social responsibility and also good public relations are achieved. Wal-Mart, the giant retailer, in response to criticisms from environmentalists and labor activists, now has a director of global ethics, who will be responsible for developing and enforcing company standards of conduct, as well as a "senior director for stakeholder engagement," whose role will be to develop a new model of business engagement that produces value for society. Similarly, clothing and apparel manufacturers, such as Nike and the Gap, in response to criticism by labor and consumer groups about exploitive working conditions in overseas "sweatshops," have ended poor working conditions, and now also report on their social responsibility efforts and achievements overseas. Business is part of society and subject to society's mandates; and if society wants more "responsibility" from business, business cannot ignore this "request" without the risk of incurring society's anger, perhaps in the form of higher taxes or more onerous government regulation. Socially responsible activities may also improve a company's reputation when viewed by external stakeholders, such as bankers, creditors, investors, and government regulators, which not only may avoid economic harm, but also may bring about economic benefits. As such an egoist and rational actor will surely see the instrumental value of a prudent degree of social responsibility and sustainability in today's global business marketplace.

The topics of social responsibility, stakeholder analysis, and sustainability emerged as critical ones for global business leaders and managers too. A global example would be the Coca-Cola's company's efforts to provide clean water to parts of the developing world, which Coke also hopes to promote goodwill, boost local economies, and broaden its customer base. Royal Caribbean Cruise Company is teaming up with a Haitian non-profit organization to build a primary school, which is located on land the company leases from the government as a stop for its ships in the port town of Labadee. Wal-Mart is now selling online handicrafts made by women artisans in developing countries, such as dresses made in Kenya and jewelry from Guatemala and Thailand. Over 500 items from 20,000 female artisans will be offered for sale, which certainly will help the female artisans but also improve the company's global image. Two excellent examples of global CSR are the Norwegian company, Yara International, the world's largest chemical fertilizer company, has sponsored public/private partnerships to develop storage, transportation, and port facilities in parts of Africa with significant untapped agricultural potential, thereby developing local agriculture, providing jobs and improved incomes for farmers, and at the same time benefiting the company through an increased demand for its fertilizer products. Second, the Nestle Company is working to improve milk production in certain regions of India, by investing in well drilling, refrigeration, veterinary medicine, and training, thereby significantly increasing output and enhancing product quality, certainly beneficial to the company, and at the same time allowing the company to pay higher prices for farmers and their employees, resulting in a higher standard of living for the local community.

The United Nations now has a business initiative on corporate social responsibility, called the United Nations Global Compact, whereby companies can join and thus voluntarily agree to make improvements in human rights, labor, the environment, and combating corruption. The World Bank, moreover, now has an Internet course on social responsibility, called "CSR and Sustainable Competitiveness," offered by its educational and training division. The corporate social responsibility course is designed for "high-level" private sector managers, government officials and regulators, practitioners, academics, and journalists. One major purpose to the course is to provide a conceptual framework for improving the business environment to support corporate governance policies and social responsibility efforts by corporations and business. The course is also designed to assist companies to formulate a social responsibility strategy based on moral and economic values as well as one with a long-term perspective.

Stakeholder Values

A *Stakeholde*r approach to values views the enterprise as a community with a number of stakeholders, that is, constituent groups that are directly and indirectly connected to the enterprise and that are dependent on its success and prosperity. These groups include employees, customers, suppliers, distributors, local communities, and especially the society or societies in which the business has operations. The stakeholder groups typically are the following: shareholders and owners, employees, customers and consumers, suppliers and distributors, creditors, community, government, unions, competition, and society. Shareholders as the owners are usually listed first. Obviously, a corporation cannot survive unless it serves and benefits its shareholders in a financial sense. However, today, shareholders may view their investment as one that benefits society too and perhaps in a direct manner by means of the social benefit corporation. Regardless, all shareholders are entitled to the honest and efficient management of their investment as well as a fair return on their investment. Employees are of course interested in obtaining and maintaining employment. They value a just wage, fair employment practices and working conditions, and job security. They also may value working for a company that is regarded as a "socially responsible" one. Customers and consumers want access to goods and services that are of good quality, at a fair price, and that come with good customer service. Suppliers and distributors want financially rewarding, long-term contractual relationships with the company. Local communities want to see the corporation located in their cities and towns in order to provide employment for the citizens and residents and to support the local tax base. The local community also values, and very well may expect, that the corporations in its presence participate in civic, charitable, philanthropic, and socially responsible activities. Creditors naturally value being repaid, and they also expect a fair rate of return as well as adequate assurances of security for the obligation. Government values legal compliance with business laws and business regulations. Government also values business as an important component of its tax base. Government also values and thus desires to promote entrepreneurship and competition. As to the competition, the competition values its own market share, yet expects in a capitalistic model "tough" and "hard-hitting" competition, but the competition also values completion that is legal and ethical. Society values its survival, of course, and also growth, prosperity for its members, and the sustainability of business and society. Members of society also value today, and thus expect, that the corporation will be a socially responsible one, particularly regarding its stewardship of the environment and efforts to improve the environment. Therefore, the goal of the business leader today is to balance and harmonize these values and thus attempt to devise corporate governance policies that maximize these values in a legal, moral, socially responsible, and practically efficacious manner, thereby resulting in "win-win" scenarios for the business and all its stakeholders and attaining a level of continual sustainable business success.

Social Responsibility and Corporate Governance

Corporate governance today has emerged as significant subject for business; and the topic of social responsibility also arises in the context of corporate governance. Initially, one may think of "corporate governance" as having strictly legal components, especially business law and regulatory law. In the traditional governance models, the corporation's primary focus is on shareholder rights, and the primary governance rule is based on maximizing shareholder value. Directors, therefore, have a duty to ensure that companies fulfill their legal obligations, protect shareholder interests, and provide accurate and timely information to investors, markets, and government regulators. Yet corporate governance also has social responsibility as well as ethical ramifications. That is, corporate governance, in the expansive meaning that the authors wish to give to this concept, means the legal, ethical/moral, and social responsibility considerations for regulating business today. Business decision-making cannot be decoupled from the responsibility – legal, ethical, and social - of business leaders for their own risk-taking; otherwise, the whole business and entrepreneurial system will be undermined.

The idea is not "just" to maximize profits by "merely" obeying the law, for example, Securities and Exchange Commission (SEC) regulations, but rather to also include ethical, moral, social responsibility, and sustainability concerns into corporate decision-making. Making profits in a legal manner is obviously an essential component to corporate governance; but the focus on "just" the law is too narrow, the authors contend. To illustrate a more expansive meaning of corporate governance, the American Law Institute in its Principles of Corporate Governance sets forth fundamental principles of corporate governance. The primary principle is for the corporation to conduct the business with an objective of enhancing corporate profit and shareholder gain. However, the corporation may take into account ethical considerations that are reasonably regarded as appropriate to the responsible conduct of business; and also the corporation may devote a reasonable amount of resources to charitable, philanthropic, humanitarian, and educational purposes; and the corporation may do so in both situations even if shareholder profit and shareholder gain are not thereby enhanced. So, although the primary focus is on the monetary value, this objective is moderated by ethical and social responsibility values. The idea is that the corporation will engage in self-governance; and thus regulate, not only by the strictures of the law, but also by morality and ethics, as well as stakeholder and societal concerns, the manner by which it generates profits. In essence, corporations will act legally, morally, and in a socially responsible manner only if those people who exercise control over the corporation, whether directly or indirectly; that is, the directors, officers, and shareholders together, have the vision to see that the collective future of the business, its stakeholders, and society as a whole is inextricably tied to the sustainability of the entity and the society and environment in which it operates and flourishes, as well as the strength of character and leadership ability to implement and act on that vision.

Corporate governance guidelines for social responsibility should be premised on fundamental principles. First the company should formulate a corporate social responsibility policy to guide its strategic planning and provide a roadmap for its CSR initiatives. Second, that policy should be an integral part of the organization's overall business policy and aligned with the company's business goals. Third, the policy should be created and framed with the participation of various level executives as well as representatives of other stakeholder groups, and the policy must be approved and overseen by the board and implemented by top management. The corporate social responsibility policy should cover the following core elements: (1) adherence to the law; (2) acting in an ethical, honest, and transparent manner; (3) consideration of the values and interests of all stakeholders, including shareholders, employees, customers, suppliers, local communities, society at large, and the environment; (4) treating all stakeholders with dignity and respect and as worthwhile means and not as mere means; (5) charitable and philanthropic activities; and (6) activities that promote sustainability and social and economic development.

A socially responsible firm, however, must also be a realistic one; that is, socially responsible, stakeholder considerations, and environmental efforts must be sustainable economically and should have some relationship to the firm's business. These prudential considerations should be reflected in the company's corporate governance polices. Employees, for example, should also be engaged directly in the company's social responsibility activities so as to engage them, inspire them, motivate them, and thereby enhance morale and productivity. Moreover, a firm's social responsibility program does not have to be a multi-million dollar effort; rather, something as simple as an employee social responsibility "suggestion box," or as straightforward as a recycling or energy saving program, will do to promote employee involvement as well as to promote and give credence to employee social values. Nonetheless, despite the size, a firm's social responsibility efforts should be publicized widely within the company, for example, in company newsletters, as well as externally, for example in company annual social responsibility and sustainability reports and on its website. Being socially responsible, therefore, is a smart and sustainable business strategy that the company's corporate governance policies must be tailored toward in order to promote this type of social responsibility.

Corporate governance emerges as a particularly challenging endeavor in the social benefit corporation considering its dual mission of profit-making and societal betterment, the concomitant trade-offs among competing stakeholders, including shareholders, of course, the ensuing competition for corporate resources, and the absence in the state legislation as to how the conflicting stakeholder demands should be balanced. Consequently, the top management team will weigh the company's social responsibility goals in light of their business objectives, and then arrive at some reasonable determination that advances profit and all stakeholder values. Moreover, to advance social responsibility accountability, it will be important that the views of management should be balanced within the company by using participatory mechanisms that allow for stakeholder representation, invite stakeholder participation, and keep internal channels of communication open and flowing. At the very least, due to the mixed mission, vague corporate socially responsible standards, conflicting stakeholder demands, as well as citizen and interest group pressure, the activities of the corporation will be, and should be, carefully monitored – principally by its management as part of their governance function, but also by company stakeholders, government legislators and regulators, and citizens.

Suggestions and Recommendations:

The authors believe and recommend that it is in the long-term, egoistic, self-interest of the corporation to be a socially responsible one and thus to be active and engaged in community, civic, and charitable activities. Accordingly, it is the job of the business leader to educate the shareholders, and perhaps corporate management as well, of the benefits that will accrue to the company and the shareholders by the company acting in a smart, shrewd, and strategic socially responsible manner. Corporate social responsibility and sustainability should be treated as an investment, not a cost, comparable to quality improvement and employee training. Business leaders, executives, and managers, therefore, must be cognizant of and appreciate the instrumental strategic value of social responsibility in its constituency and sustainability formulations. Business leaders, executives, and managers today surely are well aware of societal expectations regarding the social responsibility of their companies. Business leaders want their businesses to be successful and to sustain that success on a long-term basis. The concept of "sustainability" also has emerged, along with social responsibility and corporate governance, as important subject matters for business today. A sustainable business is one that governs itself in a long-term, stakeholder centered, and environmentally conscious manner. To be a sustainable one, the business must be concerned not "merely" with profits, but also must pay attention to, and seek to balance, stakeholder interests and environmental concerns. Sustainability has legal and ethical predicates too; and as such will result in legal and moral decision-making by companies.

For the traditional corporation some suggestions on how to structure corporate governance to maximize long-term shareholder, stakeholder, and societal value creation are as follows: empower and motivate business leaders to manage for the long-term by using incentive and compensation systems. That is, compensation should be aligned with long-term objectives, and financial rewards should be linked to the period over which results are realized. Incentive structures should also reflect a more complete measure of socially responsible performance, for example, by including environmental sustainability, in these incentive programs. The companies that make these social responsibility considerations contribute to long-term, successful, financial performance. Business leaders, therefore, must exert – leadership – to improve incentive and compensation systems as well as other aspects of corporate governance to enhance sustainability.

Conclusion

This book concentrated on one aspect of the law – tort law based on the common law – in the context of business, employment, and management. However, in addition to tort and the other manifold legal ramifications of management and business decision-making, the authors emphasized that managers today are being called upon to act not only legally, but also in a moral, ethical, socially responsible and sustainable manner. Accordingly, this chapter was comprised of two components. First, the chapter examined ethics, which is a branch of philosophy. Moreover, the authors demonstrated how ethics can be applied to management decision-making to determine if the business is acting in a moral manner. In particular, the authors discussed corporate codes of ethics and whistleblowing in the context of morally required whistleblowing. This chapter, furthermore, examined the concepts of stakeholder values, corporate governance, and corporate social responsibility, which also includes in its modern conception the notion of "sustainability," which characteristically is viewed as environmental responsibility. Accordingly, the authors discussed what it means in a modern-day management and business context for a business, particularly a corporation, to be not "merely" a legal one, but also a moral and ethical as well as a socially responsible and sustainable entity. The authors, moreover, discussed the ethical principle of Last

Resort and its relationship to social responsibility as well as the legal principle of nonfeasance.

This chapter has sought to build on the previous chapters' legal materials by introducing the readers to and examining the fields of morality, ethics, social responsibility, and sustainability, and then showing how, and why these concepts "above and beyond" the law can, and should, be applied to business today. In addition to legality, ethics and morality, social responsibility and sustainability are very important values too. Business leaders and managers, therefore, must be cognizant of these values. Furthermore, the authors stressed that today there is an emphasis on stakeholders or constituency groups as essential component of management business leadership, and corporate governance.

Managers and business leader are expected to take an "enlightened" approach to satisfying the values of stakeholders as well as being environmentally responsible in order to achieve long-term sustainable success. As emphasized by the authors, the ultimate objective is to attain "win-win" resolutions where all the company's stakeholders, including society as a whole, receive value. Social responsibility and environmental responsibility, therefore, emerge as key elements in achieving stakeholder symmetry, business success, and business sustainability. Furthermore, there is critical need for all these values for the long-term, well-being of society and the development of the economic system; and as such these values are most relevant and profound topics as well as challenges for business managers today. Business managers today, therefore, when contemplating and making business decisions, in addition to examining the financial implications, must always ask, and answer, the following questions: Is the decision legal based on the law; is it moral based on ethics; and what should a "socially responsible" and "sustainable" company be doing? Is the action legal, is it moral, is it socially responsible, and is it sustainable? That should be the management "mindset" and "drill." In order to inculcate these values into the company's leadership, management, employees, as well as decision-making and corporate governance, it is first necessary for the firm to establish an appropriate corporate culture, especially one that puts a premium on the values of diversity and respect.

CHAPTER VIII - CONCLUSION

This book described the tort law of the United States, encompassing several subcategories of negligence and intentional torts associated with this legal wrong. The book also examined and illustrated the application of tort law to business, including providing "suggestions and recommendations" to managers to avoid tort liability. Tort law itself was originally created to protect victims faced with or aggrieved by intentional or negligent physical injury and/or harm to their property, as well as to prevent future tort violations. The purposes of tort law - civil punishment, redress, and deterrence - continue to serve today. Tort law clearly impacts business, employment, and management; yet tort law also expanded into other key areas for business, especially the manufacturing business, by means of the strict liability in tort doctrine. Moreover, countries around the world have followed in the "footsteps" of the United States by developing tort and product liability laws, in order to protect persons, their property, and especially consumers. As such, managers must develop strategies and tactics to avoid legal problems with tort law. Accordingly, businesses should provide thorough education and training programs for their personnel, particularly managers, with the proper focus and examination of all the law, and specifically the laws pertaining to their type of business, and with an emphasis on how to avoid legal liability. This education and training should be done to not only protect the finances and image of the business, but also to protect people and especially customers and consumers. Managers, therefore, are obligated to acknowledge, understand, and abide by the various tort laws that exist in countries around the world in order to achieve their goals of establishing a legal, successful, and productive business.

Today, employers, managers, entrepreneurs, and employees are continually impacted by the law; and almost all human activity is affected by the law. In the business world, when contemplating a business transaction or decision, a manager not only must consider the physical, financial, personnel, and managerial aspects, but also the legal ramifications. Moreover, as the business and entrepreneurial "world" is now a truly diverse workplace, a manager must be cognizant of laws impacting his or her employees, suppliers, distributors, clients, and customers. The main purpose of this book, therefore, has been to introduce the reader to one fundamental aspect of the law affecting management and business – tort law - as well as the practical application of this *corpus* of law in the United States in the employment sector. After a brief introductory and overview chapter, the authors examined the field of intentional torts, followed by the tort of negligence, and then strict liability tort laws. Next, the authors examined the field of agency law and its relationship to tort law. Yet the authors also wanted to take the reader "above and beyond" the law by discussing other fields which a manager today must be cognizant of and prepared to handle efficaciously. As such, the authors discussed ethics as a branch of philosophy, applied ethics, morality, social responsibility, and sustainability in the context of business and management, in order to ensure that managers are conducting the business in conformity with the values of legality, morality, socially responsibility, and sustainability. The authors wanted the discerning reader, especially a management audience, to be conscious of the scope and complexity of this one body of law – tort law - affecting business. The authors, accordingly, intended to help managers recognize legal situations involving tort law in business, particularly employment; and the authors especially wanted to impart an awareness of potential legal problems pursuant to tort law, and especially to demonstrate to managers on how to avoid them.

This book, though titled as a basic "handbook," nonetheless is designed to help managers become familiar with important legal issues and concepts so they can make appropriate decisions about their company's status and functions. Managers deal with "laws of the land" every day, and consequently must be aware of its nuances and complexities in order to successfully and interdependently work with others in the organization, community, industry, and country. Thus, managers should become aware of the fundamental aspects of the legal system so they can avoid legal problems and can seek the help of experts when dealing with complex issues. *Common Law Torts in*

Business and How to Avoid Them: A Handbook for Managers has been designed to provide the foundational aspects of one component of the "American" legal system, as practiced in the United States, for current and aspiring employers, managers, as well as entrepreneurs. By reading and becoming familiar with the various tort laws presented, it is hoped that the readers will be better prepared to more effectively recognize and to deal with the legal challenges arising from tort law as applied to business, employment, and management, as well as to be better prepared to communicate with attorneys.

Common Law Torts in Business and How to Avoid Them: A Handbook for Managers introduced the reader to fundamental principles of tort law impacting business and management as well as the practical application of tort law principles in the United States. The study of this legal material will be very beneficial to all current and prospective entrepreneurs, employers, and managers, though, as the authors have emphasized, their "handbook" takes a general approach to tort law, which is predominantly state-based in the U.S., and consequently the book is not a substitute for an attorney for the pertinent jurisdiction.

Common Law Torts in Business and How to Avoid Them: A Handbook for Managers can be used academically as a supplement to a business law course or as the basis for a shorter specialized law course; yet the book was primarily designed to be used practically as an understandable legal guide and a learning tool that employers, managers, and entrepreneurs will find useful and beneficial for corporate training. Overall, the authors hope that all the stated and aforementioned objectives were attained in a stimulating, thought-provoking, and enjoyable manner; and as a result the knowledge of the reader was increased, the mental acuity of the reader was enhanced, and the mental discipline of the reader was strengthened.

GLOSSARY OF KEY TERMS

- **abuse of process** – an intentional tort based on the wrongful use of the legal process.
- **actual authority** – the power that the principal has expressly or impliedly granted to the agent to accomplish the purposes of the agency.
- **agency by estoppel** – when a person either intentionally or carelessly creates the appearance of an agency relationship.
- **agent** – a person who works for another, called a principal, but who also acts for and represents the principal in order to effectuate legal relations with third parties.
- **Anti-cybersquatting Consumer Protection Act** – the federal statute that protects Internet domain names.
- **anti-piracy agreements** – also called non-solicitation agreements; agreements in contracts that prevent departing employees from soliciting or serving the former employees' customers.
- **apparent authority** – pursuant to agency law, authority created in the agent when the principal by his or her own words or conduct manifested to third parties has misled third parties to believe that the agent is authorized to act on the principal's behalf; pursuant to the Uniform Partnership Act, the rule that an act by a partner for apparently carrying on the business of the partnership in the usual way binds the partnership.
- **assault** – an act by a defendant which causes a reasonable apprehension of fear in the victim of an immediate harmful or offensive contact to the person of the victim.
- **assumption of the risk** – a defense to negligence which arises when the defendant knowingly and voluntarily encounters a known risk.
- **battery** – an intentional act by a defendant that causes a harmful or offensive contact to the person of the plaintiff.
- **business invitees** – people invited to come on a person's land for the benefit of the landowner.
- **business sustainability continuum** – a model for a business to achieve continual success by adhering to the values of legality, morality, and social and environmental responsibility.
- **"but for" test** – pursuant to negligence law the test to determine if the defendant's careless action caused the plaintiff's injury or harm.
- **CAN-SPAM Act** – fully known as the Controlling the Assault of the Non-Solicited Pornography and Marketing Act; the federal statute which prohibits certain types of spamming activities.
- **case law** – also called the common law; law expressed by judges in court decisions.
- **Categorical Imperative** – the key ethical principle whereby morality is based not on the consequences of an action but rather on the application of a formal ethical test to the action to ascertain its morality; a three part principle to determine morality consisting of the Universal Law test, the Kingdom of Ends test, and the Agent Receiver test.

- **causation** – also known as causation-in-fact or actual causation; the presence of a causal connection between the defendant's careless conduct and the resulting harm to the plaintiff.
- **circuit courts** – "inferior" or lower courts in the state court system, possessing original jurisdiction.
- **civil law** – in the U.S. legal system, law dealing with legal wrongs committed by one private party against another private party.
- **civil lawsuit** – a lawsuit involving disputes between individuals.
- **clerk of the court** – the court officer whose function is to keep accurate records of cases and to enter cases on the court calendar.
- **codes of ethics (or conduct)** – internal rules, certain ones of which go beyond the law, which govern the professions, such as law and medicine; and now which are typically part of the corporate organization and thus an aspect of corporate governance.
- **common law** – also known as case law; law in the form of rulings in cases made by judges, which rulings serve as precedents for future cases with the same or similar facts.
- **comparative negligence** – not a complete defense to negligence, but the reduction of a plaintiff's damages based on his or her contributing fault.
- **compensatory damages** – damages awarded when there is a breach of contract and an actual loss, the purpose of which is to make the aggrieved party whole.
- **Computer Fraud in Abuse Act** – federal statute that makes accessing a computer without authority and taking confidential information a crime and civil wrong.
- **consent defense** – the defense that holds that a defendant is not liable for a wrongful act if the plaintiff has consented to that act.
- **consequential damages** – damages above and beyond compensatory damages which resulted from the breach of contract and which were foreseeable at the time of the contract.
- **consideration** – a requirement of a legally binding contract.
- **constitutional law** – law made pursuant to the U.S. federal Constitution as well as state constitutions.
- **contributory negligence** – under the old common law negligent conduct on the part of the plaintiff which amounted to a complete defense; but today replaced by the doctrine of comparative negligence.
- **conversion** – an intentional tort based on the lengthy dispossession, serious intermeddling or damage, or theft or destruction of personal property.
- **court** – a tribunal established by government to hear and decide cases and controversies.
- **court of equity** – a court empowered to issue equitable remedies.
- **corporate constituency statutes** – state statutes in the United States where the board of directors of a corporation may consider the interests of other stakeholders other than the shareholders.
- **corporate governance** – a term encompassing the mechanisms that can regulate the corporation, encompassing statutory and case law, government regulation, internal company rules, such as embodied in Codes of Ethics and Codes of Conduct, and social responsibility policies.
- **corporate social responsibility** – a concept encompassing a company acting legally and morally as well as taking an active part in civic and community activities and charitable actions; also including in some broader conceptions, "sustainability," that is, environmental responsibility.
- **corporation** – a form of business organization; an artificial legal entity created pursuant to state law upon the filing of an articles of incorporation.

- **covenants not to compete** – also called non-competition agreements; promises in contracts for the sale of a business or employment contracts in which one party promises not to compete with the other.
- **crime** – a public wrong; the violation of a public duty for which sanctions can include fines and imprisonment; known as "breaching the King's peace" in old common law days.
- **criminal law** – law dealing with legal wrongs committed against society and punished by society.
- **defamation** – the intentional tort of falsely impugning the character or reputation of another.
- **defect** – in products liability law, pursuant to the strict liability doctrine, when a product is flawed, contains an inadequate warning, or is defectively designed.
- **defective design** – pursuant to strict liability law, when a product could have been made safer with modifications that were economically and practically feasible based on the state-of-the-art when the product was made.
- **"detour and frolic"** – when an employee, while performing duties for the employer, goes out of his or her normal scope of duties to do some personal business.
- **discharge** – when contract obligations come to an end; when the contract duties of the parties are terminated.
- **district courts of appeal** – intermediate courts in the state court system, possessing appellate jurisdiction.
- **duty of care** – the existence of a legal duty to act according to a legally established standard of care.
- **duty of loyalty** – the common law rule that an employee is not to engage in any disloyal acts against his or her employer during the employment relationship.
- **duress** – forcing a person to enter into a contract by means of threats of force.
- **economic duress** – also known as business compulsion; wrongful threats of economic harm or financial ruin which force a party to enter into a contract.
- **Electronic Communication Privacy Act** – a federal statute that makes it a crime to intercept certain electronic communications.
- **employee** – a person who is employed to render services and who remains under the control of another in performing those services.
- **employer** – one who hires another to render services and who controls the manner in which those services are performed.
- **employment at-will -** where an employee is hired for an indefinite period and there is no contract or no contract provision limiting the circumstances by which the employment relationship can be terminated, then the employee can be discharged at any time, with no warning, notice, or explanation, for no reason or cause, for no good reason or cause.
- **employment by estoppel** – also called ostensible employment; created when one person either intentionally or carelessly creates the appearance that another person is his or her employee
- **Ethical Egoism** – the ethical theory that maintains that morality consists of advancing one's own long-term self-interest but in a rational, prudent, and self-enlightened manner.
- **Ethical Relativism** – the ethical theory that maintains that what a society believes is right for that society is the moral standard for that society.
- **ethics** – the branch of philosophy, consisting of ethical theories and principles, that one uses to reason to moral conclusions.

- **extrinsic values** – also called instrumental values; something good not in-and-of-itself but because, for example, money, it is a means or instrument to produce something else of value.
- **flawed product** – a defective product pursuant to strict liability in tort law when a product does not meet the manufacturer's own standards for that type of product.
- **fiduciary** - a legally recognized relationship of trust and confidence, for example in the principal-agency relationship, the breach of which is treated as fraud.
- **fraud** – the civil wrong encompassing intentional misrepresentation, also known as deceit, which is an intentional tort, negligent misrepresentation, and innocent misrepresentation.
- **fraud in the *factum*** – also called real fraud; when a misrepresentation causes a person to sign a negotiable instrument or contract or other legal document with neither the knowledge of its character nor its essential terms.
- **guests** – people who come upon the landowner's land for the primary benefit of themselves and not the landowner.
- **impact rule** – pursuant to negligent infliction of emotional distress law the requirement that the victim sustain some type of physical impact to recover emotional distress damages.
- **independent contractor** – a person who renders services in the course of an independent occupation.
- **injunction** – an order from a judge commanding a defendant to stop doing a wrongful act.
- **intentional infliction of emotional distress** – the intentional tort which arises when a defendant purposefully acts in an extreme, outrageous, and atrocious manner and thereby causes the plaintiff to suffer severe emotional distress.
- **intentional interference with contractual or business relations** – the intentional tort which arises when a defendant intentionally, knowingly, and improperly interferes with the contract, business relationship, or business expectancy of another.
- **intentional tort** – a legal wrong committed when a person or his or her property is purposefully invaded or harmed by another.
- **intrinsic values** – something good in-and-of-itself, such as happiness, without the need of explanation or justification or the need to be used as a means to produce something else of value.
- **intrusion –** one of the components of the intentional tort of invasion of privacy based on an impermissible intrusion into a person's solitude, seclusion or private place, sphere, or affairs.
- **invasion of privacy** – the intentional tort of purposefully intruding on or unduly publicizing the private life of a person.
- **joint and several liability** – the legal doctrine that holds that when there are more than one defendant who have caused the plaintiff's damages, they are equally responsible for paying the judgment, regardless of their percentage of fault.
- **judge** – the primary court officer, whose function is to preside over and manage trials.
- **judicial power** - a court's power of adjudication, judicial review, and statutory interpretation; in the U.S. Constitution, the power vested in the U.S. Supreme Court and other such "inferior" courts as Congress deems to establish.
- **jurisdiction** – the original authority of a court to hear a case.
- **jurisdiction over the subject matter** – when a case falls within a court's general, special, limited, or monetary jurisdiction.

- **jury** – the body of citizens sworn by the court to decide questions of fact and to render a verdict in a trial.
- **Kantian ethics** – the ethical philosophy of the German philosopher, Immanuel Kant, whose supreme ethical principle, the Categorical Imperative, applied a formal test to an action itself, as opposed to its consequences, in determining the action's morality.
- **Last Resort** – an ethical principle which sets forth the conditions under which one has a moral duty to act even though there is no legal duty to do so.
- **law** – the entire body of principles that govern conduct and which can be enforced by the courts or other government tribunals.
- **legal reasoning** – process of critical legal thinking that judges use to analyze and resolve a case.
- **legislative power** – the power of the U.S. Congress and the state legislatures to promulgate statutory laws.
- **libel** – written defamation.
- **libel *per se*** – a statement is defamatory on its face without the need for any extrinsic facts or explanation.
- **liber *per quod*** – when a statement is not defamatory on its fact and thus other additional facts are necessary to supply the defamatory meaning.
- **liquidated damages** – an explicit provision in a contract which fixes the amount of damages to be recovered if one party breaches the contract.
- **liquidation** – in partnership law, also known as winding up, when all partnership affairs are settled, and which ultimately leads to the partnership's termination.
- **malicious prosecution** – also called wrongful institution of legal proceedings; an intentional tort occurring when a private party wrongfully institutes civil or criminal proceedings against a party.
- **malpractice** – negligence law imposed on members of a profession, which typically requires the use of expert witnesses to explicate the pertinent standard of care.
- **market share liability** – legal doctrine that holds that damages to an injured person caused by a defective product must be apportioned based on the market share of the manufacturers who made the product when the victim cannot ascertain the exact source of the product.
- **merchant's protection privilege** – a privilege granted under the common law and statutes to protect merchants who detain a suspected shoplifter and make an investigation in a reasonable manner.
- **misfeasance** – acting in an illegal manner and violating either the civil or criminal law.
- **morals or morality** – the ethically derived conclusion as to what is good or bad or right or wrong.
- **negligence** – the name given to a civil unintentional tort lawsuit against a person for acting in unreasonable manner; also conduct which falls below the standard of care of the reasonable prudent person.
- **negligence *per se*** – the breach of a legal duty of due care which is established by a statute.
- **negligent infliction of emotional distress** – the legal wrong of carelessly causing mental anguish, usually requiring some impact on the person of the plaintiff.
- **negligent hiring** – typically based on the employer's failure to investigate or failure to do a careful investigation on the background of the employee.
- **negligent supervision** – also called negligent retention; based on the employer carelessly placing and keeping the employee in a position, or carelessly supervising the employee,

where the employers knows or should know that the employee could cause harm to a third party.

- **nominal damages** – token damages awarded when there is a breach of contract but no real loss.
- **nonfeasance** – not acting; and the general rule that holds that there is no legal liability for not acting.
- **personal property** - generally is property which is moveable and not affixed to the land; can be tangible, meaning generally that it can be seen and touched, such as a furniture, or intangible, meaning generally that it exists as a right or idea, such as a patent.
- **philosophy** – the study of thought and conduct, including the fields of ethics, logic, and metaphysics (the ultimate reality).
- **police power** – the sovereign authority that a state legislative body has to promulgate laws to promote and protect the health, safety, and welfare of the citizens and residents of a state.
- **principal** – in agency law, a person who retains another, called an agent, to represent the principal, to stand in the principal's place, in order to bring about contractual relations.
- **privity**– the existence of a contractual relationship between parties.
- **precedent** – in common law systems when a case is decided the law in the case is to be applied to future cases with the same or similar facts, thereby bringing consistency and predictability to common law legal systems.
- **premises liability** – the area of negligence law dealing with the liability of landowners to people who come upon their property.
- **preponderance of the evidence** – the standard burden of proof in a civil case.
- **private law** – law dealing with the legal problems, relations, and interests of private individuals.
- **proximate causation** – also known as proximate cause and legal causation; the legal doctrine that holds that even a carelessly acting defendant is not liable for the remote, unusual, and unforeseeable consequences of his or her wrongful act; rather, the defendant is liable only for the reasonably foreseeable consequences.
- **public law** – law affecting the people as a whole; law intended to serve the societal interest as well as to achieve justice.
- **public policy** – actions as determined by the high court of a state that promote and protect the health, safety, and welfare of the people of that state.
- **public policy doctrine** - when an employee, even an at-will employee, cannot be discharged for engaging in an activity that public policy encourages, or conversely for not engaging in an activity that public policy discourages.
- **publication** – in defamation law the required element of communication of the defamatory statement to a third party
- **qualified privilege** – also known as the conditional privilege; a defense to a defamation lawsuit if the statement though defamatory is made for a proper purpose and in a proper manner by a person who has an interest in the subject matter or a duty to communicate and to a person who has a corresponding interest or duty.
- **ratification** – in contract law, when a minor upon reaching the age of majority approves a contract made while a minor; in agency law, when a principal accepts the benefits of an unauthorized contract made by his or her purported authorized agent, thereby authorizing the contract.
- **real property** - generally considered to be land and the structures and improvements constructed upon it.

- **"reasonably prudent person" standard** – the common law standard and duty pursuant to negligence law
- **regulatory law** – law in the form of rules and regulations made by federal and state administrative agencies.
- **reliance damages** – damages which compensate the aggrieved party for any expenditure made in reliance on a contract that was subsequently breached; the purpose is to return the aggrieved party to the position he or she was in before the contract was formed.
- **rescission** – an order from a judge canceling a contract.
- ***res ipsa loquitur*** – "the thing speaks for itself"; the legal doctrine that holds that the fact that a particular injury has occurred may in and of itself establish the breach of duty element to negligence.
- ***respondeat superior*** – "let the master answer for the wrongs of the servant"; the legal principle that holds that the employer is responsible for the torts committed by the employer's employees acting within the course and scope of their employment.
- **scienter** – the requisite "evil mind" or wrongful intent needed for certain civil and criminal wrongs, such as common law fraud and securities fraud.
- **scope of employment** - when an employee acts within the normal course of his or her duties.
- **self-defense** – the use of force reasonably necessary to protect oneself or one's property from attack or harm.
- **slander** – spoken defamation
- **slander *per se*** - slander *per se* means that damage to the plaintiff's reputation is presumed; the four slander *per se* categories involve defamatory statements that: 1) a person is guilty of a serious crime of moral turpitude (and not a minor offense); 2) adversely affect a person's profession, business, or trade; 3) impute a loathsome disease to a person; and 4) historically impute that an unmarried woman is unchaste..
- **social benefit corporation** – a special type of corporation with a public benefit, which is for-profit and has shareholders, but where the board of directors *must* when making business decisions consider the interest of stakeholders and not just the shareholders and also must fulfill the public benefit.
- **social responsibility** – the doctrine that holds that a person or business should contribute to charities and take an active part in community and civic affairs; in business, typically called "corporate social responsibility."
- **stakeholders** – also at times called constituent groups; those groups, such as shareholders, employees, consumers, suppliers and distributors, local communities, and society as a whole, that have a stake in the decision-making of a business, typically a corporation.
- ***stare decisis*** – Latin for "let the decision stand"; in common law systems, the doctrine that a prior case will serve as a precedent to decide future cases with the same or similar facts.
- **state supreme court** – the high court in the state court system.
- **Statutes of Frauds** – state statutes which requires that certain types of contracts be evidenced by a writing.
- **Statutes of Limitations** – state statutes which set forth the period of time in which a law suit must be instituted.
- **Statutes of Repose** – state statutes which set forth the time period in which a products liability lawsuit must be instituted against a manufacturer or seller.
- **statutory interpretation** – the power and role of a court to interpret the meaning of a statute.

- **statutory law** – law enacted by legislative bodies, for example, the United States Congress and state legislatures, as well as county and municipal ordinances and codes.
- **statutory process** – the power that legislative bodies have as well as the processes they use to enact law.
- **strict liability in tort for products** – modern common law doctrine holding manufacturers and sellers of defective products liable without fault for harms caused.
- **"substantial factor" test** – the test used in negligence law in a multiple causation case to determine if the defendant's conduct caused the injury or harm to the plaintiff.
- **sustainability** – as a "means" thought of as environmental responsibility; and as an "ends" thought of as the objective of a business to achieve long-term financial success; attained by the business acting in a legal, moral, and socially as well as environmentally responsible manner.
- **tort** – a civil wrong; a wrongful act against a person or his or her property for which a legal cause of action may be brought.
- **trade secret** – information that is legally protected by federal or state trade secret law, particularly the Uniform Trade Secret Act on the state level.
- **transferred intent** – usually found in assault and battery cases when the defendant's intent is to harm one person, but the defendant in fact harms another who then can sue for the intentional tort.
- **trespass to chattels** – trespass to personal property as opposed to real property.
- **trespass to land** – the intentional tort which arises when a person, called a trespasser, purposefully and physically invades another's land or real property.
- **United States Constitution** – the "supreme law of the land"; the document that creates the government and provides individual rights in the Bill of Rights.
- **United States Courts of Appeals** – intermediate federal courts in the United States, possessing appellate jurisdiction only.
- **United States District Courts** – federal courts of original jurisdiction in the United States
- **United States Supreme Court** – the highest court in the United States, possessing both original and appellate jurisdiction.
- **Utilitarianism** – the ethical theory that maintains that morality is based on consequences and that holds that an action is moral if it produces the greatest amount of good for the greatest number of people.
- **values** – things that possess worth either intrinsically (in and of themselves, such as happiness) or instrumentally (because they are the means to obtain something else of value, such as money).
- **vicarious liability** – the legal principle which holds that an employer is indirectly liable for the wrongs committed by the employer's employees acting within the course and scope of their employment, regardless of the employer's fault.
- **waiver** – knowingly and voluntarily giving up a legal right
- **whistleblowing** – the attempt by people in an organization to disclose wrongdoing by their organization and/or their fellow employees.
- **whistleblowers** – people, often employees, who disclose wrongdoing by their companies or organizations, usually to government regulators, but also to the media.
- **Whistleblower Protection Acts** – federal and state statutes that provide protection to employees wrongfully discharged for disclosing to government agencies legal wrongdoing on the part of their employers but in conformity with the requirements of the various statutes.

BIBLIOGRAPHY

- *Acosta v. Scott Labor LLC,* 377 F. Supp. 2d 647 (District Court for the Northern District of Illinois 2005).
- *Acuff v. IBP, Inc.*, 77 F. Supp. 2d 914 (1999).
- *Addison v. City of Baker City*, 2017 U.S. Dist. LEXIS 101146 (District Court for the District of Oregon 2017).
- *Agency for Health Care Administration v. Associated Industries of Florida, Inc.*, 678 So.2d 1239 (Florida Supreme Court 1996).
- *Ali v. Douglas Cable Communications*, 929 F. Supp. 1362 (District Court for the District of Kansas 1996).
- *Alicia v.* Gorilla Ladder Co., 119 N.Y.S. 3d 58 (Supreme Court of New York, Appellate Division 2020).
- *Allstate Insurance Co. v. Ginsburg*, 863 So.2d 156 (Florida Supreme Court 2003).
- *Alford v. Martin & Gass, Inc.*, 391 Fed. Appx. 296 (Fourth Circuit Court of Appeals 2010).
- *American Auto. Auction, Inc. v. Titsworth*, 30 S.W.2d 499 (Arkansas Supreme Court 1987).
- *Anand Venkatrman v. Allegis Group, Inc.*, 2015 U.S. Dist. LEXIS 122409 (District Court for the District of Maryland 2015).
- *Anicich v. Home Depot USA Inc.*, 852 F.3d 643 (Seventh Circuit Court of Appeals 2017).
- *Armstrong v. H & C Communications, Inc.*, 575 So.2d 280 (Florida District Court of Appeal 1991).
- *Audio-Visual Group, LLC v. Christopher Green*, 2014 U.S. Dist. LEXIS 25413 (District Court for the Eastern District 2014).
- *Baggs, v. Eagle-Picher Industries*, Inc., 957 F.2d 268 (Sixth Circuit Court of Appeals 1992).
- *Basic Energy Services, L.P. v. Petroleum resource Management, Corp.* 343 P.3d 783 (Wyoming Supreme Court 2015).
- Baik, Jessica and Caldwell, Richard Jr. (2020). Rumberger and Kirk. *Negligence Per Se*. Retrieved April 16, 2020 from: jdsupra.com/legalnews/negligence-per-se-79300.
- *Bell, IV. v. Geraldine, et. al.* (Ninth Circuit Court of Appeals 2003).
- Boeschen, Coulter (2020a). All Law. *"Failure to Warn" in a Defective Product Case*. Retrieved April 28, 2020 from: alllaw.com/articles/nolo/personal-injury/failure-to-warn-defective-product-case.html.
- Boeschen, Coulter (2020). All Law. *Premises Liability – Injury Law Overview*. Retrieved April 26, 2020 from: alllaw.com.articles/nolo/personal-injury/premises-liability-overview.html.
- Boryga, Andrew (October 29, 2019). Woman files suit against Tesla Motors after husband's death. *Sun-Sentinel*, pp. 1B, 5B.
- *Bourgeois v. Allstate Ins. Co.*, 820 So.2d 1132 (Louisiana Court of Appeals 2002).
- *Brenden v. City of Billings*, 2020 MT 72 (Supreme Court of Montana 2020).

- *Brian A. Mastro v. Potomac Electric Power Company*, 447 F.3d 843 (Court of Appeals for the District of Columbia 2006).
- *Briggs v. Finley*, 631 N.E.2d 959 (Indiana Court of Appeals 1994).
- *Brodkin v. Novant Health, Inc*., 824 S.E.2d 868 (North Carolina Court of Appeals 2019).
- *Brown v. Kourentsos,* 2016 U.S. Dist. LEXIS 77727; No. 15 C 11076 (N.D. Ill. 2016).
- California Civil Jury Instructions (2017). *Failure to Warn – Essential Factual Elements*. Retrieved April 28, 2020 from: justia.com/trials-litigation/docs/1200/1205.
- *Cameo, Inc. v. Gedicke*, 724 A.2d 783 (Supreme Court of New Jersey1999).
- Campbell, Regina (June 26, 2019). Florida Business Litigation: What Constitutes Tortious Interference. *The Campbell Law Group, P.A.* Retrieved March 4, 2020 from: thecampbelllawgroup.com/tortious-interference-2.
- *Cape Publications, Inc. v. Reakes*, 840 So.2d 277 (Florida Court of Appeals 2003).
- *Carly Singer v. Colony Insurance Company*, 147 F. Supp. 3d 1369 (District Court for the Southern District of Florida 2015).
- *Carnegay v. Wal-Mart Stores*, 2020 Ga. App. LEXIS 63 (Georgia Court of Appeals 2020).
- *Carrington v. Carolina Day Sch., Inc*., 837 S.E. 383 (North Carolina Court of Appeals 2020).
- *Carr v. Wegmans Food Mkts, Inc*., 2020 NY App. Div. LEXIS 2129 (Supreme Court of New York, Appellate Division, 2020)
- Cassel, James (February 17, 2020). Is doing well doing good? *Miami Herald*, Business Monday, p. 15G.
- Cavico, Frank J. (2014). *Corporate Social Responsibility and Leadership*. Davie, Florida: ILEAD Academy, LLC.
- Cavico, Frank J. (2003). The Tort of Intentional Infliction of Emotional Distress in the Private Employment Sector. *Hofstra Labor and Employment Law Journal*, Vol. 21, No. 1, pp. 109-182.
- Cavico, Frank J. (2002). The Tort of Intentional Interference with Contract and Contractual Relations in the At-Will Employment Context. *University of Detroit-Mercy Law Review*, Vol. 79, No. 4, pp. 503-35
- Cavico, Frank J. (1999). Defamation in the Private Sector: The Libelous and Slanderous Employer. *Dayton Law Review*, Vol. 24, No. 3, pp. 405-489.
- Cavico, Frank J. (Winter 1997). Fraudulent, Negligent, and Innocent Misrepresentation in the Employment Context: The Deceitful, Careless, and Thoughtless Employer. *Campbell Law Review*, Vol. 20, pp. 1-90.
- Cavico, Frank J. and Mujtaba, Bahaudin G. (2020). *Business Law for the Entrepreneur and Manager* (Fourth Edition). Davie, Florida: ILEAD Academy, LLC.
- Cavico, Frank J. and Mujtaba, Bahaudin G. (2019). Defamation by Libel and Slander in the Workplace and Recommendations to Avoid Legal Liability. *Public Organization Review*. Available online at: https://doi.org/10.1007/s1115-018-0424-8.
- Cavico, Frank J. and Mujtaba, Bahaudin G. (2016). *Developing a Legal, Ethical, and Socially Responsible Mindset for Sustainable Leadership*. Davie, Florida: ILEAD Academy, LLC.
- Cavico, Frank J. and Mujtaba, Bahaudin G. (2014). *Legal Challenges for the Global Manager and Entrepreneur* (Second Edition). Dubuque, Iowa: Kendall Hunt Publishing Company.

- Cavico, Frank J. and Mujtaba, Bahaudin G. (2016). The Intentional Tort of Invasion of Privacy in the Private Employment Sector. *International Journal of Business and Law Research*, Vol. 4, No. 3, pp. 37-57.
- Cavico, Frank J., Mujtaba, Bahaudin G., Lawrence, Eleanor, and Muffler, Steven (2018). Examining the Efficacy of the Common Law Tort of Intentional Infliction of Emotional Distress and Bullying in the Employment Relationship. *Business Ethics and Leadership Journal*, Vol. 2, No. 3, pp. 14-31.
- Cavico, Frank J., Mujtaba, Bahaudin G., Lawrence, Eleanor, and Muffler, Steven (2015). Personality Tests in Employment: A Continuing Legal, Ethical, and Practical Quandary. *Advances in Social Sciences Research Journal*. Vol. 2, No. 3, pp. 60-84.
- Cavico, Frank J., Mujtaba, Bahaudin G., Samuel, Marissa, and Muffler, Stephen (2016). The Tort of Negligence in Employment Hiring, Supervision, and Retention. *American Journal of Business and Society*, Vol. 1, No. 4, pp. 205-222.
- Cavico, Frank J. Mujtaba, Bahaudin G., and Muffler, Stephen (2018). The Duty of Loyalty in the Employment Relationship: Legal Analysis and Recommendations for Employers and Workers. *Journal of Legal, Ethical, and Regulatory Issues*, Vol. 21, No. 3, pp. 1-27.
- Cavico, F.J., Mujtaba, B.G., Muffler, S.C., and Samuel, M. (2013). Social Media and Employment At-Will: Tort Law and Practical Considerations for Employees, Managers, and Organizations. *Journal of New Media and Mass Communication*, Vol. 11, pp. 25-41.
- Cavico, F.J., Mujtaba, B.G., Muffler, S.C., and Samuel, M. (2013). Social Media and the Workplace: Legal, Ethical, and Practical Considerations for Management. *Journal of Law, Policy, and Globalization*, Vol. 12(1), pp. 1-46.
- Cavico, F.J., Mujtaba, B.G., Nonet, G., Rimanoczy, I., and Samuel, M. (2015). Developing a Legal, Ethical, and Socially Responsible Mindset for Business Leadership (2015). *Advances in Social Sciences Research Journal*, Vol. 2, No. 6, pp. 9-26.
- Cavico, Frank J., Mujtaba, Bahaudin G., Muffler, Stephen, Samuel, Marissa, and Polito, Nicholas M. (2018). Manufacturer, Supermarket, and Grocer Liability for Contaminated Food and Beverages Due to Negligence, Warranty, and Liability Laws. *Economy*, Vol. 5, No. 1, pp. 17-39.
- Cavico, Frank J., Mujtaba, Bahaudin G., Muffler, Stephen, Samuel, Marissa, and Polito, Nicholas M. (2017). Restaurant Liability for Contaminated Food and Beverages Pursuant to Negligence, Warranty, and Strict Liability Law. *Global Journal of Social Science Studies*, Vol. 3, No. 2, pp. 63-100.
- Clark, Margaret M. (February 27, 2019). How to Address Negligent Hiring Concerns. *Society for Human Resource Management*. Retrieved June 15, 2020 from: https://www.shrm.org/hr-today/news/hr-magazine/spring2019.
- *Colgate-Palmolive Company v. Tandem Industries*, 2012 U.S. Dist. LEXIS 11290 (Court of Appeals for the Third Circuit 2012).
- *Colucci v. T-Mobile USA, Inc.* 48 Cal. App. 5th 442 (California Court of Appeals 2020).
- *Comet Mgmt. Co. v. Wooten*, 2020 N.J. Super. LEXIS 390 (Superior Court of New Jersey, Appellate Division 2020).
- *Conklin v. Laxen*, 2020 N.Y. App. Div. LEXIS 979 (New York Court of Appeals 2020).
- *Courtney R. Robbins v. The Trustees of Indiana University and Clarian Health Partners, Inc.*, 45 N.E.3d 1 (Indiana Court of Appeals 2015).
- *Corian Branyan v. Southwest Airlines Co.*, 105 F. Supp.3d 120 (District Court for the District of Massachusetts 2015).

- Cornell Law School (2020). Legal Information Institute. *Ultrahazardous Activity*. Retrieved April 23, 2020 from: https://www.law.cornell.edu/wex/ultrahazardous-activity.
- *Corns v. Good Samaritan Hosp. Med. Ctr.*, 2014 N.Y. Misc. LEXIS 5485 (Supreme Court of New York 2014).
- *Creditwatch, Inc. v. Jackson*, 157 S.W.3d 814 (Texas Supreme Court 2005).
- *C.R. Eng. V. Swift Transp. Co.*, 437 P.3d 343 (Supreme Court of Utah 2019).
- *Cruz v. English Nanny & Governess School, Inc. et. al.*, 2017 Ohio App. LEXIS 2231; 2017 Ohio 4176 (Ct. App. 2017).
- *CSX Transportation Inc. v. Pyramid Stone Industries, Inc.*, 293 Fed. Appx. 754 (Court of Appeals for the Eleventh Circuit 2008).
- *Curtwright v. Ray*, 1991 U.S. District LEXIS 12429 (District Court for the District of Kansas 1991).
- *Cynthia Hyland v. Ratheon Technical Services Co.* (Supreme Court of Virginia 2009); retrieved November 15, 2019 from: caselaw.findlaw.com.
- *Daniel C. Murray v. United Food and Commercial Workers International Union, Local 400*, 289 F.3d 297; 2002 U.S. App. LEXIS 9057 (Court of Appeals for the Fourth Circuit 2002).
- *Danielle Iorio v. Check City Partnership, LLC*, (2015 Nev. LEXIS 658 (Supreme Court of Nevada 2015).
- *Dawn Hahn v. Cynthia Loch, L.P.N., Lehigh Family Practice Associates, LLC, and Leroy Hahn,* 2016 Pa. Supeer LEXIS 2483 (Superior Court of Pennsylvania 2016).
- *DeLucia, et al. v. Great Stuff, Inc., et al.*, 2015 Del. Super. LEXIS 474 (2015).
- *DeLury v. Kretchner*, 322 N.Y.S. 2d 517 (New York State Superior Court 1971).
- *Denton v. Universal AM-Can, LTD*, No. 2015 L 1727 (Illinois Court of Appeals 2019).
- Devoe, Garrath A. (November 2019). Frolicking Away: Texas courts shield employers from *respondeat superior* claims. *Texas Bar Journal*, Vol. 82, No. 10, pp.786-87.
- *Devoe v. Am Eagle Energy Corp.*, 2020 ND 23 (Supreme Court of North Dakota 2020).
- *Diana Retuerto v. Berea Moving Storage and Logistics*, 38 N.E.3d 392 (Court of Appeals of Ohio 2015).
- *Doe v. B.P.S. Guard Services, Inc.*, 945 F. 2d 1422 (Eighth Circuit Court of Appeals 1991).
- *Doe v. Centennial Indep. Sch. Dist. No. 12*, 2004 Minn. App. LEXIS 1427 (Minnesota Court of Appeals 2004).
- *Doe v. Hotchkiss Sch.*, 2019 U.S. Dist. LEXIS 37483 (District Court for the District of Connecticut 2019).
- *Doe v. John Hopkins Health System Corp.* (District Court for the District of Maryland 2017); retrieved November 15, 2019 from: law.justia.com/cases/federal/district-court/Maryland.
- *Doe v. Yackulic*, 2019 U.S. Dist. LEXIS 48064 (District Court for the Eastern District of Texas 2019).
- *Dokes v. Safeway, Inc.*, 2018 U.S. Dist. LEXIS 52341 (District Court for the Eastern District of California 2018).
- *Donevant v. Town of Surfside Beach*, 811 S.E.2d 744 (Supreme Court of South Carolina 2018).
- *Dunn v. Garfield Beach CVS, LLC*, 2020 Cal. App. LEXIS 809 (California Court of Appeals 2020).
- *Drew v. Pac. Life Ins. Co.*, 2019 Utah App. 125 (Utah Court of Appeals 2019).

- *EEOC v. Day & Zimmerman NPS Inc*., 2017 U.S. Dist. LEXIS 133918 (District Court for the District of Connecticut 2017).
- *Elgin v. St. Louis Coca Cola Bottling Co.*, 2005 U.S. District LEXIS 28976 (District Court for the Eastern District of Missouri 2005).
- *Ellenberg v. Pinkerton's, Inc.* 202 S.E.2d 701 (Georgia Court of Appeals 1973).
- England, Deborah C. (2020). Assault Charges in the Workplace. *Criminal Defense Lawyer*. Retrieved March 14, 2020 from: http://www.criminaldefenselawyer.com/resources/criminal-defense/violent-crime/assault-charge-workplace.htm.
- *Feasel v. Tracker Marine LLC*, 460 P.3d 145 (Utah Court of Appeals 2020).
- Feeley, Jef (June 25, 2020). Missouri court cuts J&J talc verdict to $2.1 billion. *Sun-Sentinel*, p. 2A.
- *Fessler v. IBM*, 2020 U.S. App. LEXIS 15481 (Fourth Circuit Court of Appeals 2020).
- Find Law (2019). *What is Comparative Negligence*? Retrieved June 9, 2020 from: https://www.findlaw.com/what-is-comparative-negligence.
- Find Law (2020). *Property Owners' Legal Duty to Prevent Injury*. Retrieved April 26, 2020 from: www.realestate.findlaw.com/owning-a-home/property-owners-legal-duty-to-prevent-injury.
- *Fisher v. Nissan N. Am., Inc*., 2020 U.S. App. LEXIS 5986 (Sixth Circuit Court of Appeals 2020).
- *Flores v. Wal-Mart Stores, Tex., LLC*, 2020 U.S. Dist. LEXIS 7402 (District Court for the Western District of Texas 2020).
- *Florida Evergreen Foliage v. E.I. Dupont de Nemours & Co*., 133 F. Supp. 2d 1271 (District Court for the Southern District of Florida 2001).
- *Frank Samuels v. James D. Tschechtelin*, 763 A.2d 209; 2000 Md. App. LEXIS 169 (Maryland Court of Appeals 2000).
- *Fraser v. Nationwide Mutual Insurance Co.*, 352 F.3d 107 (Third Circuit Court of Appeals 2004).
- *Futch v. McAlister Towing, Inc*., 518 S.E.2d 591 (Supreme Court of South Carolina 1999).
- *Fry v. IBP, Inc*., 15 F. Supp. 2d 1032 (District Court for the District of Kansas 1998).
- *Gaelotti v. International Union of Operating Engineers Local No. 3*, 48 Cal. App. 5th 850 (California Court of Appeals 2020).
- *Garcia v. Duffy*, 492 So.2d 435 (Florida Court of Appeals1986).
- *George H. Larson v. United Natural Foods West Inc*., 2014 Ariz. App. LEXIS 180 (Arizona Court of Appeals 2014).
- *Gillespie v. City of Battle Creek*, 100 F. Supp. 3d 623, 628 (District Court for the Western District of Michigan 2015).
- *Gilmore v. Enogex, Inc.*, 878 P.2d 360 (Oklahoma Supreme Court 1994).
- Goguen, David (2020). Negligent Infliction of Emotional Distress Claims (NIED). *Alllaw.com*. Retrieved January 27, 2020 from: https://www.alllaw.com/articles/nolo/personal-injury/negligent-infliction-emotional-distress.html.
- *Gonzalez v. City of Chicago,* 2018 U.S. Dist. LEXIS 55141 (District Court for the Northern District of Illinois 2018).
- *Great Plains Otter Tail, LLC v. Pro-Environmental, Inc*., 953 F.3d 541 (Eight Circuit Court of Appeals 2020).

- *Gresham v. Safeway, Inc.* (District Court for the District of Oregon 2011); retrieved November 15, 2019 from: casemine.com/judgment/US.
- *Grost M.D. vs. United States,* 2015 U.S. Dist. LEXIS 112590 (District Court for the Western District of Texas 2015).
- *Gracey v. Eaker*, 747 So.2d 475 (Florida District Court of Appeal 1999).
- *Greenberg v. Alta Healthcare System, LLC*, 2004 Cal. App. LEXIS 840 (California Court of Appeals 2004).
- *Gregor v. Kleiser,* 443 N.E.2d 1162 (Illinois Court of Appeals 1982).
- *Grzan v. Charter Hosp. of Nw. Ind.*, 702 N.E.2d 786 (Indiana Court of Appeals 1998).
- *Gupta V. Eli Global, LLC*, 2019 NCBC LEXIS 40 (Superior Court of North Carolina 2019).
- Guerin, Lisa (2020). Defamation Lawsuits: Do You Have a Case Against a Former Employer? *Nolo.com.* Retrieved March 23, 2020 from: www.nolo.com/legal-encyclopedia.
- *Guobadia v. Irowa*, 103 F. Supp. 3d 325 (District Court for the Eastern District of New York 2015).
- *Hahn v. OnBoard, LLC*, Justia U.S. Law, 2:2009cv03639-Document 84 (District Court for the District of New Jersey 2011).
- Hamblen, Katie (2020). Legal Match. *Shopkeepers Privilege Law*. Retrieved June 3, 2020 from: https://www.legalmatch.com/law-library-shopkeepers-privilege-law.
- *Hansen v. Bd. of Trs. of Hamilton Southeastern Sch. Corp.*, 551 F.3d 599 (Seventh Circuit Court of Appeals 2008).
- *Hansen v. SkyWest Airlines*, 844 F.3d 914 (Court of Appeals for the Tenth Circuit 2016).
- *Harley v. City of N.J. City*, 2017 U.S. Dist. LEXIS 98808 (District Court for the District of New Jersey 2017).
- *Herlihy v. Metro Museum of Art*, 1995 N.Y App. Div. LEXIS 10035 (Supreme Court of New York, Appellate Division 1995).
- *Holliday v. Fairbanks*, 2017 U.S. District LEXIS 105566 (District Court for the District of New Hampshire 2017).
- Hurtibise, Ron (October 19, 2018). Judge OKs jury in Royal Caribbean cruise case. *Sun-Sentinel*, pp. 6-7B.
- Hussein and Webber (2020). *Criminal Defense Articles: Defense of Property under Florida Law*. Retrieved June 4, 2020 from: https://www.husseinandwebber.com/case-work/criminal-defense-articles/use-force-defense-property.
- *Huston v. Brookpark Skateland Social Club, Inc.*, 2020 Ohio 1493 (Ohio Court of Appeals 2020).
- *Hyde v. K. B. Home, Inc.*, 355 Fed. Appx. 266 (Eleventh Circuit Court of Appeals 2009).
- Ibukun, Yinka (November 18, 2019). Lagos is Facing Its Bottle Problem. *Bloomberg Businessweek*, pp.18-20).
- *I.C.U. Investigations, Inc. v. Jones,* 780 So. 2d 685 (Alabama Supreme Court 2000).
- *Ifantides v. Wisniewski*, 2020 N.Y. App. Div. LEXIS 1518 (New York Court of Appeals 2020).
- *Interim Healthcare of Fort Wayne, Inc. v. Moyer*, 746 N.E.2d 429 (Indiana Court of Appeals 2001).
- *Inthalangsy v. Wal-Mart Stores Texas*, 2020 U.S. Dist. LEXIS 32962 (District Court for the Western District of Texas 2020).
- *ISS Action, Inc. v. Tutor Perini Corp.*, 2019 N.Y. App. Div. LEXIS 1551(Supreme Court of New York, App. Div.v2019

- *Jane Doe v. Bernabei & Wachtel, PLLC*, 116 A.3d 1262, (District of Columbia Court of Appeals 2015).
- *Jane Doe v. Walmart Stores, Inc*., No. G054660 (California Court of Appeals 2018).
- *Jennifer Pawlaczyk v. Besser Credit Union*, 2014 U.S. Dist. LEXIS 150027 (District Court for the Eastern District of Michigan 2014).
- *Jews for Jesus, Inc. v. Rapp*, 997 So.2d 1098 (Supreme Court of Florida 2008).
- Jones, Andrew Milam (February 2020). Employee Monitoring: An overview of technologies, treatment, and best practices. *Texas Bar Journal*, pp. 98-99.
- *Jones Express, Inc. v. Jackson*, 86 So. 3d 298 (Alabama Supreme Court 2010).
- *Joseph v. Dillard's, Inc*. (District Court for the District of Arizona 2009); retrieved November 15, 2019 from: scholar.google.com/scholar_case.
- *Juarez v. Boy Scotts of America, Inc.*, 97 Cal. Rptr. 2d 12 (California Court of Appeals 2000).
- Justia.com (2020). Laws & Legal Resources. *Comparative & Contributory Negligence*. Retrieved June 9, 2020 from: https://www.justia.com/injury/negligence-theory/comparative-contributory-negligence.
- *Kaiser v. Raoul's Restaurant Corp*., 2008 N.Y. Misc. LEXIS 8854 (Supreme Court of New York 2008).
- *Kalmanson v. Lockett*, 848 So.2d 374 (Florida Court of Appeals 2003).
- *Kamdem-Ouaffo v. Calchem Corp*., 2018 U.S. Dist. LEXIS 157265 (District Court for the Southern District of New York 2018).
- *Kelley v. Schlumberger Tech. Corp*., 849 F. 2d 41(First Circuit Court of Appeals1988).
- Keeton, W. Page, Dobbs, Dan B., Keeton, Robert E, and Owen, David G. (1984). *Prosser and Keeton on Torts* (Hornbook Series 5th Edition). West Publishing Company: St. Paul, Minnesota.
- *K-Mart Corp. v. Trotti,* 677 S.W.2d 632 (Texas Court of Appeals 1984).
- *Konkle v. Henson*, 672 N.E.2d 450 (Indiana Court of Appeals 1996).
- *Koutsouradis v. Delta Airlines, Inc*., 427 F.3d 1339 (Eleventh Circuit Court of Appeals 2005).
- *Kubler v. Heritage Automotive Group, Inc*., 2017 U.S. Dist. Lexis 187998 (District Court for the District of Vermont 2017).
- *Kush v. Lloyd*, 616 So.2d 348 (Florida Supreme Court 1992).
- *Laba v. Chicago Transit Authority*, U.S. Dist. LEXIS 4113 (District Court for the Northern District of Illinois 2016).
- *LaBozzo v. Brooks Bros*., 2002 N.Y. Misc. LEXIS 605 (Supreme Court of New York 2002).
- *Lankford v. City of Hobart*, 27 F. 3d 477(Tenth Circuit Court of Appeals 1994).
- *La Rocco v. Harley-Davidson Motor Corp*., 2020 U.S. Dist. LEXIS 71719 (District Court for the Middle District of Pennsylvania 2020).
- Law Shelf (2020). *Abnormally Dangerous Activities*. Retrieved April 23, 2020 from: http://lawshelf.com/coursewarecontentview/abnormally-dangerous-activities.
- *Lee v. West Kern Water Dist.*, 5 Cal. App. 5th 606 (California Court of Appeals 2016).
- Legal Aid at Work, San Francisco, CA. (2020). *Assault and Battery in the Workplace*. Retrieved March 14, 2020 from: http://legalaidatwork.org/factsheet/assault-and-battery-in-the-workplace.
- Legal Aid at Work, San Francisco, CA. (2020). *Fraud or Misrepresentation in the Workplace*. Retrieved April, 2020 from: http://legalaidatwork.org/factsheet/fraud-or-misrepresentation-in-the-workplace.

- Legal Match (2020). *Negligence Per Se Laws*. Retrieved April 16, 2020 from: www.legalmatch.com/law-library/article/negligence-per-se-laws.html.
- Legal Match (2020a). *Ultrahazardous Activity Liability*. Retrieved April 23, 2020 from: www.legalmatch.com/law-library/article/ultrahazardous-activity-liability.html.
- *Levi Wilson v. Scott Lamp, State of Iowa, Jessica Dorhout-Van Engen, and John Doe*, 142 F. Supp.3d 793 (District Court for the Northern District of Iowa 2015).
- *Levinson v. Citizens Nat'l Bank of Evansville*, 644 N.E.2d 1264 (Indiana Court of Appeals 1994).
- Lewitter, Jody (2020). Siegel, LeWitter & Malkani Law Firm. *Tell the Truth or Face the Consequences: Misrepresentations in Employment Law*. Retrieved April 2, 2020 from: si-employmentlaw.com/tell-the truth-or-face-the-consequences-misrepresentations-in-employment.law.html.
- *Liberti v. Walt Disney World*, 912 F. Supp. 1494 (District Court for the Middle District of Florida 1995).
- *Liberty Mutual Insurance Company v. Steadman*, 968 So. 2d 592 (Florida Court of Appeals 2007).
- *Lipsig v. Ramlawi*, 760 So.2d 170 (Florida Court of Appeals 2000).
- Lieu, Amy (July 13, 2018). Johnson & Johnson ordered to pay nearly $4.7B to 22 plaintiffs in talcum powder lawsuit. Fox News. Retrieved October 10, 2018 from: http://www.foxnews.com/health/2018/07/13/johnson-johnson.
- *L.M. v. Karlson*, 646 N.W.2d 537 (Minnesota Court of Appeals 2002).
- *Lora v. Ledo Pizza Sys*., 2017 U.S. Dist. LEXIS 118474 (District Court for the District of Maryland 2017).
- Lorenz and Lorenz (January 31, 2020). *What is Res Ipsa Loquitur*? Retrieved April 30, 2020 from: https://www.lorenzandlorenz.com/blog/what-is-res-ipsa-loquitur/.
- *Lorfing v. Gerdau Ameristeel U.S., Inc*., 2017 U.S. Dist. LEXIS 20575 (District Court for the Northern District of Texas 2017).
- *Lorzada v. Hobby Lobby Stores, Inc*., 2017 U.S. App. LEXIS 13820 (Court of Appeals for the Eleventh Circuit 2017).
- *Love v. Southern Bell Telephone & Telegraph Co*., 263 So. 2d 460 (Louisiana Court of Appeals 1972).
- *Malphurs v. Cooling Towers Systems, Inc.,* No. 17-10170, Unpublished Opinion (Eleventh Circuit 2017), 2017 U.S. App. LEXIS 18005 (2017).
- *Manswell v. Heavenly Miracle Acad. Servs*., 2017 U.S. Dist. LEXIS 136366 (District Court for the Eastern District of New York 2017).
- *Maremont v. Susan Fredman Designs Group, Ltd*., 2011 U.S. Dist. LEXIS 140446 (District Court for the Northern District of Illinois 2011).
- *Marez v. Lyft,* 48 Cal. App. 5th 569 (California Court of Appeals 2020).
- *Markovitch v. Panther Valley School District*, 2014 U.S. Dist. LEXIS 102172 (District Court for the Middle District of Pennsylvania 2014).
- *Marrs v. Marriot Corp*., 830 F. Supp. 274 (District Court for the District of Maryland 1992).
- *McClean v. Pine Eagle School District No. 61*, 194 F. Supp. 3d 1102 (District Court for the District of Oregon 2016).
- *McManus v. Auchincloss*, 353 P.3d 17, 271 Or. App. 765 (Oregon Court of Appeals 2015).
- *McMiller v. Precision Metal Products, Inc.*, 2015 U.S. Dist. Lexis 107785 (D. Conn. 2015).

- *McLaren v. Microsoft Corporation*, 1999 U.S. LEXIS 4103 (Texas Court of Appeals 1999).
- *Mems v. LaBryere*, 2019 Mo. App. LEXIS 809 (Missouri Court of Appeals 2019).
- *Meyer v. Shearson Lehman Bros*., 1995 N.Y. App. Div. LEXIS 537 (Supreme Court of New York, Appellate Division 1995).
- *Michael Stancombe v. New Process Steel LP*, 2016 U.S. App. LEXIS 10038 (Eleventh Circuit Court of Appeals 2016).
- *Molina v. City of Pasadena,* 2018 Texas App. LEXIS 6579 (Texas Court of Appeals 2018).
- Morrison, Laura (August 2, 2016). *Edwards, Kenny & Bray, LLP*. Employment Law Essentials: Negligent Misrepresentation – pitfalls for employers in the hiring process. Retrieved April 9, 2020 from: https://www/ekb.com/employment-law-essentials-negligent-misrepresentation.
- Mujtaba, B.G., and Cavico, F.J. (2013). Corporate Social Responsibility and Sustainability Model for Global Firms. *Journal of Leadership, Accountability, and Ethics*, Vol. 10, No. 1, pp. 58-76.
- Mujtaba, B. G., Cavico, F. J., Senatip, T., and Utantada, S. (2016). Sustainable Operational Management for Effective Leadership and Efficiency in the Modern Global Workplace. *International Journal of Recent Advances in Organizational Behavior and Decision Sciences*, Vol. 2, No. 1, pp. 673-696.
- *Nettles v. Pettway*, 2020 Alabama LEXIS 53 (Supreme Court of Alabama 2020).
- *New Jersey Statutes*: Section 2C: 3-6. Use of force in defense of premises or personal property (2020).
- *Numeric Analytics, LLC v. McCabe*, 161 F. Supp. 3d 3348 (District Court for the Eastern District of Pennsylvania 2016).
- *Oakley v. Flor-Shin, Inc*., 964 S.W.2d 438 (Kentucky Court of Appeals 1998).
- *Oliver v. Walmart Stores East, LP et al*., 2017 Conn. Super. Lexis 4268 (Superior Court of Connecticut 2017).
- *Owens v. Stifel Nicolaus & Company Inc.,* 2016 U.S. App. LEXIS 9726 (Court of Appeals for the Eleventh Circuit 2016).
- *Pace v. Baker-White*, 2020 U.S. Dist. LEXIS 4984 (District Court for the Eastern District of Pennsylvania 2020).
- *Painter v. Amerimex Drilling I, Ltd*., 561 S.W.3d 125 (Texas Supreme Court 2018).
- *Pearson v. Pilot Travel Ctrs., LLC*, 2020 IL App. 5th 180505 (Illinois Court of Appeals 2020).
- Peeler, Travis (2020). *Failure to Warn Lawsuit – Product Liability Law*. Retrieved April 28, 2020 from: https://www.legalmatch.com/law-library/article-failure-to-warn-lawsuit.html.
- *Peschel v. City of Missoula* (District Court for the District of Montana 2009); retrieved November 15, 2019 from: law.justia.com/cases/federal/district-courts.
- *Pietrylo v. Hillstone Restaurant Group*, 2009 U.S. Dist. LEXIS 88702 (District Court for the District of New Jersey 2009).
- *Porietis v. Tradesmen Int'l.*, 2017 U.S. Dist. LEXIS 92 (District Court for the District of Maine 2017).
- *Postrello v. Scottsdale Healthcare Hosps.,* 2018 U.S. Dist. LEXIS 19 (District Court for the District of Arizona 2018).
- *Priore v. New York Yankees,* 2003 N.Y. App. Div. LEXIS 6119 (Supreme Court of New York 2003).

- *Quon v. Arch Wireless Operating Company,* 529 F.3d 892 (Ninth Circuit Court of Appeals 2008).
- *Raleigh v. Performance Plumbing & Heating, Inc,* 130 P.3d 1011 (Colorado Supreme Court 2006).
- Ramey, Corinne (November 16-17, 2019). The Saga of Good Government. *Wall Street Journal*, p. B4.
- *Rausman v. Baugh*, 1998 N.Y. App. Div. LEXIS 12484 (Supreme Court of New York, Appellate Division 1998).
- *Redfearn v. Trader Joe's Co*., 230 Cal. Rptr. 3d 98 (California Court of Appeals 2018).
- *Reed v. Toyota Motor Credit Corp*., 459 P.3d 253 (Oregon Court of Appeals) 2020.
- *Regions Bank & Trust v. Stone Co. Skilled Nursing Facility, Inc.,* 49 S.W.3d 107 (Arkansas Supreme Court 2001).
- Resnick Law Group (2020). *Employment Fraud and Misrepresentation.* Retrieved April 2, 2020 from: thenjemploymentlawfirm.com/employment-fraud-and-misrepresentation.htm.
- *Restatement (Second) of Torts* (American Law Institute 1977).
- *Riggs Investment Management Corp. v. Columbia Partners, LLC*., 966 F. Supp. 1250 (District Court for the District of Columbia 1997).
- Rinaldo Law Group (2020). Categories of Guest in Premises Liability Law. Retrieved April 26, 2020 from: https://www.tampainjuryaccidentlaw.com/categories-of-guests-in-premises-liability-law.
- *Saine v. Comcast Cablevision of Ark., Inc.*, 345 Ark. 492 (Arkansas Supreme Court 2003).
- *Salazar v. Golden State Warriors*, 124 F. Supp. 2d 1155 (District Court for the Northern District of California 2000).
- *Saldana v. Kelsey-Hayes Co.*, 443 N.W. 2d 382 (Michigan Court of Appeals 1989).
- *Sandra Gaynor c. American Association of Nurse Anesthetists and Brent Sommers*, 2015 Ill. App. LEXIS 2969 (Illinois Court of Appeals 2015).
- Schawneberg, Robert (August 16, 2006). Suit over loft bed falls short. *Star-Ledger*, pp. 13, 16.
- *Shamrock Power Sales, LLC v. John Scherer*, U.S. Dist. LEXIS 133650 (District Court for the Southern District of New York 2015).
- *Shanks v. Calvin Walker and Doctor's Associates*, 116 F.Supp.2d 311 (District Court for the District of Connecticut 2000).
- *Sharon Diane Waltz v. Jonathan Wade Dunning*, 2014 U.S. Dist. LEXIS 178660 (District Court for the Northern District of Alabama 2015).
- *Silvas v. Harrie*, 2018 U.S. Dist. LEXIS 203479 (District Court for the Western District of Texas 2018).
- *Smith v. Datla*, 2017 N.J. Super. LEXIS 95 (Superior Court of New Jersey, Appellate Division 2017).
- *Smith v. Library Board of Homestead*, 2018 U.S. Dist. LEXIS 72778 (District Court for the Northern District of Alabama 2018).
- *Smyth v. Pillsbury Co.,* 914 F. Supp. 97 (District Court for the Eastern District of Pennsylvania 1996).
- *Souder v. Pendleton Detectives, Inc.*, 88 So. 2d 716 (Louisiana Court of Appeals 1952).
- *Spears v. Albertsons, Inc*., 848 So. 2d 1176 (Florida Court of Appeals 2003).
- *Spenser v. Health Force Inc.,* 107 P.3d 504 (New Mexico Supreme Court 2005).

- *State Farm Fire & Casualty Co. v. Compupay,* 654 So.2d 944 (Florida District Court of Appeal 1995).
- *Steven v. Piper*, 2020 Minn. App. LEXIS 286 (Minnesota Court of Appeals 2020).
- *Stockett v. Tolin*, 791 F. Supp. 1536 (District Court of Florida 1992).
- *Sunbelt Rentals, Inc. v. Santiago Victor*, 43 F. Supp.3d 1026 (District Court for the Northern District of California 2014).
- *Stepanovich v. Houchin,* 126 N.E.3d 45 (Indiana Court of Appeals 2019).
- Stimmel, Stimmel, & Roeser (2020), *Abuse of Process – The Basics and Practicalities,* Law Offices of Stimmel, Stimmel, & Roeser. Retrieved February 2. 2020 from: stimmel-law.com/en/articles/abuse-process-basics-and-practicalities.
- *Stuart C. Irby Company v. Brandon Tipton*, 796 F.3d 918 (Court of Appeals for the Eighth Circuit 2015).
- *Sullivan v. City of Frederick*, 2018 U.S. Dist. LEXIS 72778 (District Court for the District of Maryland 2018).
- *Techno Lite, Inc. v. Emcod, LLC*, 2020 Cal. App. LEXIS 41, 44 Cal. App. 5th (California Court of Appeals 2020).
- *Terpin v. AT&T Mobility, Inc*., 2020 U.S. Dist. LEXIS 31742 (District Court for the Central District of California 2020).
- *Texas Health Resources, Trumble Insurance Company, and Texas Health Presbyterian Hospital Dallas v. Nina Pham,* 2016 Tex. App. LEXIS 8336 (Texas Court of Appeals 2016).
- *Theriault v. Genesis Healthcare*, LLC, 2017 U.S. Dist. LEXIS 59598 (District Court for the District of Maine 2017).
- *Thompson v. Johnson County Community College*, 930 F. Supp. 501 (District Court for the District of Kansas 1996).
- *Thomas v. General Electric Co.*, 207 F. Supp. 792 (District Court for the Western District of Kentucky 1962).
- *Thomas v. Hospital Board of Directors of Lee County*, 41 So. 3d 246 (Florida Court of Appeals 2010).
- *Thomas v. Stars Entertainment, LLC,* No. 2: 15-cv-09239-CAS-AFM (C.D. Cal. 2017); 2016 U.S. Dist. Lexis 25472 (District Court for the Central District of California 2016).
- *Tison v. Alachua Straw Co*., 2020 U.S. Dist. LEXIS 39196 (District Court for the District of Alabama.
- *Trahanas v. Northwestern University*, 2017 U.S. Dist. LEXIS 104098 (District Court for the Northern District of Illinois 2017).
- *Turley v. Lowe's Home Ctrs*., 2020 U.S. Dist. LEXIS 19182 (District Court for the District of Kansas 2020).
- *TXI Transportation Co. v. Hughes*, 306 S.W.3d 230 (Texas Supreme Court 2010).
- Valencia, Nick and Sayers, Devon (July 21, 2017). Florida teens who recorded drowning man will not be charged in his death. *CNN.com.*
- *Vernars v. Young*, 539 F.2d 966 (Third Circuit Court of Appeals 1976).
- *Vernon v. Medical Management Associates of Margate, Inc.*, 912 F. Supp. 1549 (District Court for the Southern District of Florida 1996).
- *Viken Detection Corp. v. Videray Techs, Inc*., 2020 U.S. Dist. LEXIS 2138 (District Court for the District of Massachusetts).
- *Virginia Stringer v. Wal-Mart Stores, Inc.*, 151 S.W.3d 781; 2004 Ky. LEXIS 245 (Kentucky Supreme Court 2004).
- *Wait v. Ohio*, 2020 Ohio 2839 (Ohio Court of Claims 2020).

- *Walter v. Jet Aviation Flight Servs.*, 2017 U.S. Dist. LEXIS 119567 (District Court for the Southern District of Florida 2017).
- *Watkins v. L.M. Berry Co.*, 704 F.2d 577 (Eleventh Circuit Court of Appeals 1983).
- *Wheeler v. Home Depot U.S.A.*, 2017 U.S. Dist. LEXIS 41783 (District Court for the Southern District of California 2017).
- *Wideberg v. Tiffany & Co.* 1992 N.Y. Misc. LEXIS 538 (Supreme Court of New York 1992).
- *Williams v. Paris Las Vegas Operating Co.*, 2020 Nev. App. LEXIS 317 (Nevada Court of Appeals 2020).
- *Wilson v. New York*, 2017 U.S. Dist. LEXIS 10492 (District Court for the Eastern District of New York 2017).

INDEX

Biographies

Frank J. Cavico is a Professor of Law, Business Law, and Business Ethics. He has taught for over 40 years at the law school, university, and college level, most recently in the undergraduate business and MBA programs at the H. Wayne Huizenga College of Business and Entrepreneurship of Nova Southeastern University in Ft. Lauderdale, Florida, where he recently retired as a Professor Emeritus after 30 years of service, though he is still teaching at Nova Southeastern as an adjunct professor. He came to Nova Southeastern to develop a graduate law and ethics course for the Huizenga College's MBA program. He holds a B.A degree in political science from Gettysburg College, a M.A. in political science from Drew University in Madison, N.J., a J.D. from St. Mary's University School of Law in San Antonio, Texas, as well as an LL.M in Torts and Product Liability from the University of San Diego School of Law. He is the recipient of several teaching honors and awards; and he is the author of several books and numerous law review and management journal articles. He resides in Lauderdale by the Sea, Florida, with his wife, Nancy, a registered nurse.

Bahaudin G. Mujtaba is currently a Professor of Management, International Management, Organizational Behavior, Leadership, and Human Resources at Nova Southeastern University's H. Wayne Huizenga College of Business and Entrepreneurship in Fort Lauderdale, Florida, United States of America. Bahaudin was awarded the prestigious annual "*Faculty of the Year Award*" in 2011 and 2005. Internationally, Bahaudin received the "Pride of HR Profession" Award at the World HRD Congress annual conference, held in Mumbai, India. Bahaudin has served as a corporate manager, trainer and management development specialist and consultant in the retail industry for sixteen years. He is a certified "Diversity" and "Situational Leadership" trainer. Bahaudin has served as Chair for national and international conferences around the globe, including in Thailand, Vietnam, the United States, China, Pakistan, Kabul of Afghanistan, Nassau of Bahama, Manaus of Brazil, Kingston of Jamaica, Malaysia, and others. Bahaudin has written and published over one hundred peer reviewed journal articles, and he has authored / co-authored over twenty books. Bahaudin was born in Khoshie of Logar and raised in Kabul of Afghanistan. He finished Fort Myers High School, then attended Edison Community College, University of Central Florida and Nova Southeastern University to achieve his academic dreams. Contact Information: Office Phone: (954) 262-5045; Email: mujtaba@nova.edu.

www.ingramcontent.com/pod-product-compliance
Lightning Source LLC
Chambersburg PA
CBHW050456190326
41458CB00005B/1313
9781936237180